THE GREAT RAID

THE GREAT RAID

RESCUING THE DOOMED GHOSTS OF BATAAN AND CORREGIDOR

WILLIAM B. BREUER

talk miramax books

HYPERION

Dedicated to
Admiral Frank B. Kelso, II (Ret.),
former Chief of Naval Operations,
whose leadership, competence, skills,
and vision have earned for him the enduring
respect and admiration of tens of thousands
of present and past members of the
United States Navy

No incident of the campaign in the Pacific has given me such satisfaction as the release of the POWs at Cabanatuan. The mission was brilliantly successful.

—*General Douglas MacArthur*
February 1, 1945

Contents

Maps

Acknowledgments

Creating this book would have been impossible without the valuable help of 306 participants—those who fought on Bataan and Corregidor and in adjacent waters, Rangers, Alamo Scouts, guerilla leaders, Death March survivors, and prisoners of the Japanese army at Cabanatuan and elsewhere during World War II. They dug out old diaries, notes, letters, drawings, newspaper and magazine clippings, decoration citations, diagrams, combat maps, unit rosters, and photographs, and sent them to me.

They probed their memories and provided recollections in face-to-face and telephone interviews, and by correspondence, by audiotape, and by fax. Many of the former POWs were able to give remarkably detailed accounts because they referred to summaries of their experiences that they had compiled after returning home and in the years ahead.

Regrettably, because of space limitations and the need to avoid repetition, many recollections had to be omitted. However, these were helpful in reconstructing the story.

While all accounts were beneficial, special thanks go to the following participants:

Leon D. Beck, Bill Begley, Robert J. Body, Charles H. Bosard, Commander Henry J. Brantingham (Ret.), Vice Admiral John D. Bulkeley (Ret.), Captain Malcolm N. Champlin (Ret.), Commander Barron Chandler (Ret.), Jerry L. Coty, Gilbert J. Cox, William Delich, Charles Di Maio, Colonel John M. Dove (Ret.), James Drewes, Cecil Easley, William R. Evans, L. Rumsey Ewing.

David Foster, Franklin Fox, Thomas E. Gage, Colonel Robert W. Garrett (Ret.), Michael Gilewitch, Major Richard M. Gordon (Ret.), Colonel Samuel C. Grashio (Ret.), Russell E. Hamachek, Harold N. Hard, Neal Harrington, Clifton R. Harris, James B. Herrick, Dr. Ralph E. Hibbs, Lieutenant Colonel Ray C. Hunt (Ret.).

Mrs. Dorothy Janson, Charles C. Jensen, Navy Captain Robert B. Kelly (Ret.), Robert W. Lapham, Captain Elmer E. Long, Jr. (Ret.), MCPO Darrell M. McGhee (Ret.), William Milne, Colonel Henry A. Mucci (Ret.), William E. Nellist, Colonel Gibson Niles (Ret.), Cleatus G. Norton, Robert W. Prince, Leland A. Provencher.

ACKNOWLEDGMENTS

Colonel Melvin Rosen (Ret.), Colonel Thomas Rounsaville (Ret.), Francis R. Schilli, Melville B. Schmidt, Brigadier General Austin C. Shofner (Ret.), Andy E. Smith, Colonel Henry J. Stempin (Ret.), Master Sergeant George R. Steiner (Ret.), August T. Stern, Jr., Leo V. Strausbaugh, Colonel Robert S. Sumner (Ret.), Alexander Troy (Truskowski), E. C. Witmer, Jr., Leon Wolf.

Tracking down 306 participants was a daunting and time-consuming task, one that could not have been accomplished without the valuable assistance of the following:

Captain Elmer E. Long, Jr. (Ret.), National Secretary, American Defenders of Bataan and Corregidor; Joseph A. Vater, editor of *Quan* magazine, publication for former POWs of the Japanese; Ms. Clydie J. Morgan, National Adjutant, American Ex-Prisoners of War; Sue Langseth, editor, *Ex-POW Bulletin*; Mrs. Gregorio P. Chua, Filipino War Veterans of America; Leo V. Strausbaugh, president, U.S. 6th Ranger Battalion Association; Colonel Robert S. Sumner (Ret.), director, Alamo Scouts Association; Donald M. McKee; and former guerilla leader Lieutenant Colonel Ray C. Hunt (Ret.).

Appreciation is expressed to other individuals and organizations who assisted the author in a variety of ways:

Archie DiFante, Historical Research Center, Maxwell Air Force Base, Alabama; Alyce Mary Guthrie, executive director, PT Boats, Inc., Memphis; Richard J. Sommers and his associates at the U.S. Military History Institute, Carlisle Barracks, Pennsylvania; Dean C. Allard and B. F. Calavante, historians, Naval Historical Center, Washington, DC; Colonel Lyman H. Hammond, Jr. (Ret.), director, Douglas MacArthur Memorial, Norfolk, Virginia; Bernard Norling of Notre Dame University, a foremost authority on Philippines guerilla actions; Colonel Samuel C. Grashio (Ret.); Kim B. Holien; and the author's wife, Vivien Breuer, for her dedicated research and coordination.

Finally, a tip of my hat to numerous qualified men who read various chapters or portions of the manuscript with the critical eye of participants and provided the author with their expert critiques.

William B. Breuer
Lookout Mountain, Tennessee

Introduction

The singular importance of the U.S. Army Ranger raid on Cabanatuan in 1945 is captured in General Douglas MacArthur's statement that "no incident of the campaign in the Pacific has given me such satisfaction." But the raid's significance endures to this day within the military, standing as a model for special operations as well as remaining one of the most remarkable and tactically studied achievements in our Army's history. The Cabanatuan concentration camp in the Philippines had witnessed the brutal deaths of nearly three thousand American POWs. They perished of disease, physical abuse, starvation, and deliberate execution during their thirty-three months of imprisonment. Another twenty-five hundred American troops had been murdered or died of thirst and exhaustion during the April 1942 Death March, which followed the final surrender of the garrisons at Corregidor and Bataan. After the Japanese forced more than ten thousand U.S. captives onto slave ships bound for Japan, China, and Korea in the waning months of the war, 511 POWs remained in Cabanatuan. They were emaciated, physically and mentally ill from years of abuse, and gripped by dread at the sure prospect that they would be murdered by their Japanese captors before the attacking divisions of General MacArthur's U.S. Sixth Army could free them.

Only fifty-four hours before it was to take effect, on January 29, 1945, a daring rescue plan by Lieutenant Colonel Henry Mucci was approved by his commanding officer. He assembled 107 Army Rangers, to be supported by more than 100 Philippine guerillas and thirteen brave soldiers of a U.S. Army commando unit called the Alamo Scouts. This raiding force of little more than two hundred fighting men slipped through Japanese lines and infiltrated thirty miles into enemy-controlled territory swarming with more than nine thousand Japanese combat troops. The terrain near the camp was open and devoid of vegetation or cover. The camp itself was directly defended by hundreds of Japanese infantry who greatly outnumbered the attacking ranger forces. The Ranger approach march would be through territory riddled also with Japanese informers and communist Huk insurgents who would turn on any U.S.-supported guerillas or U.S. units at the first opportunity. The POWs were known to be physically debilitated living skeletons. And they would have to be medically supported by this small raiding force during the dangerous firefight and subsequent night withdrawal back to U.S. lines. Crucial Air Corps support would be provided by the U.S. 547th Night Fighter Squadron, whose sixteen planes were based near Lingayen Gulf. They flew Black Widow P-61 night fighters armed with four .50-caliber machine guns and four 20-millimeter cannons. Despite enormous risks and obstacles, Lieutenant Mucci and his men performed their mission perfectly, rescuing all 511 POWs and setting the stage for the retaking of the Philippines.

As a young officer, I was privileged to be the aide-de-camp to one of these courageous Bataan Death March survivors, the late Chester L. Johnson, who retired as a U.S. Army Major General in the early '70s. His personal example of valor and honor greatly affected all of us whom he inspired, and it has proven that the legacy of Bataan and Cabanatuan is ongoing. That legacy helps explain the enormous contemporary success of U.S. special operations forces now operating in the post-September 11th global war on terror. The courage, professionalism, and incredible determination of the successful air-ground raid on the Cabanatuan POW camp is part of the historical experience for today's forty-five thousand special operations Army-Navy-Air Force troops. This successful deep penetration mission was a superb example of the special operations units who served in all the World War II theaters of war—Ranger battalions in Italy and Normandy, OSS teams, Jedburg Scouts, or Alamo Scout teams in covert operations behind enemy lines. The experience of these U.S. raiding units, as well as Allies like the British SAS, guided the subsequent development of American special warfare capabilities in Korea, Vietnam, Grenada, Panama, Desert Storm, and most recently, Afghanistan. Of all these courageous U.S. operations, the Great Raid on Cabanatuan was arguably the most dramatic, with the successful rescue of hundreds of American POWs and the annihilation of all 250 enemy infantry soldiers in the Japanese guard force.

The accomplishment of Mucci and his Rangers seems all the more remarkable for the materials and resources they didn't have. Compared to current U.S. special operations command capabilities, the 6th Ranger Battalion team had primitive technology, firepower, intelligence, and communications. The U.S. Ranger and Delta Commando Force that recently executed the night parachute assault and combat raid on a Taliban stronghold in southern Afghanistan makes a striking contrast. Almost none of these modern techniques and equipment were available to Lieutenant Colonel Mucci's World War II Rangers. Our contemporary U.S. Army special operations forces are now 100% equipped with personal night-vision goggles. Their ground combat locations are exactly pinpointed by Global Positioning System (GPS) devices that can communicate digital information. The U.S. Air Force supporting elements now have near magic night-attack capabilities to use satellite or laser-guided bombs and missiles to precisely strike enemy moving targets. The Black Widow P-61s of the Cabanatuan Raid have now been replaced by combat aircraft like the awesome U.S. Air Force AC-130s, which fire side-mounted 105 mm artillery and 40 mm and 25 mm automatic cannons with total night infrared clarity. The U.S. Army AH-64 Apache Attack Helicopter can zoom along at treetop level in pitch-blackness while hitting enemy armor at 5-kilometer ranges with the devastating tank-killing punch of the Hellfire missile system. The modern U.S. Army Ranger force has satellite-aided radios that allow extremely effective communication among both the air-ground elements of a strike force and the controlling headquarters thousands of miles away. Finally, the modern U.S. Army special operations units can carry enormously lethal and lightweight dismounted infantry firepower. By contrast, the 6th Ranger Battalion at Cabanatuan was armed to the teeth—but only with Tommy guns, BAR light automatic rifles, M1 Garand rifles, carbines, and a few 2.75 mm bazookas. I have personally carried most of these weapons in combat while serving with the Vietnamese Airborne Division in 1966–67. The World War II-era 45-cal. Thompson Submachine Gun is puny in range, accuracy, and lethality when compared to the fractional weight and enormously increased impact of modern U.S. infantry weapons like the 5.56 mm M249 Squad Automatic Weapon.

In addition, the modern Ranger will wear a Kevlar helmet and body armor as well as blast-resistant eye protection. The Ranger platoons now have medics with highly effective combat lifesaver tools and skills. And, the contemporary soldier knows the U.S. Army will not hesitate to dispatch the superb Sikorsky Black Hawk helicopters to recover wounded troopers from combat and evacuate them to our ultra-modern field surgical units. Having been personally wounded in combat three times, I learned that if we get our battle-injured infantrymen on the medevac Black Hawk helicopters alive, they are almost guaranteed to recover and eventually return to their families. For the Rangers, Alamo Scouts, and Philippine guerillas of Lieutenant Colonel Mucci's World War II combat force, there were no such assurances. A serious combat wound was a death sentence in this raiding force, which had only rudimentary medical tools and zero rapid-evacuation capabilities. Ground combat in the U.S. Ranger raid at Cabanatuan was miserable, close-range and personal.

Readers of *The Great Raid*, be they students of World War II, members or veterans of our Armed Forces, or civilians interested in our nation's history, are fortunate for William Breuer's dedication to this story and meticulous research. He has done more than merely bring together this excellent tactical combat study of the heroism and drive of the Cabanatuan Raid. He also lays out a much wider tapestry of the war in the Pacific. We learn not only of the enormous suffering and valor of the U.S. POWs themselves but also of the incredible bravery of the U.S. and Philippine men and women of the underground and guerilla forces who smuggled food, medicine, and news to keep alive the bodies and hopes of the Bataan survivors.

Finally, William Breuer gives us some fascinating snapshots of the wider war in the Pacific and in particular the genius, personality, and complexity of General Douglas MacArthur, who fulfilled his stirring promise of "I shall return." One of the great personal honors of my own service career was to be present as a young cadet in the West Point Mess Hall in May 1962 when the old general gave his hauntingly beautiful and important "Farewell Speech to the Corps." In my opinion, General MacArthur's speech should be required reading by all young Americans. MacArthur has been viewed by historians with widely varied conclusions ranging from abject hero worship to disdain. There is, however, little disagreement that he was perhaps the most physically courageous military officer of either World War I or World War II. He was also a strategic genius whose victories saved the blood of our military by the indirection and cleverness of his tactics. There are many who focus exclusively on the monumental ego and lifelong towering ambition that makes his detractors so vehement in their hatred of this complex personality. However, many of us strongly believe that MacArthur, despite his flaws, was one of the most effective and brilliant officers of the nation's history. In this current era of the global terror threat to the American people and our allies, MacArthur's gripping and poetic eloquence will again capture the hearts and minds of our people.

The Great Raid is an important book for our current military and political leaders to read. It reminds us of the awful consequences of battlefield defeat. This book also speaks to the power of the human spirit in its illustrations of the way U.S. soldiers will sacrifice their own precious lives so that others may survive and live free. The raid by the 6th Ranger Battalion at Cabanatuan did far more than underscore the bravery and skill of the soldiers and airmen involved. The battle payoff was much greater than the salvation of the 511 liberated U.S. POWs. The raid at Cabanatuan is a continuing metaphor for the strength of the American soldier's spirit. The modern Ranger Creed captures the values of these heroes of Luzon: "I volunteer as a Ranger, fully knowing the hazards of my chosen profession...Readily will I display the intestinal fortitude required to fight on to the Ranger objective and complete the mission though I be the lone survivor." And survive they did.

General Barry R. McCaffrey, USA (Ret.)
January 2002

1

Deep in
Hostile Territory

A broiling sun began its ascent into the cloudless blue skies over Luzon, the largest of the Philippine Islands, when Lieutenant Colonel Henry A. Mucci, the scrappy leader of the U.S. 6th Ranger Battalion, convened a powwow of his officers in the barrio (hamlet) of Plateros. Mucci and 107 of his Rangers were in a perilous situation, for they had infiltrated thirty miles behind Japanese lines on one of the most audacious missions of the war in the Pacific and had been holed up in Plateros for twenty-four hours. It was January 30, 1945.

Only a mile and a half to the south of the barrio was the notorious Japanese prisoner-of-war camp known as Cabanatuan, named after the largest nearby town. Earlier in World War II, there had been as many as twelve thousand Americans penned up in the huge stockade under the most brutal and primitive conditions, but thousands of them had been shipped to Japan and Manchuria to provide slave labor for Japanese war production. Buried in shallow, unmarked graves just outside the camp's barbed-wire fence were twenty-six hundred other American POWs—ones who had been murdered by Japanese guards or had died of starvation, disease, despair, or maltreatment.

Now only 511 POWs, mostly Americans, who had endured thirty-three months of captivity, remained in the Cabanatuan hellhole. They were a pitiful lot. Most were living skeletons. Some were blind. Many could not walk. Others were missing one or more arms and legs. A few had taken leave of their senses.

Three weeks before Colonel Mucci and his Rangers reached Plateros, General Douglas MacArthur's forces had stormed ashore at Lingayen Gulf, sixty-five miles northwest of Cabanatuan. Soon, U.S. intelligence officers received frightening news from guerillas in the region: When MacArthur's spearheads drove closer to the POW compound, vengeance-seeking Japanese soldiers would probably slaughter the helpless prisoners.

As a result of this information, Mucci and his Ranger force had been given the daunting task of slipping through Japanese positions for thirty miles to assault the Cabanatuan stockade, kill the sizable number of enemy troops in the compound, rescue the POWs, and escort them back through Japanese territory to American positions.

Among the officers now conferring with Henry Mucci in Plateros were twenty-five-year-old Captain Robert W. Prince, leader of the 6th Rangers' Charley Company, who would be in direct charge of the stockade assault; Lieutenant John F. Murphy of Springfield, Massachusetts, who had been a star quarterback at Notre Dame University; Filipino guerilla Lieutenant Carlos Tombo; and three lieutenants of the Alamo Scouts, William E. Nellist of Eureka, California; Thomas J. Rounsaville of Atoka, Oklahoma; and John M. Dove of Hollywood, California.

Few in number, the Alamo Scouts had been formed in New Guinea more than a year earlier to infiltrate Japanese territory and nail down facts about enemy troop strengths and movements. Nellist, Rounsaville, and Dove were veterans of numerous hair-raising reconnaissance raids in New Guinea and its offshore islands.

"We've got to hit the Japs tonight!" Colonel Mucci declared grimly. "Intelligence says there are nine thousand Japs in this region. So we can't stay right in the center of all this Jap activity indefinitely without being discovered."[1]

Despite the urgency, the thirty-three-year-old Mucci, a West Pointer and son of a Bridgeport, Connecticut, horse dealer, was convinced that more detailed information about the POW camp would have to be collected or the rescue operation could result in a catastrophe for the Rangers and the Alamo Scouts—and no doubt spell doom for the prisoners.

"We've got to get someone up close to the front gate," the Ranger commander declared. "We're going to bolt through that entrance, so the gate is the key to the entire operation."[2]

Selected for this crucial snooping job were the Alamo Scouts lieutenants Bill Nellist and Tom Rounsaville. They had been handed a tall order. The terrain around the POW camp was flat and void of trees; it would be broad daylight, and Japanese sentries at the gate could see anyone approaching for a half mile.

"I don't care how you get the dope," the colonel declared solemnly. "Just get it!"

Compounding the seemingly impossible task was the strict time limitation. Mucci stressed that the Scouts would have to send back their intelligence no later than 3:00 P.M.—less than six hours away—in order to provide a couple of hours for Captain Prince to put the finishing touches on an assault plan.

Two hours later, Bill Nellist and one of his Alamo Scouts, Private First Class Rufo Vaquilar of Fresno, California, were lying flat on a low knoll some seven hundred yards from the prison's massive front gate. Between them and the stockade was a nipa hut that was less than three hundred yards from the camp entrance.

William Nellist remembered: "The nipa hut would make an excellent observation post. From there we could get a clear view of the gate. But the problem was, how could Vaquilar and I get to the hut with Jap guards looking in our direction?"[3]

Nellist and Vaquilar rustled up some native clothes and quickly donned them. A key feature of their disguise were the straw, wide-brimmed buri hats of the type worn by countless Filipinos. Their pistols were stuck in belts under the garments, and Nellist also concealed an aerial photograph of the camp layout.

Three other Alamo Scouts watched their two comrades put on the native garb and were deeply concerned over their safety. If the Japanese captured them in civilian garb, the two Scouts most certainly would be tortured, then beheaded as spies.

Private First Class Gilbert Cox, who had played football at Oregon State University, recalled: "The clothes fit Bill and Rufo okay, and so did the big hats. What worried us was that there were not many Filipinos as tall as our two fellows, so the Japanese might grow suspicious. There was no doubt that the Japs at the gate would see them, for Bill and Rufo would be in plain view."[4]

Between Nellist and Vaquilar and the targeted hut were large fields growing an assortment of plants. Strolling leisurely from a bamboo thicket, the two Scouts ambled across the fields, their wide-brimmed hats covering their faces, and pretended that they were farmers inspecting their crops. Adrenaline was pumping; hearts were beating faster. Nellist and Vaquilar could almost feel Japanese eyes boring into them.

William Nellist remembered: "We finally reached the hut with no indication that the Japs were suspicious of us. It was not unusual for Filipino farmers to be strolling around the region. It was a little unsettling to be so close to the front gate, however.

"Some distance to the rear of the spy hut were other shacks in which natives were living. I had Vaquilar, still wearing his native garb, bring me people who had worked in and around the camp. I had them point out things I wanted to know. How many guards? Where were they located? Which way the front gate swung to be opened? It seemed as though anything I wanted to know, Vaquilar found a native who could come up with the answer and explain it to me."[5]

When Bill Nellist and Rufo Vaquilar had been in the hut for about an hour, they spotted a young Filipina, her shiny black hair flowing in the breeze, sauntering along the road toward the front entrance. The two Scouts felt a surge of concern when the woman walked up to the gate and began talking with the guards. Was she tipping them off that Nellist and Vaquilar were holed up in the hut only a short distance from the gate and that other Scouts were lying in rice paddies while keeping the camp under surveillance? Or was she telling them that the Rangers were encamped at nearby Plateros?

William Nellist recalled the tense situation: "She seemed to be talking forever, but perhaps it had only been fifteen or twenty minutes. Rufo and I were watching intently and were worried. Finally, she left and walked on down the road and out of sight. After a half hour or so when we saw there was no stir among the Japs in the camp, we assumed that she had not spilled the beans."[6]

Only much later would the Alamo Scouts learn that the young woman had been sent to the front gate by guerilla Lieutenant Carlos Tombo to pick the Jap guards' brains for the latest information on what was taking place inside the enclosure.

Lieutenant Nellist scrawled on a pad detailed information about the front gate. It was wooden, about nine feet high, and opened in the middle, either frontward or backward. A huge padlock about four feet from the ground secured the gate. That padlock would play a crucial role if the impending raid were to be a success.

As planned earlier, the Alamo Scouts and Lieutenant Tombo's guerillas sent their up-to-the-minute intelligence back to Colonel Mucci in Plateros by 3:00 P.M., four and a half hours before the Rangers were to hit the stockade.

Robert Prince recalled: "Our forward scouts did a magnificent job. They plotted the exact location of the watchtowers and found out how many Japs were in each one and the type of weapons they had, which buildings held the tanks, where two pillboxes were located, which barracks the transient Japanese troops were in, and which were the guards' quarters. They also told us that there were two hundred and twenty-five to two hundred and fifty enemy soldiers in the enclosure."[7]

Within an hour of receiving the current intelligence, Captain Prince, along with Lieutenant John Murphy, the leader of a platoon, finalized details of the rescue operation. Each Ranger, Alamo Scout, and Filipino guerilla was briefed on his specific task, as well as on the overall plan. Total surprise, stealth, and speed would be crucial. When night fell, the Rangers would assault the compound—with fury and deadly skill. There would be no second chance should they fail.

A short distance from where Bob Prince and his men were shouldering their weapons to head for the stockade, an undercurrent of foreboding rippled through the Cabanatuan camp. Private First Class Cecil "Red" Easley, Jr., of Houston, Texas, was in his hut chatting grimly with his two closest pals and fellow Texans, Cecil Hay of Arlington and Jimmy Pittman of Dublin. Hay was so weak that he could not walk, Pittman was almost blind from malnutrition.

Cecil Easley remembered: "All of us were fearful. Tension of late had been thick enough to cut with a knife. Even the Jap guards were jittery. From clandestine radio sets hidden in the camp, we knew that General MacArthur's troops had landed in Lingayen Gulf, but most POWs felt the Japanese would embark on a murderous rampage against us at any moment as our forces drew closer to Cabanatuan."[8]

For Red Easley and the 510 other gaunt POWs still remaining at the Cabanatuan hellhole, fright and agony long had been a way of life. They had suffered incessant torments of the damned as helpless captives of the Japanese army. Their excruciating ordeal had its roots in an evolving chain of events that had been triggered by a crucial strategic decision reached at the highest levels of the U.S. government more than three years earlier.

2

Roosevelt Abandons the Philippines

A week after a woefully unprepared America was bombed into global war at Pearl Harbor, Hawaii, and in the Philippines, an obscure brigadier general named Dwight D. Eisenhower arrived by train at Washington's Union Station. Army Chief of Staff George C. Marshall had summoned the affable, chain-smoking Eisenhower from Fort Sam Houston, Texas, where he had gained a glowing reputation as a staff officer. It was Sunday, December 14, 1941.

Wartime Washington was grim, cold, and nervous. Two nights earlier, a trigger-happy soldier manning an antiaircraft gun atop a downtown office building had fired a round at a nonexistent low-flying bomber. Whizzing across the city at treetop level, the projectile exploded against the front of the historic Lincoln Memorial, knocking a huge hole in the concrete facade.

Rumors were rampant and a wave of near hysteria flowed over many government officials in the capital. One prominent senator telephoned the White House, declared that the West Coast of the United States could not be held against a certain Japanese invasion, and demanded that American forces establish a defensive line in the Rocky Mountains. Secretary of the Navy Frank Knox, a former newspaper publisher and the token Republican in President Franklin D. Roosevelt's cabinet, looked up as an excited aide bolted into his office.

"Mr. Secretary," the man almost shouted, "A Japanese army is landing in California!"

Hysteria heightened in the capital when J. Edgar Hoover, the director of the Federal Bureau of Investigation, warned the public to be on guard against enemy spies and saboteurs who were roaming the United States. Civilian law enforcement agencies in Washington were ordered to arrest "any suspicious looking person," leaving it up to the individual police officer to decide who looked suspicious and who did not.

Much to the disgust of President Roosevelt, a pair of antiaircraft guns, relics from World War I, were placed on the roof of the White House. In his front yard were posted three soldiers manning an ancient machine gun, which may or may not have been in condition to fire against would-be presidential assassins. The Secret Service, whose job it was to protect Roosevelt, frisked nearly everyone who entered the White House grounds on business.

Against this backdrop of gloom and frenzy, Ike Eisenhower caught a Yellow Cab at Union Station and was soon standing before silver-haired, fifty-nine-year-old General Marshall in the Munitions Building. Eisenhower was awed: Every army professional knew that the chief of staff was aloof and austere, although most respected him. After a short greeting, Marshall tersely briefed Eisenhower on the dreary situation in the Pacific.

Eisenhower was shocked to learn from the chief of staff that America had suffered the worst military debacle in her history in the Pacific. At Pearl Harbor, the U.S. Pacific Fleet had been caught napping by an early morning Japanese sneak air assault and had been virtually destroyed. A few hours later, powerful Japanese bomber forces, based on Formosa, inflicted a "Second Pearl Harbor" on the Philippines, five thousand miles west of Hawaii.

In one fell swoop, the Japanese had bombed, strafed, and pulverized the key U.S. air bases on Luzon: Clark, Nichols, Nielson, Iba, Vigan, Rosales, La Union, and San Fernando fields. For all practical purposes, American air power in the Philippines no longer existed. Two days later on December 10, elements of Lieutenant General Masaharu Homma's Fourteenth Army stormed ashore in northern Luzon and began driving southward in the direction of Manila.*

Recognizing that the Japanese had struck with overpowering strength, General Douglas MacArthur, the U.S. commander in the Phil-

---

*The Philippines are on east longitude time. At 6:00 A.M., December 10, on Luzon, it was 11 A.M. December 9 in Hawaii.

ippines, prepared to execute War Plan Orange 3. That operation called for a combined American-Filipino force under U.S. Major General Jonathan M. "Skinny" Wainwright to confront the invaders, then pull back southward, phase line by phase line, into the mountainous, jungle-covered landmass of Bataan, a peninsula that formed the western shore of Manila Bay.

General Marshall then ticked off other facts concerning the situation in the Pacific: the size and strength of Japanese land, sea, and air forces; intelligence estimates of Japanese intentions; the condition and battle-readiness of the U.S. Army and its Filipino units in the Philippines, and the capabilities of America's British allies in the Far East.

One more crucial point had to be factored into the Philippines equation: Nazi Germany. Four days after Japanese bombers hit Luzon and Pearl Harbor, Adolf Hitler, the German dictator who had conquered most of Europe during the past two years, declared war on the United States. A few hours later, Hitler's crony, bombastic Italian strongman Benito Mussolini, followed suit.

All the while General Marshall had been talking, Ike Eisenhower was furiously scribbling notes. Suddenly the low-key chief of staff demanded: "All right, Eisenhower, what should be our general line of action?"

Eisenhower was stunned. All he knew about what was going on in the Pacific was what he had read in the newspapers, heard over the radio, and picked up from Marshall's short briefing. Moments later, Eisenhower replied, "Give me a few hours, sir." Marshall agreed.

Such was the niggardly prewar budget provided the War Department by Congress that Ike Eisenhower had no staff, not even a secretary, and he had to use his hunt-and-peck system on a battered old typewriter he had borrowed. Before he hit the first key, he knew that the Philippines could not be saved, and the course of action should be to build up troop strength and bases in Australia for an eventual offensive toward the Japanese home islands, four thousand miles to the north.

Eisenhower found himself in a curious situation. Between 1935 and 1939, he had served as an aide to General MacArthur in the Philippines. There had been no love lost between the two men. On his return to the United States, Ike had quipped to cronies: "I studied theatrics for four years under Douglas MacArthur."

Now, Eisenhower had in his hands the power to influence the destiny of his one-time boss and his troops in the Philippines.

It was nearly dusk when Eisenhower returned to Marshall's office with his recommendations. Although he stressed that it was too late to get reinforcements to MacArthur, he felt that an effort should be made to supply him because the prestige of the United States was at stake in the eyes of tens of millions of people in East Asia.

"I agree with you," Marshall replied evenly.[1]

Impressed by Eisenhower's analysis and recommended course of action, the chief of staff immediately appointed the one-star general to be in charge of the Far East Section of the War Plans Division.

Forty-eight hours later, President Roosevelt, on the unanimous recommendation of his joint chiefs of staff—General George Marshall of the army, General Henry H. "Hap" Arnold of the air corps, and Admiral Harold R. "Betty" Stark of the navy—agreed to a global strategy whereby Nazi Germany would be defeated first and the Philippines would be abandoned. This grand design meant that twenty-three thousand American soldiers, sailors, airmen and marines, along with ninety-eight thousand Filipino regulars and draftees in the Philippines, would be written off as expendable, pawns of war on a world chessboard.

Douglas MacArthur, the American commander who would be most impacted by this hallmark decision, was kept in the dark about it.

Although the leaders in Washington were concentrating on Europe, public focus was upon Douglas MacArthur. In times of danger and adversity, America needs a hero: They found him in the flamboyant, upbeat, highly decorated general in Manila. MacArthur had become a symbol of national defiance. "Old Mac will show those dirty Japs a thing or two!" rang out across the land.

At age sixty-one, MacArthur looked twenty years younger. His dark hair had receded and his piercing blue eyes either mesmerized those he was seeking to woo or scared the hell out of those who had gained his displeasure. He walked with a brisk step that had aides scrambling to keep up with him. MacArthur always looked as though he had just emerged from a tonsorial parlor: In the stifling heat of Manila, his uniforms were crisp and neatly pressed at all times. Few knew that he had thirty-one uniforms and changed them three times each day.

Newspapers and magazines in the United States faithfully reported his every move and utterance. When he told worried America, "My message is one of serenity and confidence," home-front morale skyrocketed.[2]

American citizens insisted on peering at the new war through rose-colored glasses. The Japanese treachery at Pearl Harbor and in the Philippines had stuck in their craw, but within days, their mood switched from disbelief to anger. Old tendencies to sneer at anything Japanese surfaced. Now, the home front agreed, Japan was going to be taught a quick lesson: Any red-blooded American soldier could lick at least ten Japs.

Few Americans realized how dismally unprepared for war the United States was. General John Dill, who had fought the mighty German army in France as a corps commander two years earlier and now was the British liaison officer to the U.S. War Department, cabled London:

> This country (the United States) is soft and highly organized for peace. Their armed forces are more unready for war than it is possible to imagine. . . . The whole military organization belongs to the days of George Washington.[3]

Back in the Philippines, Douglas MacArthur was trying to stem the onrushing Japanese tide with a hodgepodge of partially trained, ill-equipped troops armed largely with obsolete weapons. Their ammunition was so old that four out of five grenades were duds, and five out of six artillery shells failed to explode. His total force of some 120,000 men, most of whom were on Luzon, Corregidor, and the southern island of Mindanao, included 98,000 drafted Filipinos, who were reluctant warriors at best.

These native conscripts were mainly farmers, taxi drivers, street peddlers, and manual laborers. Their primary military skills were saluting (usually with the correct arm) and being on time for meals. Twenty percent of the Filipino draftees were illiterate, as were many of their sergeants and corporals. They spoke eight Far Eastern languages and eighty-seven dialects, so there was mass confusion when orders were given in English by their American officers or in the dialects of their native noncoms.

Late in December, MacArthur declared Manila, long known as the

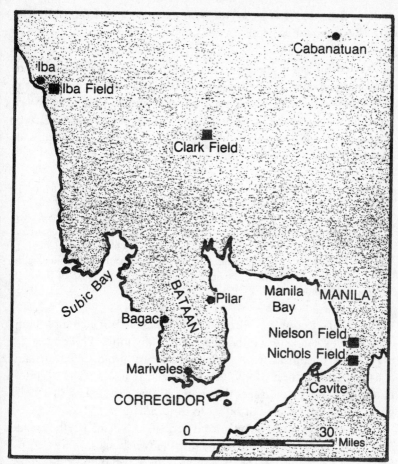

The Manila Bay Region

Pearl of the Orient because of its majestic buildings and palm-lined thoroughfares, to be an "open city" (meaning it would not be defended), and by January 5, 1942, all of his forces on Luzon had pulled back into Bataan. Footsore, hungry, and exhausted, the American and Filipino soldiers felt a faint surge of relief.

"We've run long enough," they told one another. "Now we're going to stand and fight until the promised reinforcements and warplanes arrive."

No one knew that Bataan, a harsh, forbidding locale hardly

changed from the Stone Age, would be a gigantic trap from which the only escape would be capture or death.

Meanwhile, in far-off Washington, President Roosevelt sat before a microphone in his White House study and beamed by shortwave radio an upbeat message to the American and Filipino troops, who were slugging it out with the Japanese in scores of pitched battles on Luzon. A Corregidor radio station, dubbed "The Voice of Freedom," rebroadcast the president's remarks throughout the Philippines:

> The resources of the United States have been dedicated by their people to the utter and complete defeat of the Japanese warlords. I give to the people of the Philippines my solemn pledge that their freedom will be redeemed and their independence established and protected. The entire resources, in men and material, of the United States stand behind that pledge. . . . The United States Navy is following an intensive and well-planned campaign which will result in positive assistance to the defense of the Philippine Islands.[4]

Within hours, Roosevelt realized that he had pulled an incredible blunder. There was no substantial help on the way to the Philippines. So Steve Early, the president's cagey press secretary, promptly began damage-control operations. Reporters were told that they had misinterpreted Roosevelt's message, that not too much emphasis should be given to the immediate but rather to the ultimate.

Then Early rushed Senator Tom Connally, chairman of the Senate Foreign Relations Committee, before the Washington press corps. Somberly, Connally declared that things looked bad in the Philippines. However, from a military point of view, the islands had long been looked upon as more of a liability than an asset, he added.

A few hours later, a clutch of reporters besieged President Roosevelt in the Oval Office. Did these gloomy remarks by Senator Connally mean that the Philippines were being abandoned and American forces there written off? For once, the articulate Roosevelt fumbled for words. He stuttered, hemmed, and hawed.

From his command post on Corregidor, Douglas MacArthur continued to bombard Washington with urgent requests for reinforcements and supplies for his beleaguered men on Bataan, who were on half rations because of a shortage of food. Soon General George Marshall began sending encouraging messages listing the weapons and equipment earmarked for the Philippines. MacArthur was notified that one hundred and twenty-five P-40s and fifteen B-24 heavy bombers were aboard ships sailing westward. What the chief of staff did not say was that the convoy would be diverted to Australia, twenty-five hundred miles south of the Philippines.

"We are doing our utmost . . . to rush air support to you," Marshall cabled. "The President has seen all of your messages and directs navy to give you every possible support in your splendid fight."[5]

A few days later, Marshall advised that Roosevelt, British Prime Minister Winston S. Churchill, and their combined chiefs of staff were "looking toward the quick development of strength in the Far East so as to break the enemy's hold on the Philippines. Our great hope is that the development of overwhelming air power in the Malay Barrier will cut the Japanese communications south of Borneo and permit an assault in the southern Philippines. . . . A stream of four-engine bombers is en route. . . . Another stream of similar bombers started today from Hawaii. Two groups of medium bombers leave next week. Pursuit planes are coming on every ship we can use."[6]

Douglas MacArthur and his key commanders were elated. However, they apparently misinterpreted the precise intent of these cables. Had Marshall meant to convey that these bombers and fighter planes were bound for the Philippines, or that they were heading for Australia, where strength would be built up for an *eventual* return to the Philippines? Or had Marshall deliberately intended to mislead MacArthur so that the men who now called themselves "The Battling Bastards of Bataan" would fight on and thereby buy precious time?

Based on these seemingly heartening communications from Roosevelt and Marshall, MacArthur composed an upbeat message to his fighting men and ordered every company commander on Bataan to read it to his troops:

> Help is on the way from the United States. Thousands of troops and hundreds of airplanes are being dispatched. The exact time of arrival of reinforcements is unknown, as they will have to fight their way through the Japanese. It is imperative that our troops hold until these reinforcements arrive.
>
> No further retreat is possible. Our supplies on Bataan are ample. A

determined defense will defeat the enemy's attacks. It is a question now of courage and determination. Men who run will merely be destroyed but men who fight will save themselves and their country. I call upon every soldier in Bataan to fight in his assigned position, resisting every attack.[7]

This exhortation was warmly received by the Filipino soldiers, who had long worshiped MacArthur. But many Americans were cynical. They hooted and jeered. Ample supplies? They were already on half rations. Their grenades and shells were no good. And how could help be on the way if the U.S. Pacific Fleet had been wiped out at Pearl Harbor? A hard-bitten colonel shrugged off the message to the troops as "one of MacArthur's ghost stories."

MacArthur's trapped troops on Bataan were confronted by not one, but two implacable foes—hunger and the Japanese soldier. Before sailing for the Luzon invasion, many of General Homma's soldiers had mailed to loved ones in Japan locks of hair or fingernail clippings. For if they ever returned to their homeland, it probably would be in the form of ashes in an urn. They also studied carefully the Imperial Japanese Army directive handed to them on the transports:

> When you encounter the enemy after landing, think of yourself as an avenger come at last face to face with his father's murderer. Show him no mercy.

The typical Japanese fighting man was keenly disciplined, highly motivated, and tenacious. There was no greater honor for him than to die in battle for the emperor. Their allegiance to the emperor was reinforced almost daily when they faced in the direction of Tokyo and recited parts of the "Imperial Rescript to Soldiers and Sailors," proclaimed by Emperor Meiji in 1875. The Rescript contained the Code of Bushido which demanded "honor, obedience, and valor." It told what was expected of the samurai warrior: "The soldier and sailor should consider loyalty their essential duty . . . and duty is weightier than a mountain, while death is lighter than a feather. . . . Never by failing fall into disgrace and bring dishonor to your name."

Japanese soldiers underwent training that was considered harsh, even brutal, by Western standards. Long forced marches with no water were common. Those who fell to the wayside were ostracized by their comrades; only through glorious death in battle could the miserable derelict regain his honor. It was routine for a superior to beat a sub-ordinate for minor faults; more serious shortcomings could result in the miscreant being clubbed senseless.

Meanwhile in Washington, Dwight Eisenhower was laboring through fourteen-hour workdays, seven days a week, struggling with an awesome array of problems. As chief of the Far East Section of the War Plans Division, Eisenhower drafted all replies to the barrage of cables that MacArthur had been and was firing at Washington. Since MacArthur and Eisenhower had been conducting a subtle feud for years, it no doubt was galling to each man that they had been cast into this cuddly relationship.

In one cable, MacArthur demanded that the navy be ordered to sally forth from Hawaii and break through the Japanese blockade of the Philippines. Eisenhower replied that the Japanese had seized the Pacific islands of Guam, Wake, the Marshalls, and the Gilberts, which gave their land-based planes air superiority, so the navy was helpless to rush to MacArthur's assistance.

In his tiny office in Malinta Tunnel on Corregidor, a tiny island perched in the mouth of Manila Bay, MacArthur was furious after read-ing the cable from his former aide. His tired, filthy, hungry, and ill men on Bataan were battling for their lives with obsolete weapons and in-sufficient or faulty ammunition. The thought of immaculately tailored, well-fed, and comfortably housed staff officers in Washington was maddening to MacArthur, and to his commanders.

MacArthur ranted to aides that "faceless staff officers" in Wash-ington (meaning Eisenhower) were deliberately deceiving him and his beleaguered troops. Had there been more determination in the War Department, he declared, supplies and reinforcements could reach Ba-taan and Corregidor.[8]

For his part, Ike Eisenhower filled his diary with scathing de-nouncements of his one-time boss. On January 19: "In many ways, MacArthur is as big a baby as ever. But we've got to keep him fighting."[9]

A few days later, a message was received from MacArthur in which he recommended his chief of staff, General Dick Sutherland, to be his successor "in the event of my death." Revealing his lack of appreciation for the perilous situation in the Philippines, Eisenhower scrawled in his diary: "Douglas likes his bootlickers" (meaning Sutherland).[10]

On January 29, after receiving a MacArthur cable calling again for the navy to break the Philippines blockade, Eisenhower's diary entry declared: "MacArthur refuses to look facts in the face, an old trait of his." And he suggested that MacArthur was "losing his nerve."[11]

While the blizzard of cables was flying between Corregidor and Washington, on the stifling hot morning of February 8, 1942, General Masaharu Homma was conferring with his staff at San Fernando, a sugar center forty miles north of Manila. A fifty-two-year-old native of Tokyo, Homma was the most westernized of top Japanese generals. He had studied in Great Britain and later was a military attaché in London, receiving a British decoration.

A soft-spoken, incisive commander, Homma now was gripped by deep anguish. The master plan for Japanese conquest in the Pacific had given him sixty days to seize the Philippines, but this day was the deadline—and Bataan and Corregidor were holding on doggedly. So he vented his anger and frustration on Imperial General Headquarters in Tokyo.

The Fourteenth Army commander ranted that he had been provided with flawed maps of the Philippines and grossly inaccurate intelligence reports. These documents held that the Filipino soldiers would turn on their American "exploiters" once Homma had landed on Luzon and MacArthur would be confronted by a war within a war. Homma even suspected that General Hideki Tojo, the chief warlord, wanted him to fall flat on his face in the Philippines so that Homma would have to return to Japan in disgrace. It was well known among Japanese military professionals that no love had been lost between Homma and Tojo.[12]

Now, with Bataan and Corregidor still holding out, the question before Homma and his staff was: What should be the next course of action? Some officers suggested that the forces on Bataan dig in and wait for MacArthur's men to starve. Homma promptly rejected that proposal because it might take months to achieve.

For several hours, the conference rambled on in the humid, ninety-five-degree heat. Homma finally decided that he would undergo the loss of even more "face" by asking Tokyo for large numbers of reinforcements in order to launch a final, all-out assault on the Bataan defenders.

Just as the session was about to break up, a junior officer handed a telegram to Homma. It was from Imperial General Headquarters—meaning Hideki Tojo. The chief warlord was immensely unhappy over Homma's seeming lethargy. Everywhere there was victory, except in the Philippines. Hong Kong, the British jewel in the Far East, had fallen. Singapore, hailed by the Brits as an "impregnable" fortress, was about to be taken by burly Lieutenant General Tomoyuki Yamashita, who would gain the sobriquet "Tiger of Malaya."

Homma, his face etched in agony, buried his head in his hands as his staff members slipped quietly out of the room.

3

Legion of the Living Dead

On February 23, 1942, Douglas MacArthur, who had taken a personal vow to die with his men if need be, received a cable from President Roosevelt ordering the general to go to Australia to "assume command of all U.S. troops." MacArthur was anguished. He told aides that he had been put in a no-win situation. If he disobeyed Roosevelt's direct order—an option he was considering—he could be court-martialed for disobedience. If he complied with the order, he would be looked upon as a general who deserted his hard-pressed fighting men.

MacArthur saw only one way out of his personal predicament: He would resign his commission in the United States Army and volunteer to fight on Bataan as a private. That night he dictated his resignation, but confidants persuaded him not to submit it to Washington.

MacArthur's aides pleaded with him to go to Australia, pointing out that this course was the best hope for salvaging the situation in the Philippines. Clearly, they stressed, MacArthur was being sent to Australia to lead an army back to Luzon and rescue the Battling Bastards.

Still, MacArthur could not bring himself to go. On March 6, he received a prodding from Roosevelt: "The situation in Australia indicates desirability of your early arrival there." Three days later, the general reached a gut-wrenching decision: He would shift his base of operations to Australia, take charge of the army there, and return to the Philippines—hopefully by July 1 in time to save the Bataan garrison. But MacArthur was trapped on Corregidor; how would he get through the Japanese air and naval blockade?

Meanwhile, the Battling Bastards of Bataan were steadily growing weaker and dwindling in number. Quinine was exhausted. Some five hundred malaria cases entered the two field hospitals each week. These were the most severely ill men. The remainder of the sick soldiers, perhaps one-third of the total force, stuck to their foxholes. With no means for resupply, the food situation had gone from serious to desperate. All the monkeys, cats, dogs, lizards, and iguanas had been killed and eaten. MacArthur ordered rations to be cut from half to three-eighths. He himself had lost more than fifteen pounds since the food rationing began two months earlier.

On Bataan, there remained only one source of food, the horses of the U.S. 26th Cavalry Regiment. One of these animals was Joseph Conrad, General Jonathan Wainwright's own beloved horse, who had been awarded many medals in the United States as a prize jumper. Even while burdened with unsolvable problems on Bataan, the old cavalryman periodically found time to visit Joseph Conrad and stroke his once glossy neck.

Now, the general told a quartermaster officer, "You will begin killing the horses at once; Joseph Conrad will go first." Then Wainwright turned and walked away, his eyes brimming with tears.

Weakened by the relentless bouts with hunger and debilitating tropical diseases, the Americans' minds were prey to doubt, fear, and outlandish rumors. One report that spread like wildfire across a dry prairie was that a huge convoy was on the way to the Philippines, bringing a cavalry division of black soldiers who would charge the Japanese mounted on snow-white horses. Many believed that the convoy indeed would arrive, but instead of black troops, it would carry a special division of Tennessee squirrel-shooters led by Sergeant Alvin York, the famed World War I hero.

Soon, these incredible rumors became standard jokes among the bitter men on Bataan. Only the most naive now felt that a relief convoy was coming. Soldiers scrawled the letter "V" on their helmets—not the Allied "V for Victory" slogan, but rather "V" as in victim. They composed angry poems denouncing President Roosevelt and Douglas MacArthur, passing the salty creations from foxhole to foxhole.

Those on Bataan and Corregidor who had access to shortwave radios listened avidly to a powerful station broadcasting from San Francisco, California. One commercial message urged listeners to hurry to their friendly neighborhood grocery and bring home a generous supply of mouth-watering cheese. At a company command post in the green hell of Bataan, a lieutenant shouted: "Goddamn it, America, stop making cheese and send us bullets and airplanes!"

One of the station's news announcers invariably touched off obscene outbursts on Corregidor. From the safety of his perch in the plush Fairmont Hotel, the news announcer would often "dare" the Japanese to bomb and shell Corregidor. "*We* can take it!" the announcer boasted.

In the meantime, Douglas MacArthur and Navy Lieutenant John D. Bulkeley, a thirty-year-old skipper of a PT-boat squadron, were walking alone in an open, bomb-pocked field on Topside, the highest elevation on Corregidor. The four-star general wanted to be away from prying ears.

John Bulkeley remembered: "As we strolled side by side, General MacArthur revealed that President Roosevelt had given him a direct order to go to Australia. He indicated that he hoped to lead the army there back in time to rescue his force on Bataan. General MacArthur said he wanted my four remaining PT boats to break through the Jap sea and air blockade and carry him and a small party some six hundred miles south to Mindanao. There he would hook up with a couple of planes flown up from Australia for the final leg of the trip.

"All of this he was telling me was top-secret stuff—I wasn't to say a damned word to anyone about it until it was about time to shove off. Finally, the general asked: 'Well, Johnny, do you think you can pull it off?' Having been young, cocky, and brash, I replied, 'General, it'll be a piece of cake!'

"Not only would we have to dodge Jap ships and patrolling aircraft, but those six hundred miles of largely uncharted waters, with unseen, jagged coral reefs waiting to rip apart our thin-skinned boats, with much of the distance covered at night and with only primitive compasses with which to navigate; those facts alone should have warned of impending danger."[1]

Malcolm N. Champlin, who, while serving as an aide to Admiral Francis Rockwell, the Philippines' navy commander, had seen the PT-boat squadron skipper almost daily, remembered: "John Bulkeley was a wild man. Daring, courageous, and admirable in many ways, but still a wild man. He reminded one on first glance of a swashbuckling pirate. He wore a long, unruly beard and carried two ominous pistols at his side. His eyes were bloodshot and red-rimmed from constant night patrols and lack of sleep, but his nervous energy never seemed to give out. He walked with a cocksure gait, and one could always count on him to raise particular hell with any Jap he met."[2]

A few days later, MacArthur summoned Jonathan Wainwright, put an arm around his old friend, and said in a voice choked with emotion, "If I get through, you know I'll be back as soon as I can with as much as I can."

In the background could be heard the angry roar of Japanese guns on Bataan. Then Wainwright replied softly, "You'll get through, Douglas."

MacArthur quickly responded: "And back!"

At dusk on March 11, Douglas MacArthur, wife Jean, little son Arthur and his Filipina nanny, Ah Cheu, and sixteen key military men began climbing aboard John Bulkeley's PT-41 as a sinking sun purpled the South China Sea. Some carried a few personal belongings. MacArthur did not have an ounce of personal luggage, not even a razor (he had slipped a toothbrush into his pocket).

MacArthur was the last to board. For long moments he stood on the shell-torn North Dock—a lonely figure, a tragic symbol of America's failure to be militarily prepared. In the gloaming, MacArthur heard a voice ask:

"What's the Old Man's chance of getting through, Sarge?"

And the gruff reply: "Dunno. If lucky, maybe one in five."[3]

Bulkeley's craft shoved off, rendezvoused with his other three PT boats in Manila Bay, and raced off for Mindanao, as far from Corregidor as Chicago, Illinois, is from Buffalo, New York. The crews and passengers on the mahogany-hulled plywood boats were perched on powder kegs. The deck of each craft was crowded with twenty steel drums, each holding fifty gallons of high-octane gasoline. An enemy's incendiary bullet could ignite the fuel fumes in a drum and instantly turn the craft into a raging inferno. Engines were meant to be changed every few hundred hours, but after three months of heavy use without adequate maintenance, the boats had already quadrupled the engines' normal life span.

Bulkeley's boats were not equipped with a pelorus (a navigational instrument having two sight vanes), so a course was followed by the use of simple compasses (much like the ones Boy Scouts use), dead reckoning, and the stars—techniques used by the ancient mariners.

After thirty-five grueling hours on the often angry sea, dodging Japanese warships, without sleep for three days and two nights, navi-

MacArthur's Escape from Corregidor (U.S. Navy)

gating by primitive means, John Bulkeley hit the target—Cagayan Point on Mindanao—right on the nose, a near-miracle of seamanship.

After General MacArthur congratulated the PT boaters and shook each man's hand, Bulkeley walked up to him and asked, "Sir, what are my orders?"

MacArthur pondered the question momentarily, then replied: "You will conduct offensive operations against the Empire of Japan in waters north of Mindanao."

John Bulkeley remembered: "In essence, I, a lowly lieutenant, had been appointed commander of the United States fleet in the Philippines. We had lost one boat on the way and I arrived with only three. A thought struck me: 'That's a hell of a lot of water for my three-boat fleet to cover!' "[4]

Douglas MacArthur and his entourage were met on Mindanao by a pair of B-17 Flying Fortresses. The refugees from Corregidor landed at an airstrip fifty miles from Darwin in northern Australia. There, the general was jolted by the most shocking news of his military career: The "army" that he thought he was to lead back to the Philippines to rescue the Battling Bastards of Bataan did not exist. Counting Australians, there were only thirty-two thousand Allied troops in the entire land, and nearly all of them were noncombat types. There were fewer than one hundred serviceable airplanes, most of them obsolete and timeworn, and not a single tank was to be found in all of Australia.

For one of the few times in his life, Douglas MacArthur was near despair. When given this scandalous news by his aide, Richard Sutherland, MacArthur's jaw clenched and he whispered hoarsely: "God have mercy on the United States."[5]

Traveling southward by rail from near Darwin to Melbourne, a trek of a thousand miles, MacArthur paced the aisle of the decrepit, dusty, stifling hot, and fly-infested wooden coach. His mounting fury was directed at "Washington," meaning President Roosevelt, who, the general was convinced, had betrayed him by implying in a series of messages that significant help was on the way to the Philippines. This had led MacArthur, in turn, to unknowingly deceive his besieged men on Bataan. Never again would the general trust Roosevelt.[6]

Arriving at a Melbourne station, a cheering crowd of thousands buoyed the general's spirits. In a wrinkled, ribbonless, khaki bush jacket, he told the throng: "The President of the United States ordered me to break through [the blockade]—for the purpose, as I understand it, of organizing an offensive against Japan, a primary objective of which is the relief of the Philippines. I came through . . . and *I shall return*!"[7]

On embattled Bataan, many junior officers and enlisted men were angry and scornful about MacArthur's departure. Bitter poems about "Dugout Doug" were passed around, one of which read in part:

> In Australia's fresh clime,
> he took out the time
> to send us a message of cheer.
> My heart, he began,
> Goes out to Bataan,
> But the rest of me's
> Staying right here.

Senior officers and noncommissioned officers with long service in the army realized that MacArthur would be far more valuable to the war effort by taking command of an army in Australia and leading it back to the Philippines than he would be as a dead general on Bataan or Corregidor. They knew, too, that cowardice was not a factor: The general had proven countless times on the battlefields of France in World War I and on Luzon and Corregidor that he was brave to the point of foolhardiness.

Douglas MacArthur's new title would be Supreme Commander, Southwest Pacific, while Jonathan Wainwright became leader of a new unit designation, United States Forces in the Philippines (USFIP). He held no illusions that there would be a miraculous rescue of his trapped men on Bataan, nor that they could hold on much longer. He had inherited a Legion of the Living Dead.

Eighty percent of his soldiers, sailors, and airmen were physically unfit for combat. They were racked by malnutrition, scurvy, dengue fever, beriberi, avitamioisis, malaria, and dysentery. Because many were too weak to climb from foxholes, they lived in their own excrement.

The Battling Bastards were saturated in sweat, filth, and lice. They were unshaven and their hair was matted. Their uniforms—tattered, torn, and caked with mud and dried blood—draped loosely from their skeletonlike frames, causing once sturdy men to resemble scarecrows. Field hospitals removed shabby uniforms from the wounded and dying, then sent them to the front lines for reissue. Food was almost nonexistent, and the famished men took to gnawing on roots.

The Filipino troops were in equally wretched shape. One-fourth of them had no shoes. None had mosquito nets or pup tents. For helmets, they had hollowed out coconut halves and clamped these improvisations on their heads to deflect shrapnel.

Medical supplies were gone. Minor ailments like a head cold could flatten a soldier and make it impossible for him to get up. As many as fifty Americans and Filipinos a day were found dead in their foxholes, victims of disease and starvation.

Shortly after MacArthur departed for Australia, General Homma apparently was convinced that the Bataan defenders were ripe for surrender. So hundreds of empty beer cans were dropped from airplanes on and behind American-Filipino lines. Much effort had gone into painting the cans red and white, the Japanese colors. Inside each container was a message to Wainwright—a surrender ultimatum—that said, in part:

> Your Excellency:
> We have the honor to address you in accordance with the humanitarian principle of Bushido, the code of the Japanese warrior. You have fought to the best of your ability. What dishonor is there in avoiding needless bloodshed? What disgrace is there in accepting honorable defeat?
> The International Law will be strictly adhered to by the Imperial Japanese forces and Your Excellency and those under your command will be treated accordingly. If a reply is not received by noon, March 22, 1942, we shall consider ourselves at liberty to take any action whatsoever.
>
> *Masaharu Homma*
> *General, Commanding*

Jonathan Wainwright, his face tired and drawn, remarked dryly to aides: "At least the bastards could have sent a few full cans of beer!" He made no reply to the ultimatum.

As the deadly slugfest continued on Bataan, disease, hunger, gunfire, and bombing whittled down American and Filipino companies to platoon size, so the ranks were augmented by air corps pilots and ground crews without planes and by navy men without boats or ships. One of these "instant infantrymen" was Sergeant Bill Begley of the 34th

Pursuit Squadron. Begley remembered: "Three days before being committed to the front line, my comrades and I were issued Springfield rifles from wooden crates marked 'World War I—Condemned.' My rifle had a faulty bolt, which was so loose it flopped each time I handled the weapon. A bandoleer of bullets, that is, a sort of long pouch that was thrown over your shoulder, was issued and I was told, 'Now don't shoot any of these!' I wondered what in the hell I was supposed to do with the bullets if they weren't to be fired."[8]

Michael Gilewitch, a former 31st Infantry Regiment sergeant, recalled how the combat troops had to scrounge to obtain adequate weapons: "My company got hold of some air corps riot guns and shells. These were excellent for shooting Jap snipers, who would climb up into tall trees thick with foliage and take potshots at us. We couldn't see them, so we used these riot guns to spray the upper foliage with three or four rounds and that usually did the job. Just to be sure, we'd blast all other trees in our vicinity with riot-gun shells. Soon, we caused rear area ordnance officers to be stricken with apoplexy. Riot guns were against international law, they declared, and they ordered us to collect and turn in all riot guns. I'm sure the Jap snipers were happy over that."[9]

On the night of April 2, the Bataan killing grounds were ghostly quiet. Unseen by the Americans and Filipinos, fifty thousand fresh, well-fed, heavily armed Japanese soldiers—most of them the reinforcements imported by General Homma—stole noiselessly through the tangled jungle into jump-off positions.

So cocksure was Homma of rapidly crushing Bataan's weakened defenders that an announcement was made that night over Japanese-controlled Radio Manila: "We are starting an all-out offensive to crush the American imperialists . . ."

At ten o'clock the next morning, many of the Americans and Filipinos were silently reciting prayers, for it was Good Friday. Suddenly, the silence was shattered. A few hundred Japanese heavy guns began a thunderous bombardment, the mightiest barrage of the war in the Pacific. It continued for more than six hours. All the while, Japanese warplanes roamed unchallenged, saturating the defenders with hundreds of bombs and clusters of incendiaries. Leaves and vegetation burst into flames, converting the jungle into a roaring inferno. Frenzied Americans and Filipinos, too feeble to struggle out of foxholes, were cremated.

While scattered bands of exhausted Americans and Filipinos fought desperately to stem the Japanese avalanche, U.S. Army Lieutenant Hattie Brantley was working countless hours tending to an increasing flow of wounded men at Hospital Number 1 at Limay, at the southern tip of the peninsula. When Brantley arrived at the hospital in late December 1941, she found, to her dismay, that it consisted of thirty long nipa (palm) structures, all empty and covered with thick dust. Medical supplies in the warehouse were wrapped in 1918 newspapers. Then the nurses were issued new clothing. Brantley received heavy GI shoes and a size forty-two pair of coveralls that draped her slender frame.

That first afternoon of the full-blooded Japanese assault to wipe out the stubborn defenders of Bataan, Hattie Brantley, her face caked with perspiration and dust, her body nearly numbed by fatigue, stood outside a hospital shack and squinted into the sun as a flight of Mitsubishi bombers circled overhead. She felt reasonably safe, however, because white bed sheets with huge red crosses were spread on the ground, plainly marking the hospital.

Then there were weird fluttering noises and, moments later, explosions rocked the ground. A bomb hit the mess hall and the doctors' and nurses' quarters. Cots began to crumble in the wards packed with the ill and the wounded. Helpless patients began screaming.

Above the din, Hattie Brantley heard yet another bomb explode, this one raising a cloud of dust and smoke over a ward that had been set up in an open space and roofed by burlap. More piercing screams. Scores must be dead or dying, she was convinced. She dashed into the orthopedic ward for help. There, panic was on the verge of erupting. Then she saw the chaplain, Father James Cummings, standing on a desk. Above the roar of the airplanes, the explosions and the shrieks of the wounded, his voice could be heard: "Our Father, who art in heaven . . ." Calmed by the prayers, the patients quieted.

One hundred and one American and Filipino patients—and two wounded Japanese soldiers—had been killed in the bombing.

After darkness fell, Japanese tanks clanked forward. Hard on the monsters' heels were swarms of infantrymen, brandishing bayonet-tipped rifles and shouting, "Banzai! banzai! ban-zaaiii!"

One of those hit by the assault was twenty-year-old Lieutenant William Galos, an army engineer who had been hurled into the front lines to fight as a rifleman.

Galos remembered: "Our lines broke. It was a mess. Killed men piled up for others to run over. It was so dark you couldn't see in front of your face. You bumped into trees, slashing your exposed skin with razor-sharp cogan grass. Brush was like barbed wire, ripping your clothes and skin. Men shouted in the jungle trying to find their outfits. Sometimes we were in front of the Japanese, sometimes in back of them.

"The stench of bodies, decomposed in the sun from days before, was very strong, as though the corpse wanted you to remember him. It was a stink that was hard to forget. I wondered if my body would be bloated and stinking to remind somebody later."[10]

Bedraggled Americans and Filipinos were pouring southward ahead of the onrushing Japanese. Mass confusion reigned. Mariveles, the town at the tip of the peninsula, was a madhouse. Large mobs of disorganized, confused, and exhausted troops milled about listlessly. They had the haunted stare of men who had just escaped from the jaws of death, unable to comprehend that a monumental debacle was taking place.

Now Mother Nature decided to perpetrate a cruel act on the beleaguered men of Bataan. She touched off a moderate to severe earthquake on the southern portion of the peninsula. The ground shook and trembled for perhaps three minutes.

"It's the end of the world!" one hysterical GI screamed.

Meanwhile on Corregidor, General Wainwright had been getting only scraps of confusing and conflicting information. By radio, he managed to get in touch with Major General Edward King, Jr., to whom Wainwright had turned over command of all forces on Bataan.

"Launch a counterattack," the Philippines' commander ordered.

An able and courageous officer, the sixty-year-old red-haired King realized that Wainwright had no true conception of the chaotic situation on Bataan. So he called in his chief of staff, Brigadier General Arnold Funk, and his operations officers, Colonel James Collier. For three hours, the men mulled over every possible action to reverse the battlefield picture. All agreed that the Rising Sun flag would be flying over Mariveles within twenty-four hours.

Finally, King said grimly, "I have decided to surrender Bataan."

It was the only decision that a realistic commander could make. Yet it stunned the three officers: King, Funk, and Collier broke out in tears.[11]

With the fall of Bataan a certainty, Lieutenant Earleen Allen Francis, a thirty-one-year-old army nurse of Jacksonville, Illinois, and nine other nurses were put aboard an amphibian PBY airplane bound for Australia. As the winged craft lifted off, Lieutenant Francis looked back at burning Bataan with deep emotions. Somewhere in that tangled jungle, Lieutenant Colonel Garnet P. Francis, her husband of only a few months, had been fighting the Japanese. Was he dead? Alive? Wounded?

During a brief lull in the fighting, Colonel Francis and Lieutenant Allen had been married on Bataan by a chaplain in an old house near the front lines. He read the ceremony by flashlight. Music was furnished by a GI playing a harmonica. Just as the newlyweds were entering their honeymoon cottage, a native hut spruced up for the occasion, Japanese shells began exploding in the locale. That broke up the honeymoon. The bride returned to her hospital duties, the groom rushed back to the front. They had not seen one another since.

Now, winging toward Australia with the other nurses, Earleen Francis's PBY crash-landed on Mindanao, where it was going to refuel. Unbeknownst to her, Colonel Francis was taken prisoner on Bataan at the same time that her airplane went down.[12]

In less than an hour after the surrender of Bataan, a column of Japanese tanks, trailing a plume of thick dust, clanked to a halt in front of the U.S. Army Hospital Number 2, where some forty-two hundred American and Filipino soldiers were being treated for serious illnesses and battle wounds. Located on the southern slope of Mount Mariveles, Hospital Number 2 was only a half mile from Hospital Number 1, which had been heavily bombed two days earlier.

Standing in the doorway of the shack that served as his headquarters, Colonel James W. Duckworth of San Francisco, California, the hospital commandant, looked on impassively as the enemy tanks aimed their guns at each of his buildings. Moments later, a Japanese lieutenant colonel scrambled out of the hatch of a tank and walked briskly toward Duckworth.

"I understand you have wounded Japanese here," the Japanese officer declared, speaking flawless, unaccented English.

"That is true," Duckworth replied. "Forty-two of them."

At his request, the Japanese officer was escorted to the ward where his countrymen were being treated. After speaking to them, he returned to Duckworth.

"Our men tell me they have been given good treatment," the Japanese said. "We are going to bivouac on your grounds and will make certain that you and your staff are not harmed until you can be sent to a prisoner-of-war camp."

Perhaps emboldened by the solicitous tone of the Japanese colonel, Jim Duckworth broached the subject of the bombing of Hospital Number 1 that left more than a hundred American and Filipinos dead.

"Oh, that was a mistake," the Japanese responded airily.

"Mistake, hell!" Duckworth snapped. "There were at least five large red crosses on the ground!"

Only a few hours before the conquerors stormed into Mariveles, hundreds of American and Filipino soldiers, sailors, and airmen had set out for the haven of Corregidor in anything that would float. In desperation, many pushed off clinging to boards. Some men lashed bamboo poles together to form makeshift rafts. Hundreds, all weak from disease and hunger, tried to swim the two and a half miles in shark-infested waters. On Bataan's shore, Japanese riflemen vied to see which one could pick off the most bobbing heads.

Untold scores of Americans and Filipinos drowned or were killed, but perhaps two thousand of the refugees reached Corregidor. Hardly any of them were combat soldiers, so they would be of negligible value in defending the Rock from invasion. Rather, they were merely many more mouths to feed from a dwindling food supply.

In Malinta Tunnel, the Voice of Freedom broadcast a final salute to the Battling Bastards:

> The Philippine-American troops on the war-ravaged and bloodstained peninsula have laid down their arms. With heads bloody but unbowed, they have yielded to the superior force and numbers of the enemy . . . The world will long remember the epic struggle that Filipino and American soldiers put up in the jungle fastnesses. Besieged on land and blockaded by sea, cut off from all sources of help in the Philippines and in America, these intrepid fighters have done all that human endurance could bear.[13]

On April 9, an aide slipped into Douglas MacArthur's office at his new headquarters in Melbourne and saw the general seated at his desk, tightly gripping the message informing him that the final bloody curtain had been drawn on Bataan. MacArthur's eyes were brimming with tears—tears of sorrow for his men on Bataan, tears of anger over the Washington politicians he was convinced had betrayed him.[14]

4

Sixty Miles
of Atrocities

While General Masaharu Homma had been gearing up for a final all-out offensive to overrun Bataan in late March 1942, Colonel Toshimitsu Takatsu and a bevy of aides and armed soldiers pulled up in front of Camp O'Donnell, sixty miles north of Bataan in Tarlac Province. As logistics and administration chief for Homma, Takatsu's task was to locate confinement facilities for the expected twenty-five thousand American and Filipino soldiers that remained on Bataan.

O'Donnell, which Douglas MacArthur had ordered to be hastily built to train Filipino recruits, consisted of largely ramshackle barracks, bahai (shacks), and a barely adequate hospital building. After inspecting O'Donnell for an hour, Colonel Takatsu climbed back into the dusty Dodge sedan that had been captured from the Americans and, along with his entourage in other cars and trucks, headed for Cabanatuan in Nueva Ecija Province, forty miles to the northeast.

By Philippine standards, Cabanatuan was a fairly large town and a bustling one. Its main commercial activities centered in the marketplace where vendors tried to eke out a living by selling their goods in scores of shabby stalls. Passing through the marketplace, Takatsu's convoy headed northeast for four and a half miles to another abandoned Philippine army training camp near the barrio of Pangatian. Since hardly anyone on Luzon had ever heard of Pangatian, the former military post was customarily referred to as Cabanatuan camp after the larger city. Again, Colonel Takatsu strode through the dust on his inspection tour, then departed, satisfied that O'Donnell and Cabanatuan camp would be able to easily hold the expected twenty-five thousand prisoners.

With the two POW enclosures selected, Major General Yoshikata Kawane, the Fourteenth Army's chief of transportation who was responsible for moving the anticipated captives, rapidly drew up a plan. Prisoners were to march northward, lugging their own food rations, along Bataan's east coast road to the border of Pampanga Province. There, the captives would climb into two hundred waiting trucks and be driven on northward to the railhead at San Fernando, where trains would carry them on to the town of Capas, eight miles from O'Donnell. From Capas, it would be a routine foot march to the prison camp.

General Kawane's precisely formulated prisoner evacuation plan was about the only thing that went right in the days that would follow. Almost at once, chaos developed in Japanese leadership ranks. Within hours of the capitulation of Jonathan Wainwright's Legion of the Living Dead, Colonel Yoshi Imai, a field commander on Bataan, received a radio message: "Kill all prisoners!"

Imai could not believe his ears, so he instructed his radioman to ask for the message again. Back it came: "Kill all prisoners!" The colonel promptly fired back his own message, declaring that he would not carry out the order unless it came in writing over General Homma's signature. As Imai had suspected, this order had not originated from the commander of the Fourteenth Army, but rather from zealous associates.

Only a few days earlier, a clique of hard-line officers from General Hideki Tojo's headquarters in Tokyo had visited the battlefront on Luzon and had preached a sermon of hatred to junior officers. The Pacific war was a racist clash, Tojo's emissaries had declared, stressing that the "white devils" must be wiped out. Many Japanese officers bought this logic, resulting in the kill-all-prisoners edict.

With the mass surrender on Bataan, the Japanese were confronted by a major logistics problem that had not been envisioned: Instead of capturing twenty-five thousand Americans and Filipinos, some seventy-two thousand of them were prisoners. This situation meant that General Kawane's painstakingly conceived POW evacuation plan already had gone awry.

As soon as word spread through American and Filipino ranks that the war was over on Bataan, twenty-three-year-old Lieutenant Samuel C. Grashio of Spokane, Washington, a pilot with the U.S. 21st Pursuit Squadron, and four comrades climbed into a dusty staff car in southern

Bataan and headed hell-bent for Mariveles. They had heard a report that a submarine might be waiting there to take the pilots off in order for them to continue the war from a base farther south. Reaching the chaos of Mariveles shortly after dawn on April 10, Grashio learned that the submarine was just another myth.

Unsure of their destination, Grashio and the others drove away and soon met a Japanese tank and staff car. The Americans halted, climbed out, threw up their hands, and waved white handkerchiefs. A Filipino turncoat with the Japanese contingent began hollering that the Americans were violating surrender instructions because they were wearing sidearms. Then a Japanese officer got out of the staff car, approached six-foot two-inch Lieutenant William "Ed" Dyess, and, without a word, began mercilessly beating him.

Samuel Grashio recalled how he first learned of the unpredictable and mercurial sides of the Japanese soldier: "After beating up Ed Dyess, our squadron commander, the Jap stole two rings of mine, a crash bracelet, and a pen-and-pencil set. Then he motioned for us to get back into our car and resume driving. As we proceeded, this same Jap caught up with us, pulled his car close to our vehicle, stuck his head through the open window, smiling broadly, and threw my jewelry back into the car. Minutes later, some other Japs halted us and stole my possessions all over again."[1]

Not far away, an American major refused to give up his wedding ring to a pair of Japanese soldiers. They beat him to the ground, then stole his ring by cutting off his finger with a bolo knife.[2]

Nearby, a Japanese officer pilfered a ring from Sergeant Mario G. "Motts" Tonelli of Skokie, Illinois, who had been a star fullback at Notre Dame and later played professional football with the Chicago Tigers (which would become the Chicago Cardinals) in the late 1930s. Inscribed on the ring were the words "Notre Dame."

"What year did you graduate?" the Japanese officer asked in perfect English.

"Nineteen thirty-five."

"I graduated from the University of Southern California that same year," the Japanese replied. As both men well knew, Notre Dame and Southern California long had had a fierce football rivalry. Without a word, the enemy officer handed back the ring to Tonelli.

Even before what would become known as the Bataan Death

March began, Japanese soldiers were running amok with hardly any effort by superiors to control their excesses and brutalities. In one instance, twenty-year-old Leon D. Beck of the U.S. 31st Infantry Regiment and about twelve members of his antitank company were herded into a bare field near Mariveles. They were ordered to put all their personal possessions on the ground and strip down to their shorts. Then the captors stole everything they wanted, including used toothbrushes. Lieutenant Colonel Peter D. Calyer, executive officer of the 31st Infantry, foiled the captors, however. He tied his West Point class ring around his penis and testicles and let it hang down his shorts. This innovative hiding place resulted in his keeping the sentimental piece of jewelry.[3]

A short distance away, Japanese soldiers, wielding long bamboo sticks, burst into the U.S. Army's Hospital Number 2, where there were six thousand ill and wounded men, mainly Filipinos. The captors drove the feeble patients from their cots, out the front gate, and along the road, where they were ordered to march. Many of the captives, some with only one leg, were on makeshift crutches. As they staggered along, bandages unwound, and the guards ripped off casts, causing massive hemorrhages. Large numbers of Filipinos keeled over and died in the ditches before they had gone a mile.

At Hospital Number 1, which the Japanese had bombed a few days earlier and now was charred ruins, sick and wounded Americans, clad in hospital pajamas, were wandering around in a daze. They were rounded up and prodded by rifle butts and bamboo sticks into a passing line of marching POWs. They tried to walk, but most fell by the wayside where they were left to their agonies and eventual death.

Seemingly endless columns of American and Filipino soldiers, along with U.S. sailors, airmen, and some forty-five marines—perhaps as many as seventy thousand altogether—were shambling northward along the east coast road on the first leg of a nightmarish sixty-five-mile trek to Camp O'Donnell. Already sapped by dysentery, beriberi, malaria, and starvation, the prisoners were scorched by the boiling sun. Almost constantly, they gasped for breath because of the exertion and the swirling clouds of choking dust. Eyes became glazed and vision blurry.

Major Richard M. Gordon, one of the marchers, recalled: "No design or plan for the exodus to prison camp ever materialized. Each sunrise the Japanese, shouting and shooting, would assemble anyone they could to make up marching groups of about one hundred men. As a result, individuals often found themselves among perfect strangers, even if they were fellow Americans. Consequently, a dog-eat-dog, every-man-for-himself attitude soon prevailed. Few helped one another.

"During the march, volunteers were sought to carry a stretcher containing an American colonel wounded in both legs and unable to walk. Four men offered to help. After hours of carrying the colonel in a blazing sun with no stops and no water, they asked for relief from other marchers. No one offered to pick up the stretcher. Soon, the original four bearers put down the man and continued on their own. The colonel was last seen by the side of the road, begging to be carried by anyone."[4]

On the first day of the trek, Lieutenant William Galos, who had been assistant superintendent of a gold mine in Baguio when bombs started falling and volunteered for the army, was in a group halted and told to form alongside the road. A Japanese officer demanded that all engineers take a step forward, and Galos and eight or nine others identified themselves and were led off. Galos thought they were going to be murdered. Instead, the engineers were subjected to a brutal interrogation.

William Galos recalled: "The Japs thought there was a water line running from Bataan to Corregidor, and part of their plan, we learned much later, was to starve the garrison on the Rock and deny them water. So the Japs wanted us engineers to shut off the water. As it turned out, there was no such water line, but no amount of denials would convince the Japs.

"They kicked us and kicked us with their hobnailed boots so that by the time we got out of there, my shins were like raw hamburger. The blood stuck to my pants and dried, so by the time we reached Camp O'Donnell, I had a hard time taking the pants off."[5]

Meanwhile, in the marching column, Sergeant Leon Wolf of the 14th Ordnance saw a Japanese lieutenant dash up to an American captain who was a tank commander. Wolf held his breath: It appeared that the captain had somehow offended the Japanese officer. To the sergeant's astonishment, the Japanese, beaming broadly, hugged the American—they had been classmates at the University of California at

Los Angeles (UCLA). After chatting for a few minutes, much as they no doubt had done on campus in better times, each man moved off in opposite directions.[6]

As the prisoners hobbled on, the Japanese ferocity grew. Captives were clubbed brutally for halting briefly to drink muddy water from the footprints of *carabao* (water buffalo). Staff Sergeant Michael Gilewitch of Frackville, Pennsylvania, and the 31st Infantry Regiment, was among a group halted by the guards for yet another looting search.

Michael Gilewitch recalled: "Anything Jap found on a prisoner resulted in death or torture for the victim. On the man next to me, they found a cigarette lighter with 'Made in Japan' stamped into the metal. That was considered to be taken from a dead Jap soldier. My comrade was forced to hold his arms outstretched and shoulder high. One Jap pointed his rifle at the helpless American while another Jap drew his samurai sword and lopped off the man's arm. Blood gushed from the stump. It was something of a game. The idea was to see if the sword-wielding baboon could hack off the second arm before the pitiful wretch fell to the ground, where he died in excruciating agony."[7]

Neither age nor rank was respected. For the first time in history, several American generals were trudging toward a prison camp. Pedaling ahead of them on a bicycle was a Japanese private who seemed to take delight in halting regularly and shouting at the American generals to hurry up.

At the whim of the captors, gray-haired chaplains were beaten, clubbed, and bayoneted along with teenage infantrymen. The guards were no longer content with merely mauling stragglers or pricking them in the buttocks with bayonets. Now the thrusts were intended to kill.

Michael Gilewitch remembered: "The first killing of a helpless victim I saw made me sick and it was all I could do to keep from rushing to his aid—which would have gotten me bayoneted or clubbed to death. To make more 'sport' of it, the Japs rolled the weak victim onto his back and bayoneted him once in the stomach. They didn't want him to die too quick. This made the poor wretch scream and groan in agony in the blazing sun. The Japs laughed with glee and mimicked the writhings and contortions of the dying man."[8]

Major Emil P. Reed, a thin, bespectacled native of Dallas, had to leap to one side numerous times to keep from getting hit by Japanese vehicles, which were moving southward toward Bataan along the same narrow road. Reed, whose father was a prominent Oklahoma City physician, was regimental surgeon of the 26th Cavalry. He recalled: "Many times I saw the Jap drivers try to run over our men as we marched along. Other Japs made great sport of leaning out of passing trucks and trying to knock off the prisoners' hats with rifle butts or long poles. When their aim was poor, the soldier on the receiving end was usually knocked senseless, his face a bloody pulp."[9]

While the POWs were trudging along, General Albert Jones, who had led a corps on Bataan, was brought back to near Mariveles. Soon he was ushered into the office of General Susumu Moiroka, his old foe who led the 16th Division. There were several minutes of conversation. Then Moiroka asked: "Who's going to win the war, General Jones?"

"We are, of course,"

Moiroka smiled and replied, "Well, *you* won't."

"Not me, maybe," the American replied. "But I have four boys at home who will!"[10]

As the long trail of atrocities continued, the roadside became littered with the corpses of Americans and Filipinos.

Michael Gilewitch remembered: "Some bodies were swollen to monstrous size by the heat, and they turned a blackish hue. Eyeballs popped out and hung by their cords. Many cadavers were pecked open by big birds (crows, I believe), and while feasting on the corpses, the birds were fighting with one another. Other bodies were covered with buzzing hordes of fat green flies and by swarms of maggots. Along one stretch, I counted thirty-two headless corpses, and since all of them had turned black from the boiling sun, the only way I could guess their nationalities was that the taller ones were probably Americans, the shorter ones, Filipinos."[11]

William Begley, known to friends as Wild Bill, who had fought as an infantryman during the final days of Bataan when his 34th Pursuit Squadron was hurled into the front lines, recalled: "Some guys reached the end of their endurance and committed suicide. An American chaplain, who was delirious, jumped off a cliff. An officer rushed to help and a Jap bayoneted him."[12]

Like many others in the march of death, Begley doubted if he could survive, so he hid in the underbrush when the guards' backs were turned. Stumbling and crawling, he reached a turnip patch and holed up there for two days. Famished, he devoured raw turnips and drank great gulps of muddy, polluted water in a ditch. Although half crazed, he staggered inland, where he was intercepted by a group of Japanese who proceeded to "beat the hell out of me." A few hours later, he was back in the marching columns.

Repeated horrors were witnessed by Bill Begley: "There was a little Filipino boy of about ten, ragged, skinny, and his ribs sticking out from hunger. As we passed, he gave the V for Victory sign. That infuriated the Japs. They ran a bayonet through the little boy. His crying mother tried to rush to his side as he lay bleeding to death, and the Japs bayoneted her, too. Both corpses were left to rot alongside the road."[13]

Men began having hallucinations, conjuring up images of glistening springs of bubbling water at each side of the road. As the Legion of the Living Dead staggered and stumbled along, its members suffered from excruciating thirst, yet their guards refused to give them water.

Leon Beck recalled: "They'd deliberately halt us in front of the artesian wells along the road, and let us get close enough to see the water. But they kept us from drinking. Anyone who made a dash for the well risked being shot or bayoneted."[14]

During the sixteen-mile trek between Orani and Lubao, a great number of prisoners reached the limit of their endurance at about the same time: They collapsed in twos and threes. Skulking along behind contingents of marchers were the "buzzard squads," groups of Japanese whose job it was to murder those who had fallen. Members of these clean-up bands would stoop over each huddled form, then shoot the victim in the head, bayonet him, or kill him with rifle butts.

One marcher, Major Alvin C. Poweleit, was a medical officer in a tank unit, and he had once possessed an imposing physique—thick chest, broad shoulders, large biceps. He had worked his way through medical school as a professional boxer and had a knockout punch in each fist. Now, after long weeks of starvation on Bataan, he was a gaunt scarecrow. Only Poweleit's flaming spirit remained intact. Jovial and placid by nature, Major Poweleit suddenly was infuriated when he spotted a limping American straggler being beaten viciously by a Japanese guard's rifle butt.

Poweleit recalled: "I uncorked a right and caught the Jap flush on the jaw. It lifted him off his feet. He dropped to the ground without a sound. I dove for him and twisted his head until I could feel the cervical vertebrae grate and slide over each other. Then I tossed the body into a bamboo thicket, picked up the battered GI, and moved on up the road. It was my good fortune that there were no other Japs on the scene at that time."[15]

News of the Death March had reached Lubao, a town of thirty thousand, by Bamboo Telegraph, the label Americans had given to the rapid spreading of information by Filipino couriers to outlying locales. When the shambling column struggled through the residential area, sympathetic Filipinos stood on the sidewalks, tossing scraps of bread, rice cookies, pieces of chocolate, and lumps of sugar—even cigarettes— into the POW ranks. The Japanese guards went berserk, slugging, beating, and lunging wildly with bayonets against the Good Samaritans. Then the captors turned their rage on the Americans.

There were occasional American minor triumphs. One Japanese, while conducting a "security search," grabbed a bottle of sleeping pills that Captain Sidney Stewart had been given in a hospital.

"*Yorishi* (are they all right)?" he asked.

"Yes, indeed," Stewart replied, "Very good!"

The Japanese gulped down two handfuls. A few minutes later, he went into convulsions and died in agony. His puzzled Japanese comrades were at a loss to understand what horrible affliction he had been stricken with.[16]

Leon Beck recalled: "I begged my buddies to escape with me because misery wants company. You need someone to help you. But what I kept hearing from them was, 'Bullshit, the American army will be back here within six months and retake us, and we'll be free and gone. We can do six months in prison standing on our heads.' It was just stupid bullheadedness, but I wasn't going to be a prisoner any longer."[17]

When Beck and his group reached Lubao, they were penned up in a stifling old warehouse. With escape in mind, Beck tried to crawl out through a sea of legs and was caught. The Japanese beat him unconscious. Later, his first sergeant saw that they had placed Beck in a row of American corpses that were being carried across the road by the Japanese and hurled into a mass grave.

Beck's guardian angel was hovering overhead. Just before it was his turn to be picked up and buried alive, he regained consciousness and crawled away. Since groups of POWs were kept in Lubao for two or three days, Beck regained sufficient strength to rejoin the marching column.[18]

On the final leg from Lubao to San Fernando, there was virtually no shade and the road's asphalt, churned by tanks and heavy trucks, had been melted into goo by the broiling sun. To thousands of men with no shoes, and countless others whose shoes were ripped to shreds, it was much like walking endlessly over hot coals.

During this stretch, a few thousand Filipino captives managed to escape, and the Japanese guards did nothing to stop them. For Americans, escape was a high-risk venture. Few, if any, knew the countryside, hardly any spoke Tagalog, and their height and white skin made them conspicuous.

Leon Beck remembered making his move: "My buddies said they'd watch the Japs for me, and then they said 'hit it.' I just rolled off the road and got under the first clump of small bushes. I just laid there until this group of prisoners marched away from me. Then I got up and said, 'Dear Lord, don't let my feet stick in the mud,' and I started pickin' 'em up and layin' 'em down. Later, exhausted, I reached a shack with a lot of lumber in it, and I wriggled in under the wood and stayed there for two days—a free man."[19]

Not far away, air corps Sergeant Ray C. Hunt, Jr., of St. Louis, Missouri, also decided to make a break, even if it meant his death. Disease and starvation had plummeted his weight from one hundred and sixty pounds to an estimated one hundred pounds. As his column of POWs crossed a bridge, Hunt dashed into a deep ditch and hid in some foliage. He remembered: "I heard a POW say, 'Don't look! Do you want him to get shot?' The Japs didn't see me, and soon the column was out of sight. I began crawling along the ditch and came upon two Americans, face down and scared to death. One was a captain and the other a corporal. Before too long, we spotted two Filipino farmers and they led us, at the risk of their lives, to a small shack from where we could watch other marchers go past. Some Filipinos brought us water, rice, and sugar. A few days later, they loaded us into a cart, covered us with hay, and a carabao pulled us up into the Zambales Mountains."[20]

Finally, the captives hobbled into San Fernando, the headquarters of General Homma's Fourteenth Army. There the men were given small amounts of water and balls of rice, then they were penned up in the

Blue Moon Dance Hall, old factories, school buildings, open fields, and a cock-fighting arena.

During the next few days, the POWs, in groups of about five hundred, were marched to the railroad station and ordered to climb into small boxcars, which were only thirty-three feet long and seven feet wide. There was room for perhaps forty POWs, but the guards shoehorned 115 men into each boxcar.

Among those crammed into the cars was Private Robert J. Body, a native of Sarnia, Canada, who had served as a machine gunner with the 31st Infantry and had enlisted in the U.S. Army at age sixteen and turned seventeen on Bataan.

Body remembered: "Both boxcar doors were slammed shut. We had to stand in the ovenlike interior, for there was no room to move. There were only cracks for fresh air. The stink from sweaty, unwashed bodies, along with festered sores that covered most of the captives, created an almost unbearable stench.

"As the train moved along the countryside, we felt we were suffocating. Many did. They remained upright in death, for we were packed in like sardines and they couldn't fall.

"There were screams of 'Let me out!' and loud weeping and moaning. Gripped by dysentery and malaria, many men defecated on themselves and others nearby. Others urinated where they stood and some vomited on those next to them."[21]

After what seemed to the POWs like the passing of centuries—the rail trip had lasted about five hours—the train chugged into Capos and halted. Boxcar doors were thrown open, and the captives spilled out, gulping in huge amounts of fresh air. Formed into straggly columns, the captives marched for eight miles in the torrid heat, not having had food or water in two days. They limped through the gate of a collection of rough-hewn buildings and nipa huts. This was their new home—Camp O'Donnell.

Even while the men of Bataan were marching northward, an article splashed across the front page of the Japanese-controlled, English language *Manila Tribune* on Sunday, April 19, declared:

If in spite of the humane treatment the Japanese are giving these prisoners, they are too weak to reach their destination, there is only to blame the generals of the American forces for surrendering when many of their men were already terribly weakened by lack of food and by disease.

In the days ahead, thousands of the Legion of the Living Dead poured through the gates at O'Donnell. Of the seventy-thousand Americans and Filipinos who had started the march, some fifty-four thousand reached the POW camp. An estimated ten thousand had died of hunger, disease, or brutality, or were murdered along the way.[22]

5

"Situation Fast Becoming Desperate"

General Masaharu Homma had no inclination to gloat over crushing the stubborn defenders of Bataan. Tokyo had given him sixty days to conquer the Philippines, but one hundred and twelve days had passed—and Corregidor was holding out defiantly despite the hopeless predicament of its trapped garrison. In recent days, Field Marshal Count Hisaichi Terauchi, commander of the Southern Army and Douglas MacArthur's opposite number, visited the Philippines and demanded that Corregidor be seized—rapidly. Homma, Terauchi implied, was jeopardizing the entire Japanese timetable for conquest in the Pacific.[1]

Long known as the "Gibraltar of the Far East," Corregidor is three and a half miles long and one and a half miles wide at its widest point. It is shaped like a tadpole, with its large head pointing west toward the South China Sea. The tadpole's eastern (tail) section is sandy, wooded, and little more than 150 feet above Manila Bay at its highest elevation. At the center of the island, Malinta Hill rises abruptly to a height of 350 feet, and into this promontory was burrowed the 1,200-foot-long Malinta Tunnel.

At his headquarters in San Fernando on April 8, 1942, General Homma gave the order to deluge Corregidor with a colossal tonnage of shells and bombs. If that bombardment did not bring surrender, then Japanese troops would storm ashore.

Late that afternoon, Japanese artillery on Bataan unleashed a torrent of shells, pounding the Rock from Topside to the tip of the tail. The roar of the big guns echoed for miles across Manila Bay. After the

43

barrage lifted, wave after wave of Mitsubishi bombers dropped hundreds of tons of explosives. Except for the Rock's obsolete pom-poms (antiaircraft guns) that blasted away at the intruders, Corregidor could do nothing to halt the onslaught.

In the week ahead, Japanese bombers were over the Rock almost constantly during daylight. Casualties on Corregidor would have been much heavier had it not been for Colonel Stuart "Stu" Wood, Wainwright's chief intelligence officer, who had learned the Japanese language while serving as a military attaché in Tokyo a few years earlier. Electronically monitoring Japanese radio traffic at Luzon airports, the colonel knew when bombers were taking off to pound Corregidor, and he could even hear Japanese air controllers cursing and yelling, "Get those damned carabao off the runway!" Although the flights to Corregidor required only a few minutes, Wood's electronic snooping gave the defenders time to take cover.

Members of the U.S. 4th Marine Regiment also put great faith in the advance warnings given by Private First Class Soochow, who had an uncanny instinct for sensing when bombers were on the way to hit Corregidor. Soochow was a small mongrel dog that had been adopted as a mascot by the 4th Marines in Shanghai, China, in 1937. He had become a legend in his own time, riding around teeming Shanghai in rickshaws, and eating sirloin steaks and guzzling beer with the other marines in his own tailor-made uniform.

When the 4th Marines shipped out to the Philippines shortly after war broke out, Private Soochow was smuggled aboard. On reaching the Rock, his two-legged pals soon discovered that when Japanese warplanes were approaching, the mongrel would start yapping and dancing around in circles. Then, when the bombings were about to begin, Soochow hit the foxholes with his buddies.[2] There were eleven thousand American and Filipino military people on the Rock, but only the fifteen hundred men of Colonel Samuel L. Howard's 4th Marines were trained for ground combat and they would be the backbone of the beach defenses. Except for some aging World War I veterans of Belleau Wood fame, and a handful of men who had fought rebels in Nicaragua in the 1930s, none of the marines had tasted combat.

Augmenting Howard's force was a motley collection of twenty-five hundred beached sailors, grounded airmen, Filipino aviation cadets, supply soldiers, and a handful of retired Filipino mess boys (as they were known) of the U.S. Navy who had been recalled to active duty when war broke out. Most of these men had rifles, but many had never fired one. The main antitank weapons were Molotov cocktails.

In far-off Australia, an anguished Douglas MacArthur held no illusions about the ultimate fate of Corregidor. On April 13, he radioed General Marshall in Washington: "The life of this fortress is definitely limited and its destruction certain unless sea communications can be restored. . . . You must be prepared for the fall of Corregidor."[3]

MacArthur also made it clear to Wainwright that no troops, planes, food, ammunition, or weapons were on the way: "I cannot tell you how anxious I am to bring you relief," MacArthur radioed. "My resources are practically negligible. I have represented to the War Department that the only way in which you can be reinforced is by use of the Pacific Fleet. I have had no reply."[4]

Three weeks into the siege of Corregidor, Colonel Stu Wood, the Japanese language expert, reminded Jonathan Wainwright that Wednesday, April 29, was the birthday of Emperor Hirohito, the diminutive, mild-mannered father of six, who most Japanese revered as a god.

"You can count on the Japs here to give us a rousing celebration," Wood declared.

By now, General Homma had 116 big guns arrayed along the southern tip of Bataan and near Cavite seven miles across Manila Bay to the east. The largest of these weapons were 240-millimeter monsters that fired thousand-pound shells. When one of these huge projectiles was making its downward flight, its terrific noise sounded to the Americans like a freight train racing through a tunnel.

Masaharu Homma's "celebration" of Hirohito's birthday began just after daybreak when eighty-three Mitsubishis unloaded hundreds of bombs. Malinta Tunnel was a particular target, presumably on the premise that Wainwright and his staff would be cowed into surrendering.

Twenty-four hours later, a 240-millimeter shell penetrated an underground magazine where sixteen hundred artillery powder charges, each weighing sixty pounds, were stored. A gargantuan explosion seemed to lift Corregidor out of the water as though a huge, supernatural force had grabbed the island by its tail and was madly shaking it. Soldiers near the blast were tossed high into the air like rag dolls. A score or more were killed instantly from the concussion without a mark on their bodies. Hundreds of yards from the blast, men in the open were knocked down, stunned, but otherwise unhurt. Chunks of stone and debris landed as far as two miles away. A sixty-ton slab of concrete was hurled a thousand yards. Ten-ton mortar barrels were flung into the air as though they were Ping-Pong balls. The explosion seemed to intensify the psychosis of fear and doom that gripped many on Corregidor.

On May 2, Wainwright cabled George Marshall in Washington: "Corregidor subjected to continuous shellfire, the heaviest concentration yet experienced. During one five-hour period, twelve 240-millimeter shells fell per minute for a total of thirty-five hundred hits in only one (gun-battery) area of Topside."[5]

That day, two PBYs managed to elude the air and sea blockade and landed on Manila Bay south of Corregidor. After a medicine shipment and a few mechanical fuses were unloaded, thirty nurses, three civilian women, and seventeen military officers scrambled aboard. Soon the flying boats skimmed across the bay and lifted off for Australia.

On Lake Lanao, Mindanao, the PBYs landed for refueling. Staff Sergeant Jerry L. Coty of the U.S. 19th Bomb Group and a few comrades were assigned the task of pumping gasoline into the aircrafts' thirsty tanks. A short time later one PBY, while preparing for takeoff, hit a submerged object, ripping a hole in one of its pontoons. Crew and passengers climbed out of the damaged aircraft and rapid repairs were made. However, the plane's load would have to be lightened because of the damage.

Jerry Coty recalled: "Much to our disgust, several of the male officers, including a few West Pointers, pulled rank and bumped several lady nurses. These men got flown to safety and the nurses were left behind."[6]

Early in the afternoon of May 3, the twenty-fifth day of Homma's all-out effort to blow Corregidor off the map, Americans on Topside, peering through high-powered telescopes, detected an alarming development: The Japanese had collected scores of motorized landing barges along the Bataan shore. Clearly, an amphibious assault against the Rock would be launched soon. At the same time, Wainwright penned in his report: "Corregidor experienced its 287th bombing (today) since the war began."[7]

Then Wainwright cabled MacArthur: "*Situation here fast becoming desperate*. The island is practically denuded of vegetation and trees, leaving no cover, and all structures are leveled to the ground. . . . Terrain pockmarked like craters in the moon. . . . Casualties since April 9 (from bombings and shellings) approximately six hundred."[8]

Although Malinta Hill and the thick concrete roof and walls provided immunity from bombs and shells for Jonathan Wainwright and his staff and communications technicians, the tunnel was a subterranean Hades. Along with the military people, the excavation was crammed with two thousand Philippine civilians, who were too terrified to go outside, so they defecated and urinated on the floors and walls. The heat and humidity were stifling. Unwashed bodies gave off a horrendous odor. Huge black flies and cockroaches were everywhere. When bombs or shells crashed above the tunnel, the lights flickered, then went out, plunging the tomb into inky blackness. Unless one had a watch, he did not know if it were night or day at any given time.

In the tunnel's hospital lateral, wounded men were tenderly cared for by American nurses, who came to be known as the "Angels of Corregidor." These young women moved from cot to cot, consoling the dying, calming the wounded, administering injections, bandaging, giving water to those who were paralyzed, feeding those with no arms. Wearing GI coveralls or khaki shirts and slacks or skirts, the Angels often had to cover their faces and those of the patients with improvised masks of wet gauze as shields against the thick dust generated by crashing bombs and shells above them on Malinta Hill.

In charge of the operating room was Lieutenant Eunice F. Young, a native of New York. She had joined the Army Nurse Corps in 1939, and, after two years at Letterman Army Hospital in San Francisco, volunteered for overseas duty, arriving in Manila in August 1941. When the Japanese struck at Corregidor, Lieutenant Young and other nurses organized the operating room in Malinta Tunnel and staffed it twenty-four hours a day as the violence swirled around and on the Rock.

Young remembered: "We never seemed to be without wounded men waiting for surgery. We put in eighteen-hour workdays, seven days per week."[9]

Early in the morning of May 4, Corregidor shook under a monstrous deluge of bombs and shells, possibly the heaviest cascade of explosives on such a small area that history had known to that time. Within a few hours, an estimated sixteen thousand shells streaked onto the Rock, and then the Mitsubishis winged overhead, unopposed as usual, to drop their lethal cargos.

After enduring an almost ceaseless avalanche of explosives for more than three weeks, untold numbers of men on Corregidor reached the limits of their endurance. While bombs were raining down, a few GIs leaped from foxholes and scrambled around in circles, babbling incoherently. Others stood stonelike in the open, staring sightlessly. A few shot themselves deliberately in the foot or hand, hoping to be taken to the temporary safety of the Malinta Tunnel hospital. Some put the muzzles of rifles or pistols to their heads and squeezed the trigger, forever ending their dreadful ordeal.

On the dark night of May 5, a spooky silence blanketed the Rock. Along the shoreline, the tense men of Colonel Sam Howard's beach-defense force peered seaward, trying vainly to split the blackness with their eyes. Just past 9:00 P.M., alarming news reached the waterfront: The electronic "ears" on the Rock had picked up the sound of barges starting their engines on the Bataan shore.

Minutes later, the eerie hush was fractured. Japanese guns across the bay began to roar, and countless shells screamed into Corregidor. For two hours, the barrage was so heavy that the island shook and quivered as though an earthquake were in progress. Thick clouds of black smoke covered the Rock, and the pungent odor of cordite fumes filled nostrils. Howard's beach defenders clung to the bottoms of their foxholes, foreheads and palms sweaty, stomachs knotted, hearts pounding furiously, mouths dry. Many were praying, some to themselves, others out loud. Abruptly, as though shut off by a switch, the bombardment lifted. Silence returned. It was 11:10 P.M.

A few minutes later, a squad under Sergeant John F. Hamich, dug in near Cavalry Point on the north shore of Corregidor's curving tail, discerned the shadowy contours of many barges approaching.

One of Hamich's men called out: "Here come the bastards!"

Nearby, a GI searchlight flashed a long finger of illumination across the black seascape, bathing in its glare the faces of hundreds of Japanese soldiers packed into the landing craft. Hamich's squad, along with Americans to either side, sent a blistering fusillade of machine-gun and rifle fire into the oncoming barges.

Above the ear-splitting crescendo, the Americans could hear the screams of Japanese soldiers as bullets tore into fragile flesh and bone.

Perhaps half of the first wave was killed, wounded, or drowned. However, a large number of the invaders, led by Colonel Gempachi Sato, scrambled ashore and headed westward along Corregidor's tail toward Malinta Tunnel.

Sharp, confused clashes erupted in the darkness.

Despite the stubborn resistance put up by Corregidor's marines, soldiers, sailors, airmen, and Filipinos, the invaders kept pouring reinforcements ashore. In a lateral of Malinta Tunnel, Corporal Irving Strobing, an army radio operator, was broadcasting to Honolulu station WTJ a play-by-play account of the death throes of Corregidor:

> We are waiting for God only knows what. Lots of heavy fighting . . . Shells were dropping all night faster than hell. Too much for guys to take. Corregidor used to be a nice place but it's haunted now.[10]

Just past 10:00 A.M., General Wainwright received the crushing news that he had been expecting but dreaded to hear: Japanese tanks were ashore. His men had neither tanks nor antitank guns. The death knell had sounded for doomed Corregidor.

Gripped by anguish and bitterness, the Old Cavalryman remained silent for several minutes. Never in history had an American general been confronted by his predicament. Months earlier, Washington had sacrificed the Philippine garrison on the altar of global strategy. Nearly all of the Rock's big guns and mortars had been blasted into twisted metal. His men were outnumbered, emotionally spent, ill-equipped, and lacking in firepower. Homma, on the other hand, could bring in fresh, fully armed reinforcements, and his 240-millimeter howitzers and warplanes could pound the American-held portion of the Rock at will. If Wainwright attempted a last-ditch stand, thousands of Americans and Filipinos would be slaughtered. Was there any military logic in continuing the grossly uneven struggle when the Japanese were going to overrun the entire island within forty-eight hours?

His gaunt face contorted by distress, Jonathan Wainwright turned to an aide, Brigadier General Lewis C. Bebee, and said, "Lou, I hope I am doing the right thing."

Then the Philippines commander called in Colonel Theodore "Tiger" Teague, his communications officer. Calmly Wainwright said, "Tell the Japanese we'll cease firing at noon."

Then he sent a final message to Douglas MacArthur in Australia:

> We have done our full duty to you and for our country. We are sad but unashamed. I have fought for you to the best of my ability from Lingayen Gulf to Corregidor, always hoping that (reinforcements) were on the way. Goodbye, General, my regards to you and our comrades in Australia. May God strengthen your arm to insure ultimate success of the cause for which we have fought side by side.[11]

Next, Wainwright, by the flickering light of a candle, scribbled a message to be sent to President Roosevelt:

> There is a limit to human endurance, and that limit has long since been passed. Without prospect of relief I feel it is my duty to my country and to my gallant troops to end this useless effusion of blood and human sacrifices. . . . With profound regret and with continued pride in my gallant troops, I go to meet the Japanese commander. Goodbye, Mr. President.[12]

Promptly at noon, Corregidor's guns fell silent. Radio equipment was destroyed, small arms smashed, codes burned. More than two million pesos in Philippine paper money was slashed into confetti with scissors. It was the lot of Colonel Paul D. Bunker, a West Point classmate of Douglas MacArthur, to carry out the ignominious task of hauling down the American flag and replacing it with a white flag of surrender.

Bunker, who twice had been named an all-American football player while at the Point, had been strolling from battery to battery during the past week, building up the crews' morale and inspecting the guns, ignoring the bombs and shells that were exploding around him. On these hazardous jaunts, the sixty-year-old colonel wore an old campaign hat, carried a walking stick, and was followed by his little mongrel dog, Colin.

Now, shortly before noon, Bunker tucked a white sheet under one arm and walked toward the ninety-foot flagpole beside the parade ground on Topside. Colin trotted along at his heels. Solemnly, the colonel lowered the Stars and Stripes and ran up the white flag. An aide noticed that tears trickled down the tough old soldier's ruddy cheeks.[13]

In Malinta Tunnel, Corporal Irving Strobing was radioing a final account to the Honolulu radio station:

The jig is up. Everyone bawling like a baby. They are piling dead and wounded in the tunnel. Now I know how a mouse feels caught in a trap and waiting for men to come along and finish him up.[14]

Tiger Teague established radio contact with Japanese headquarters on Bataan and arranged for Wainwright to meet with Masaharu Homma to surrender Corregidor.

Even in the midst of the debacle, GI humor had not vanished. Scrawled on the wall of a damaged building were the words: "Corregidor Still Stands! Under New Management."

Two days after Corregidor fell, Sergeant Thomas Gage of the 34th Pursuit Squadron and several other POWs were taken on a work detail from Camp O'Donnell to the town of Tarlac to haul timber for rebuilding a bridge. There, the Americans were told by the Japanese that they would not have to work that day because it had been declared a holiday to celebrate the capture of Corregidor.

Thomas Gage recalled: "The Japs kept us in a schoolyard surrounded by a chain link fence. We were told that there was going to be a parade in Tarlac and that we could see it. Here came the parade. In front was a Jap officer on a white horse, saber, boots, and all. Behind him was a Filipino band (which had been ordered to take part). Just as the Jap on the horse got in front of where we were watching, the band broke into "Stars and Stripes Forever." We went nuts, jumping and yelling. The Jap officer thought our demonstration was for him and he was beaming. Of course, he had never heard the "Stars and Stripes Forever." The little Filipino bass drummer was looking at us, grinning from ear to ear."[15]

6

"You Are Enemies of Japan!"

Seventy miles north of doomed Corregidor in late April 1942, Camp O'Donnell was bursting at the seams with thousands of survivors of the Bataan March of Death. Each new group of POWs that hobbled into the vast enclosure was greeted by the camp commandant, Captain Yoshio Tsuneyoshi, who was fifty-one years old, far overage for his modest rank. Most of his classmates at the Imperial Military Academy were now colonels and generals.

Tsuneyoshi had been rushed to take charge of O'Donnell only a week before the first POWs arrived, an assignment most Japanese army officers considered to be highly undesirable. Always the scenario was the same. Bareheaded, exhausted contingents of new prisoners were forced to stand in the blazing sun for two hours. Finally, a stubby figure clad in sun helmet, baggy trousers, and wrinkled shirt bustled into sight and climbed onto a large box: Yoshio Tsuneyoshi.

Promptly dubbed Baggy Pants by the captives, Tsuneyoshi had his spiel down pat: America's long exploitation of the people of the Pacific had ended; Japan was now taking control and establishing the Greater East Asia Co-Prosperity Sphere; American soldiers were soft and cowardly; President Roosevelt and General MacArthur would be hanged as war criminals when Emperor Hirohito ruled the United States from the White House in Washington.

As his tirade droned on, Tsuneyoshi became angry. His face was flushed and contorted. His voice rose to a shout. "You are enemies of the Japanese Empire, and we will fight you for a hundred years!" the commandant bellowed. "You are not honorable prisoners of war, you are captives, and you will be treated as captives. You must obey all orders or you will be severely punished. Forget that you have names, forget that you have parents, wives, and children. Your loved ones no longer care and have forgotten about you—just as Roosevelt and your generals have forgotten you. Anyone trying to escape will be shot."

Seemingly drained of energy, his uniform soaked with perspiration, Baggy Pants scrambled from his pulpit and strode back inside his headquarters building. The POWs were forced to remain standing on the scorched ground for another hour.[1]

If ever the Black Angel of Death had a cauldron of victims ready for him, it was Camp O'Donnell. The mile-square compound was located on a treeless plain and surrounded by a thick expanse of tall cogan grass. Compressed into the enclosure were some forty-five thousand Filipinos and nine thousand Americans. About one hundred and fifteen POWs were squeezed into sixty-foot-long barracks that had been intended to hold forty Filipino army recruits before hostilities broke out. A prisoner's bed was often the earthen floor.

Without mosquito bars and quinine to fight malaria, thousands of POWs were stricken with raging fever, racking chills, and chattering teeth. Bodies broken in the Death March, many POWs deprived of adequate food, shelter, and clothing, overwhelmed by isolation, and with no hope of early recapture, lost the will to live. They turned their gaunt faces to the wall, refused rice and water, and soon died.

Those who were critically ill were hauled by other POWs on improvised stretchers to the camp hospital, which was staffed by American doctors, who also were racked by disease and the ravages of hunger. The sick patients were deposited in whatever space was available in the overcrowded facility. Often they had to be put down in the mud under the elevated floor.

Most patients seemed to die during the starlit hours. Each morning the doctors wearily disentangled the dead from the living. This gruesome task was difficult. The pulses of the barely living were so feeble and respirations so shallow that it required careful diagnoses to determine which ones were dead.

One of the American physicians assigned to the hospital, Major Emil Reed, was known to the POWs as "Doctor Rigor Mortis." Since the Japanese demanded that a specified number of prisoners report each day for work details, Reed, so the POWs declared grimly, had to send nearly everyone to perform manual labor unless rigor mortis had set in.

Thirty-five-year-old Major Reed, who had practiced medicine in Brownsville, Texas, before being called to active duty in 1940, was surgeon for the 26th Cavalry when captured on Bataan. He had rapidly exhausted the tiny amount of medicine he had been able to slip into camp in field medical kits.

Emil Reed recalled his deep frustration: "It was most discouraging to stand weakly and listen to the pitiful complaints of the men and then have no medicine to give them. Pleas to the Japanese for medicine were ignored. The Japs were evidently determined to do nothing for the prisoners. On one occasion, Jap officers made a formal inspection (of the hospital) and were evidently disturbed by the large number of ill men. So they 'solved' that situation by ordering us doctors not to allow so many cases (of illness) to occur."[2]

During the first two weeks at O'Donnell, the Americans and Filipinos were fed little food, partly because of the lack of cooking facilities. Then the prisoners used shovels made from mudguards of abandoned cars and dug clay from nearby rice paddies to construct stoves large enough to hold iron containers about four feet in diameter. On these primitive ovens rice and water steamed, stirred by bamboo poles, to create the staple dish *lugoa* (rice gruel). Twice a day, POWs stood in the broiling sun or in torrential rains for many hours to get their small portion of the tasteless lugoa.

There was one outdoor spigot for about one thousand prisoners. Long, straggly lines of prisoners waited impassively, canteen cups in hand, for their modest amount of water. Their drawn faces showed no anger over the ordeal. There was no banter, no loud voices, no cursing. Silently they stood, portraits of resignation.

Camp O'Donnell rapidly became a gargantuan sewer. Plumbing was nonexistent. Latrines were open trenches buzzing with billions of large, black flies. Clouds of these insects were everywhere. They crawled into the mouths and open eyes of men in comas or those too weak to shoo them away. They swarmed on open arm and leg ulcers.

Death soon became the norm. Most POWs were skin and bone, had pipestem legs and arms, and there was no flesh on buttocks. Bare chests and faces were tanned nut-brown, scorched by the sun hanging high in the cloudless heavens. Lungs loaded with tissue fluid fell easy prey to pneumonia. Hearts weakened by prolonged starvation suddenly dilated and stopped beating. Men standing shakily in chow lines toppled over dead. Some straddling latrines slithered down into fecal graves, too weak to extricate themselves. Others hobbled back from long work details, lay down on their filth-covered pallets, and died. Men were carried to the burial grounds, but a twitching eyelid or a quivering finger signaled that they were not yet dead, so the stretcher bearers brought them back for a few more hours of life.

Despite the macabre situation, the POWs showed glimpses of grim humor. They called those who died "lucky stiffs."

Early on, the American and Filipino prisoners had been segregated into different areas of the complex. After six weeks, a hundred Americans were succumbing each day. In the Filipino section, they were dying at the rate of two to three hundred every twenty-four hours. There were so many corpses that the Japanese designated a large building as the morgue and labeled it the 00 Ward or Double Zero Ward. Cadavers were hurled haphazardly into the structure until bodies were piled three feet deep.

As soon as a man died, POWs had to strip the tattered clothes off the corpse, wash the garments, and turn them over to the Japanese guards, who sold the rags to Filipino civilians living in the region and pocketed the money.

Japanese soldiers continued to inflict brutalities upon the POWs, regardless of age or rank. General Edward King, who had surrendered the Bataan force, was badly beaten and received two black eyes for merely pleading for food, water, and medicine for the prisoners. An air corps colonel was pounded with thick bamboo sticks and fists because he refused to disclose to the Japanese details of America's supersecret Norden bombsight, about which he knew nothing.

Japanese bayonets were thrust into arms and legs to inflict excruciating pain. Bones were broken with clubs. Hoses were inserted in mouths or rectums and the water turned on, often causing bellies to burst. POWs were staked out naked in the torrid sun for as long as five days without food or water, a torture that usually resulted in the victim screaming to be killed.

While the Legion of the Living Dead was undergoing the torments of the damned at Camp O'Donnell, seven thousand Americans and five thousand Filipinos on Japanese-held Corregidor were awakened by shouting guards in Malinta Tunnel on the second night after the Rock's surrender.

Prodded by bayonets, the prisoners were taken outside and ordered to start marching. All of the wounded who could walk were forced to join the trek. Just after dawn, the POWs reached Kindley Field, the small airstrip on the eastern tail, where they were congregated on a patch of ground barely one hundred yards square.

For seven days, the prisoners were kept there, unprotected from the pot-boiler sun. No food was provided. The men had to line up for twelve hours to get a canteen of water from the lone spigot. They fainted by the score. Each morning, a hundred or more unconscious POWs were hauled away to unknown fates. A few hundred American and Filipinos were taken from the site each day to toil for twelve hours clearing the Rock of debris, salvaging damaged and discarded weapons, collecting shells and ammunition, and tidying up the premises for the new Japanese proprietors.[3]

Late on the afternoon of May 11, nearly all of the POWs were marched to the Corregidor docks and stuffed into the airless, putrid holds of three old freighters, some four thousand men to a ship. That night the vessels crossed the bay and anchored just off Dewey Boulevard in Manila. At noon, during the most severe heat of the day, the hatches were finally opened, the prisoners climbed out and were loaded into barges for the four-hundred-yard trip to the shore, where large numbers of silent Manilans had gathered.

Although the barges easily could have run onto the beach, they stopped a hundred yards short and the POWs were ordered to jump into the water, which came up to their necks. After wading ashore, the disheveled captives were formed into columns, four men abreast. All were drenched, hungry, and thirsty. Many weaker ones could hardly stand. Among the POWs was Captain Austin F. Shofner of the 4th Marines, who had been a star lineman on the University of Tennessee football team a few years earlier. Because of his rugged build and passion for physical fitness, the twenty-five-year-old marine withstood the grueling ordeal in the POW enclosure on Corregidor better than had most others.

Shofner recalled: "The Japs began marching us through Manila. Although the destination, Old Bilibid prison, was two miles away, the route would cover five miles so the most Philippine civilians possible could see us being humbled and humiliated. It didn't work. Many of the Manilans lining the streets wept openly, and the others, at great personal risk, silently held up two fingers—the V for Victory symbol.

"Although it was hot as hell and most of the POWs were in feeble condition, we were allowed no rest stops. Gravel and sand had collected in our wet shoes, and painful blisters soon developed, causing even young men to hobble."[4]

The shuffling column passed the former residence of the Philippines high commissioner, now the main headquarters of General Masaharu Homma. In downtown Manila, the POWs trudged past a large building, where, unbeknownst to them, an agonized General Jonathan Wainwright was watching from a window on the fourth floor where he was being held by the Japanese.

After nearly five hours of marching, the captives, most of them dazed, blurry-eyed, and near delirium from the scorching sun and exertion, were within two blocks of Old Bilibid. Up near the front of the column, a frail, older American lieutenant colonel collapsed and lay unconscious on the hot pavement, disrupting the line of march. Japanese guards shouted for two American prisoners to pick up the senseless officer and drag him along. The lieutenant colonel was dead when the column entered the gate of Old Bilibid, the notorious jail where Filipino murderers, rapists, and violent criminals were held by the government. Many of these dregs of humanity had been freed by the Japanese to make room for the captives.

Most of the Corregidor men were kept in Old Bilibid for two or three days. Then they were marched to a Manila railroad station where freight trains were waiting. More than 115 POWs were packed into each boxcar. With the human cargo sealed inside, the trains began chugging northward. After jolting along for seemingly endless hours, the trains screeched to a halt. Boxcar doors were thrown open, and the numb prisoners piled out to inhale large gulps of fresh air. A sign on the dinky railroad station read "Cabanatuan."

Formed into uneven columns, the POWs began marching; ten hours and some five miles later, they reached their new "home"—godforsaken Cabanatuan prison camp. It was late May 1942.

Years earlier, the Cabanatuan campsite had been a U.S. Department of Agriculture station, and after that, a training center for Philippine army draftees. Circling the camp was an eight-foot-high barbed-wire fence, and tall wooden towers were spaced along it at even intervals. Usually, four Japanese, manning machine guns and armed with rifles, stood watch at each tower.

New groups of Corregidor POWs were met by the camp commandant, forty-six-year-old Lieutenant Colonel Shigeji Mori, who had been a classmate at the Imperial Military Academy of the chief warlord, General Hideki Tojo. Rumor spread among the Americans that Mori had operated a bicycle shop in Manila for several years before being called to Tokyo and active army duty.

Colonel Mori told the incoming POWs that the war was over for them, that they must cooperate with the guards, and that anyone trying to escape would be shot to death or beheaded.

Had their predicament not been so dreadful, the Americans would have regarded Shigeji Mori as a comical figure. As it was, this short, squat officer had life or death control over them. Bedecked with medals the Americans quipped had been awarded to him for slaughtering helpless prisoners, Mori wore a Hitler-like mustache, which was the POWs' target for countless obscene jokes. He strutted around the compound, always escorted by a covey of flunkies, in a gait that reminded the Americans of the famed Hollywood movie comedian, Charlie Chaplin. His samurai sword, carried in a scabbard at his side, was so long that it dragged in the dust.

Colonel Mori had a large garden planted near his living quarters and a miniature Mount Fuji built in its center. Most nights, it was rumored, Mori stumbled around the garden clad in a black kimono, roaring drunk.[5]

Meanwhile at Camp O'Donnell, forty miles southwest of Cabanatuan, American and Filipino POWs from Bataan were continuing to die by the hundreds each week. Then, in early June, word flashed by grapevine through the camp that the American POWs were going to be moved to another prison.

"Guess we aren't dying fast enough to satisfy the Japs," twenty-five-year-old Sergeant William "Bill" Delich, who had been in charge of a searchlight squad on Corregidor, told comrades. For once, the rumor proved to be true.

Two days later, thousands of Americans began stumbling out through the gates of O'Donnell and marching back along the same road that they had taken from Capas two months earlier. Destination unknown. This time, the guards seemed to want the prisoners to finish the long, hot, tortuous trek.

Michael Gilewitch remembered: "We could not believe what was taking place. There was no prodding with bayonets, shouting, or urging a faster pace. Even leaning on each other did not cause a rumble. However, there were deaths. Some of those being carried in blanket slings succumbed, and other walkers simply let out loud moans and fell down dead. At the Capas railroad station, they again crammed us into those stifling little boxcars where we could hardly move, much less sit down. Again the slamming of the doors, the stink, the thirst, the hunger, the ovenlike heat, the struggle to breathe.

"I was one of those who passed out, although I was wedged in and remained upright, for I didn't remember the train even moving. The next thing I felt was the jolt on hitting the ground, where I had been shoved by air-starved men in the boxcar when the doors were opened. When I partially regained my senses, I saw a sign on the railroad station that said 'Cabanatuan.'"[6]

After a punishing march of eight miles, the Bataan POWs joined the Corregidor captives behind barbed-wire in the Cabanatuan hellhole. Before the month of June was over, the compound held from seven thousand to twelve thousand prisoners, but the population fluctuated as POWs deemed able to work were regularly shipped to slave labor camps in Formosa, Manchuria, Japan, and elsewhere in the Philippines. In direct violation of the Geneva Convention, the POWs sent elsewhere were forced to support Japan's war effort—toiling in the coal mines, building airfields, unloading ships, and laboring in factories that produced weapons.

In the meantime, the O'Donnell death camp had turned into a ghost camp. All of the surviving members of the Legion of the Living Dead from Bataan had been shipped to Cabanatuan camp, and the Japanese had released some forty-five thousand Filipino POWs (six thousand more had been imprisoned after the fall of Corregidor).

Camp O'Donnell had been one of history's largest death factories. Since April 11, 1942, a total of 30,172 captives had died of disease, brutality, and hunger, or had been murdered by the Japanese. These figures were recorded by an American prisoner who had been assigned to work in the commandant's office. The dead included 1,602 American soldiers, 49 U.S. sailors, 3,182 Philippine Scouts, 24,492 men of the Philippine army, and 847 civilians who had worked for the U.S. armed forces.[7]

Guards at Cabanatuan were as brutal as they had been at O'Donnell and on the Death March. Atrocities were a daily occurrence.

William Delich recalled: "We hadn't been at Cabanatuan long when four men tried to escape and were recaptured. We were all assembled and had to watch our fellow Americans. They were tied to posts and the Japs beat the hell out of them with fists and clubs. Then the four men were forced to dig their own graves—we still had to watch—and a firing squad of eight Japs cut them down as they stood in their graves."[8]

A few days later, large posters were put up throughout the camp. Printed in English were large letters that said: "Ten prisoners will be shot to death for every one that escapes." The proclamation was signed by Colonel Shigeji Mori, the camp commandant.

William Delich remembered: "Those in camp were grouped in tens. This brought our ten closer than ever. All were constantly checking, counting, and keeping together as best we could in case one of us decided to make a break for it. Sleep was difficult. We were concerned that one of our ten might try to slip through the barbed-wire fence at night. It was agreed that if one man wanted to flee, the other nine of us would try also. At least that way we would have a fighting chance, instead of merely being hauled out, beaten viciously, and then shot."[9]

The harsh edict from Colonel Mori failed to halt escape attempts by those who could no longer endure the barbarities. A week later, the POWs were rousted from their barracks by shouting guards and hustled into a large field. There had been an escape attempt by two Americans, who were dragged out of a small building. Their faces had been beaten to bloody pulps, and their hands were tied behind their backs. Then eighteen other POWs, escorted by Japanese soldiers brandishing rifles with fixed bayonets, were lined up along a fence, together with the recaptured escapees. These were the two groups of ten.

Among the watching Americans, a hushed voice was heard: "My God, they're going to kill them all!"

A volley of shots rang out. The twenty GIs crumbled to the ground in pools of their own blood. They were left lying where they had fallen for two days.

Cabanatuan prisoners were classified by the Japanese into light duty or heavy duty categories. Light duty men, those especially enfeebled, cut tall cogan grass to feed the herd of carabao that wallowed in a man-made lake near the gate. Heavy duty POWs toiled outside the camp on a three-hundred-acre spread known as Farmer Jones's Garden. Farmer Jones—no one knew his first name—was a retired U.S. army soldier who had farmed on Luzon for many years. Those on work details had to go barefooted as a hedge against escapes.

Perhaps three thousand POWs were hoeing, planting, and hauling water in buckets to grow corn, squash, beans, rice, and other vegetables. Farmer Jones was held responsible for growing this produce despite the fact that there had been an undercrust of lava ash deposited in the region thousands of years earlier when Mount Aryat exploded.

William Delich remembered vividly those seemingly endless days in the broiling sun: "We were slaves. They hustled us off to the farm early each morning. That's when the trouble began. The Japs were always shouting '*speedo, speedo*' at us. If you didn't walk fast enough, a guard would crack you with a bamboo club. On the farm, we worked on our knees, planting and picking. The way you found out the rules was when you broke one. You were supposed to bow to the guards. I couldn't get it into my bull head to do that, so I was always getting the hell beat out of me.

"Our Jap farm boss was a real mean bastard we called Air Raid— when he descended on you with his club, you felt as though you had been bombed. Air Raid ordered us to plant four seeds in each hill. I deliberately put three in, and he caught me and began screaming. Then Air Raid bombed me good."[10]

All the produce went to Japanese army units in the region. Work in the field was harsh, hot, debilitating. Sick men had to toil under the burning sun for twelve hours each day. There were no plows or tractors. The skeletal figures scrubbed around in the dirt with their bare hands, sharp sticks, and hoes they fashioned out of scraps of metal. A hungry prisoner did not dare to return to camp at sundown with a vegetable hidden in his ragged clothes. If detected, he would receive a severe beating, even a beheading, depending upon the whim of an individual guard at that particular moment.

POW morale plunged when word circulated that the Japanese had a five-year plan for expanding Farmer Jones's Garden, meaning the

Americans could expect to remain at Cabanatuan at least that long—provided they survived.

Grudgingly perhaps, the Japanese commandant gave lip service to the Geneva Convention by paying POW enlisted men and junior officers the equivalent of ten cents per day and officers above the rank of major double that amount. This money was supposed to be in return for their labor, but it was only a fraction of the sum called for by international law. Most higher ranking officers pooled their daily twenty cents with the ten cents of the enlisted men and junior officers so that all could share equally in buying small amounts of the onions, rice flour, or duck eggs that might be available on occasion in the camp commissary, a ramshackle room supervised by Lieutenant Colonel Harold K. Johnston, an infantry officer.[11]

Occasional work details away from Cabanatuan camp provided a respite from laboring on the farm or cutting wood. One of these details resulted in two thousand Americans being carefully selected as extras in a Japanese version of a Hollywood-type movie extravaganza. This propaganda film, which would be shown in Dai Nippon and elsewhere in the conquered Far East, was titled *Down with the Stars and Stripes*. The invincible Japanese Imperial Army were the knights on white horses and the GIs were the bad guys.

These two thousand POWs, handed ancient Enfield rifles (without bullets) and clad in American uniforms taken earlier from dead and wounded on Bataan and Corregidor, were ordered by an excitable Japanese film director to act their roles convincingly. The implied threat should they try to do otherwise was not lost on the hapless POWs. The central theme of the crude production was the mass surrender of cowardly American soldiers who had been pillaging and raping in the Philippines until the commonwealth was "saved" by the noble soldiers of the Imperial Japanese Army.

Scavenging for food was a constant among the famished prisoners. A coveted work detail was one going into Cabanatuan town, four and a half miles away, with a Japanese escort to clean out a rice-storage warehouse.

Charles Di Maio, who had been a U.S. Navy petty officer, recalled: "There were always a few busted sacks, so when the Japs weren't looking we stuffed handfuls of rice in our pockets. There were lots of mice scurrying around. We would grab them, strangle them, hide them in our G-strings, and smuggle them into camp. We bribed a Jap guard—the bastards were always on the take—to get us some cooking oil, and we boiled the mice with the rice, making a mice stew. It was quite a delicacy; the small rodents were very tender."[12]

One day, the POWs were told that a Japanese three-star general was going to inspect the camp, and they were warned sternly that no captive was to speak to the visitor unless spoken to by him first. Marine Lieutenant Colonel Howard Beecher, a square-jawed, two-fisted fighting man, was designated to accompany the general. Beecher had no intention of remaining silent.

"We have many sick here," Beecher declared.

Speaking precise English, the Japanese general replied, "Why?"

Beecher pointed to a mess shack nearby, where a skimpy noonday meal of white rice and thin carrot soup was being served.

"There is why," the American replied. "We are all starving to death!"

"That will be enough!" the general barked. "Your men are not starving. What they need is more exercise."

By July 1942, seven months after the Japanese armed forces struck in the Pacific, they had conquered the Philippines, Singapore, Hong Kong, the Dutch East Indies, Malaya, Borneo, the Bismarck Islands, Siam, Sumatra, the Gilberts, the Celebes, Timor, Wake, Guam, most of the Solomons, and half of New Guinea. Japanese bombers had pounded the key Australian port of Darwin, and citizens of Brisbane, Melbourne, and Sydney feared an imminent invasion. The Japanese Empire now radiated for five thousand miles from Tokyo in nearly every direction, and owlish Emperor Hirohito reigned over one-seventh of the globe.

Banzai!

In Washington, gloom contended with chaos. Generals George Marshall and Henry Arnold, along with Admiral Ernest J. King, the new navy chief, were astonished by the unexpected power, speed, and skill of the Japanese blitz. The brass and gold braid reached a shocking conclusion: With full mobilization of manpower and resources, and at a frightful cost in American casualties, it would require at least ten years to reconquer the Pacific and prepare for an invasion of the Jap-

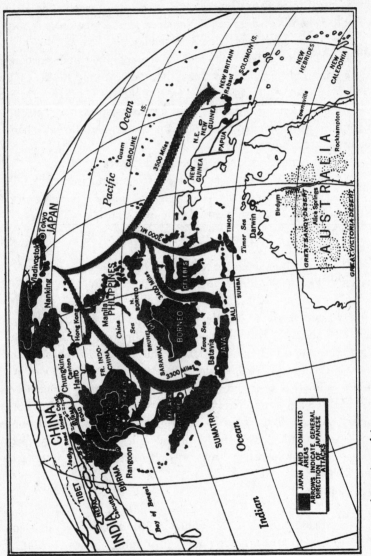

Japan and Dominated Areas

anese home islands. With luck, the bloodbath in the Pacific could conclude successfully by 1954.

When two partially trained U.S. divisions reached Australia in
June 1942, filling in what had been a paper force, General Douglas
MacArthur vowed to take the offensive. On July 20, he moved his headquarters fifteen hundred miles closer to the Philippines at Port
Moresby, New Guinea. He would be hacking his way back on a shoestring. Washington, which months earlier had set a Hitler-first strategy,
would provide MacArthur with only 12 percent of America's military
manpower and accoutrements of war.

Despite these meager resources, the general launched what he
called a "hit-'em-where-they-ain't" campaign of speed and surprise,
aimed at leapfrogging up the thirteen-hundred-mile spine of primitive
New Guinea, bypassing Japanese strongholds and leaving them to
starve. Always, Douglas MacArthur's thoughts were on the Philippines,
where he planned to liberate American prisoners, avenge Bataan and
Corregidor, and restore tarnished American prestige in the Pacific.[13]

7

Miss U and Her Underground

Frightened chickens scurried off the weedy trackbed as an ancient, wheezing locomotive pulling three passenger cars jerked to a halt next to the decrepit railroad station in Cabanatuan town. Stepping down from one car was petite Naomi Flores, a black-haired Filipina who had operated a beauty shop in Manila. Times were hard, so she closed down her business, sold her equipment, and decided to eke out a living in Cabanatuan as a roasted-peanut vendor. It was August 1942.

Clutching a threadbare valise in which she kept her few belongings, Naomi felt her heart pound furiously, for her true purpose in coming to Cabanatuan was to reconnoiter the town and the POW camp for a new underground network based in Manila. Code-named Looter, the twenty-three-year-old beauty had been warned to steer clear of the notorious turncoat, Godofredo Monsod, who had been appointed by the Japanese as chief of their puppet Philippine Bureau of Constabulary in Cabanatuan.

Struggling to appear casual, Naomi began walking toward the marketplace in the center of town when, suddenly, she felt a white-hot surge of fear. Strolling directly toward her was Chief Monsod. Naomi was convinced that he would arrest her, after which the Japanese would torture and then behead her. Silently, she murmured the Lord's Prayer. Then came a flash of exultation: Monsod walked on past as if she hadn't existed.

Naomi had no way of knowing that Monsod, far from being a Philippine traitor, was pro-American and hated the Japanese occupiers. He had been a major in General MacArthur's army, was captured on Bataan, and survived a long stretch in Camp O'Donnell before being released. He had accepted his present job in order to deftly pry secret information from his Japanese masters and pass it on to guerillas in the nearby mountains.[1]

Monsod had filled his constabulary with Filipino junior officers who had fought on Bataan and also were secretly pro-American. His top assistant, Mario Garcia, had been a lieutenant in the 88th Field Artillery, Philippine Scouts, and had survived the Death March and O'Donnell. Monsod's principal courier, who sneaked his messages to the outlying guerillas, was Juanito Quitives, who had been a junior officer in the Philippine Scouts. In the daytime, Quitives went through the motions of being a Cabanatuan constable; at night, he was the leader of a guerilla force that conducted hit-and-run raids against Japanese outposts.[2]

In this strange and dangerous town, Naomi Flores, a gentle woman, felt isolated and frightened. But she banished dark thoughts of her fate should her true role be discovered, and walked into the countryside in the direction of the POW camp. Only a half mile from the gate of the enclosure, she knocked on the door of a small wooden house badly in need of repair. Before leaving Manila, Looter had been told that the two women living there had husbands in the POW camp.

Answering the summons at their door, the two Filipinas invited Naomi inside, where she quickly established her true identity. Eager to strike a blow against the Japanese, the two women agreed that Looter could live in their house indefinitely. The Filipinas became valuable cogs in the underground machinery; they could mosey around the camp gate while reconnoitering the situation without attracting the suspicions of the Japanese, who knew that their husbands were prisoners there.

Founder and driving force behind the Miss U underground network was thirty-four-year-old, blonde Margaret Utinsky. A native of St. Louis, Missouri, Margaret, then a widow with a small son, had come to the Philippines for a six-month visit in 1934. She loved the beauty and the serenity of the islands and decided to remain. Shortly after arriving, Margaret was introduced to a handsome engineer, John "Jack" Utinsky, who worked for the U.S. government on Corregidor. After a whirlwind courtship, the couple was married. For several years, they had enjoyed the good life, one filled with fun, gaiety, and the easy comradeship with friends in Manila and on Corregidor.

Suddenly, this idyllic mode was shattered. America was at war. Jack Utinsky, who held a reserve commission as a captain in the U.S. Army, was promptly called to active duty and ordered to report to Bataan. After the victorious Japanese poured into Manila in late December 1941, Margaret hid in her apartment for several months, always dreading a heavy knock on the door that would mean the Japanese had discovered an American was holed up there. One night her world crashed: A Filipina neighbor slipped into Margaret's apartment and told her that Bataan had fallen.

Margaret was determined to get to Bataan and see if she could learn of the whereabouts of Jack. But how could an American woman, conspicuous by her white complexion, travel through Japanese-controlled territory without being caught and jailed? There was but one solution: Margaret Utinsky would vanish. In her place would be born a woman of another nationality and background.

Jack Utinsky had been a native of Virginia, but his ancestors had emigrated to the United States from the Baltics generations earlier. Margaret found that one of those countries, Lithuania, did not have a diplomatic consul in Manila, so there would be no convenient record of Lithuanian citizens living in the Philippines. Margaret became an instant "Lithuanian."

A phony, but plausible, background was needed. Since Kovno was one of the few Lithuanian cities whose name she could pronounce, Kovno became her birthplace. Neither Margaret nor Peggy (as she was known to friends) was a Lithuanian name, so she became Rosena. She painstakingly scoured her apartment and belongings, destroying every scrap of personal identification.

Now, reborn Rosena Utinsky needed a Japanese pass in order to travel to Bataan. Recalling a Filipino acquaintance of her husband who was an expert in penmanship, she paid him twenty-five pesos ($12.50) to forge a pass. The forger was an expert. He even reproduced a precise signature of an authentic Japanese officer.

Masquerading as a nurse, Rosena Utinsky joined a Philippine Red Cross unit, which was working under the direction of the Japanese and was leaving for Bataan to set up emergency clinics for sick and wounded civilians. Along with the real doctors and nurses, she arrived in Bataan in the wake of the Death March and was shocked and sickened by the grotesque sight that greeted her eyes. Massive slaughter had taken place along the road leading northward toward Camp O'Donnell. Hundreds of stinking, often mutilated corpses of American and Filipino soldiers were strewn about—alongside the road, in ditches half-filled with stagnant water, in rice paddies.

For several weeks, while laboring as a Lithuanian nurse in a Bataan emergency clinic, Rosena Utinsky made subtle inquiries about the fate of her husband. Much to her relief, she learned that he had survived the Death March, reached Camp O'Donnell, and later was transferred to the Cabanatuan prison. Shortly after returning to Manila, she opened a note that had been smuggled out of Cabanatuan by a POW, Lieutenant Colonel Edward C. Mack, and was delivered to her by a Filipino courier.

"Your husband died here recently," Mack wrote. "He is buried here in the prison graveyard. . . . You may be told that he died of tuberculosis. That is not true. Our men say he died of starvation. A little more food and medicine, which (the Japanese) would not give him, might have saved him."

Margaret Utinsky, loving wife, shed no tears. She was too numb. Instead, she was gripped by a fierce resolve to save other American prisoners from Jack's fate. She began to write a note to Colonel Mack and thank him for the news about her husband. But how would she sign the message? If the Japanese intercepted the note—a distinct possibility—and her true or adopted name was on it, her life could be forfeited. After a few moments' reflection, she signed the message "Miss U." Thus was born the Miss U underground of southern Luzon. Her goal was to smuggle food, medicine, clothing, shoes, and money to the desperate men inside Cabanatuan camp.

As soon as Naomi Flores (Looter), Miss U's emissary, reported back from her reconnaissance of Cabanatuan in August, Margaret was stunned by the enormity of the task she had undertaken. Instead of the two thousand POWs she had heard were penned up at the camp, Looter had discovered that there were nine thousand to twelve thousand of them.

Miss U knew that an underground organization would require two things: money and members. So she sold her Spode and Wedgewood china for $200 and her silver service for $400—only a fraction of their true value. Her rings, pearls, and bracelets were bought for $600 by a Manila jeweler, and her apartment's electric stove went to a Philippine couple for $195.

In the days ahead, the modest treasury dwindled. So items she could no longer afford to buy, she begged for. She had learned many of the Cabanatuan prisoners were barefoot, so she began to round up old shoes. An Irish priest, Father John Lalor, a friendly, silver-haired man fifty-five years of age, joined her in pounding the hot, dusty streets of Manila, pleading with anyone they thought they could trust for old shoes. After collecting several hundred pairs, they were confronted with the need to find storage space until the shoes could be smuggled into Cabanatuan.

Father Lalor came up with the solution. The large garage at the Malate Convent, in a fashionable suburb of Manila, would be used as a warehouse. Lalor and three other Irish priests were in charge of the convent, which also included a centuries-old church of Spanish architecture, a school that had become a part-time medical clinic, and a neatly manicured garden. Japanese suspicions would not be aroused by the loads of supplies going in and out of the garage, Father Lalor pointed out, because the four priests were citizens of neutral Ireland.

Neutral or not, Father Lalor (code name Morning Glory) held no illusions about his fate should his underground role be discovered by the Kempei Tai, the dreaded Japanese secret police. Yet he plunged into the smuggling business with enormous enthusiasm and dedication.

As time passed, Miss U recruited a large number of members to her underground network. They represented a wide array of American sympathizers—Spanish, Swiss, Irish, Chinese, Italian, Russian, and Filipino. To each recruit, she assigned a code name. A group of Maryknoll sisters (code name Angels) salvaged hundreds of pajamas from a closed Manila hospital where they had worked. These garments were cut up, and each one was converted into two pairs of pants and a T-shirt for the Cabanatuan prisoners. Two Manila pharmacists (one Swiss, one Chinese) covertly provided Miss U with quinine and sulfa, as well as the vaccines used to fight cholera, typhoid, and dysentery—diseases that had already killed hundreds at O'Donnell and Cabanatuan. The two pharmacists were code-named Medicine Men.

One entire Filipino family joined up. Joaquin D. Mencarinis was code-named Rocky; his wife, Augustias, was Boots; the couple's daughter, Elvira, was Little Boots; the older son, Manuel, was Hotshot; and the younger son, Ralph, was Skeezix (named after a popular American comic-strip character).

Curly Top was a jovial, heavyset Swiss named Kurt Gantner, who was a leader among the large number of his countrymen living on Luzon. The Swiss were especially valuable to the network; as neutrals, they could move about freely with minimum danger of being arrested. Gantner's wife was code-named Screwball Number Two; her sister, Marceline Short, wife of an American major imprisoned at Cabanatuan, was Screwball Number One.

Two Russian citizens, Zenia Jastin (code name Bakala) and Herman Roles (Fancypants) played key roles in the underground. Zenia's husband, Walter Jastin, was an American civilian penned up at Cabanatuan, while Roles was a cashier in a large Manila restaurant. His tiny office served as a "mail drop" for receiving and sending secret messages. Roles had a remarkable memory and never accepted or dispatched written notes. Instead, he passed along each message to a courier by word of mouth, a considerable feat since his brain might be loaded with up to twenty communications at any given time.

Mr. X was Brother Xavier of De La Salle College in Manila, and his closest helper was Scatterbrain, whose real name was Madeline Cripe. Her husband, an American sailor, was a POW at Cabanatuan. Lovely Nati Ashborn, a young Spanish woman, had been married to U.S. Army Lieutenant Walter Ashborn for only a year when he was captured on Bataan. For weeks, Nati had anxiously awaited word about Walter's fate. Then she heard through the Manila grapevine that Miss U had compiled a list of American servicemen who had died at Cabanatuan, so she hurried to call on the underground leader. Lieutenant Ashborn was indeed on the list: He had died of dysentery and starvation. Nati fought back the tears, then rolled up her sleeves and went to work carrying messages for the underground. She was given the moniker Trixie.

Middle-aged Elizabeth Kummer was among the handful of Americans permitted to roam Manila at will; her husband, Max, was a German, and Adolf Hitler's Third Reich was a Japanese ally. Max had been the German counsel in Manila, but he had been booted from that position after the bigwigs in Berlin learned that he had never joined the Nazi Party.

Through her husband's connections, Elizabeth Kummer was acquainted with numerous Japanese officers in Manila. One day while walking with Miss U, Elizabeth bumped into one of her Japanese acquaintances, and she introduced her companion as "a Lithuanian nurse, Miss Rosena Utinsky." Miss U found herself in the strange ritual of smilingly shaking hands with one of her underground's enemies.

Japanese officers trusted Elizabeth, since her husband Max was an "ally." So from conversations with them, she was often able to warn Miss U that one of her covert operatives was under suspicion and in danger of being arrested by the Kempei Tai. The underground suspect would lay low or else flee into the rural area to hide out until the heat was over.

Another American, Ernest Johnson, a civilian who had been an executive of the Maritime Service, was confined to a Manila hospital with a serious injury he had suffered prior to the Japanese capture of Corregidor. The Japanese paid no attention to Johnson, presumably believing that he was immobile (which was true) and unable to cause them any mischief (which was untrue).

Ernie Johnson, code-named Brave Heart, conducted his underground business from his hospital room. An outgoing, friendly type, he had many friends in Manila, and each time one would visit him, he would persuade the visitor to make a cash contribution. While the money was being exchanged, Japanese officers often were strolling up and down the corridor outside Brave Heart's room.

When Brave Heart had information or money to pass along to Miss U, he would send a Filipino boy with a bottle of rum. This was the signal that he wanted to see her. If the courier were to be stopped and grilled by the Japanese, he could not give away the conspiracy about which he knew nothing. All he knew was that Johnson had paid him a few pesos to deliver the bottle to a Lithuanian nurse, presumably with romantic intentions.

Known in the code book as Per, Enrico Paravino was Italian by birth but had Philippine citizenship. Per collected funds from Italian citizens living in Manila, an especially dangerous act since Benito Mussolini's Italy was on the side of the Japanese and any Italian he approached might squeal on him. Per also served as a courier of secret messages.

One of Miss U's most effective agents was Ramón Amosategui (code name Sparkplug), a dashing former Spanish naval officer and now a wealthy property owner in Manila. Sparkplug kept in contact with Miss U through Bert Richey, a part-time guerilla, whose peg leg failed to slow him down. Richey's apt moniker was One Slipper. Also in the network was Sparkplug's beautiful Spanish wife, whose code name was Screwball Number Three.

In the early weeks of the underground, when it was especially strapped for cash, Sparkplug and his wife invited a large number of Spaniards to a secret meeting at their palatial home so that Miss U could make a pitch for financial contributions. Later, Sparkplug set up a shortwave radio in a Manila cemetery, and each night, he slipped behind the graveyard's circular stone wall to take down in improvised shorthand the latest news broadcast from San Francisco, California. It was risky business: Detection would have meant the loss of his head.

After a session or two in the blackness of the cemetery, Sparkplug would take his scribbling to Miss U at her apartment (which was code-named Auntie), where she typed his notes into narrative form on an ancient machine that had belonged to her husband. Then the typed sheets were reproduced by a friendly Filipino printer, and scores of them were sneaked inside Cabanatuan camp. This news pipeline enormously boosted POW morale. "The Cheer" was the name given by the prisoners to the typed news reports.

Soon Miss U dispatched a second operative to Cabanatuan town to assist Naomi Flores in reconnoitering the prison camp. She was Evangeline Neibert (Sassie Susie), a pert young woman who was the daughter of a former member of the Philippines Bureau of Education. Her father had come to the islands years earlier and married a Filipina schoolteacher. Sassie Susie was intensely dedicated to her secret activities: Her American boyfriend was one of the living skeletons in Cabanatuan camp.

Dressed in old clothes with dirty shawls worn over their heads, Looter (Naomi) and Sassie Susie strolled around the marketplace in Cabanatuan town, disguised as roasted-peanut vendors. They also made frequent trips to reconnoiter the gates at the POW camp. As a result of their spying, Miss U had to alter her plans for slipping food, clothing, and medicine inside the enclosure. She had planned to sneak these commodities through the gates in the back of Filipino trucks and ambulances, which she had thought made routine trips in and out of the camp. That procedure was dropped after Looter and Sassie Susie reported that no Filipino vehicles were allowed to enter the compound.

In light of this new intelligence, Miss U concluded that supplies would somehow have to reach the prisoners through native contacts in Cabanatuan town. Her main contact would have to be one already deeply imbedded in the fabric of the town, so that he did not attract undue attention from the Japanese. His job would be coordinator and expeditor for the clandestine distribution of materials to the camp prisoners.

Sassie Susie and Looter singled out a likely prospect, a Filipino named Juan Maluto, who operated several merchandise stalls in the marketplace. Each week, he routinely traveled to Manila in a battered old truck to bring back goods from his warehouse. Secretly, he hated the Japanese; they had brutally murdered his only son.

Cautiously, Looter approached Maluto and told him that "Rosena Utinsky," a Lithuanian nurse, wanted to talk with him about an extremely important matter. Could he call at her apartment the next time he was in Manila? Maluto was suspicious and hesitated, but finally agreed.

A few days later, the Filipino was seated in the sparsely furnished living room at Miss U's apartment, listening to her briefing on the work of her clandestine organization and its goals. Then she told him of his prospective role: using his several stalls in the Cabanatuan marketplace as a covert distribution center for smuggling goods, money, medicine, and food to the American POWs.

Maluto was frightened. His hands trembled. Detection by the Kempei Tai would mean unspeakable torture and eventual beheading. His wife and daughter might undergo the same harsh fate. Despite his deep fears, Maluto agreed to become the underground's key operative in Cabanatuan town. Miss U told the Filipino that his code name would be Savior.

Now Miss U and Father Lalor were confronted by yet another vexing problem: how to get the supplies from the Malate Convent garage to Cabanatuan town. A wealthy Filipino, Juan Elizalde, owner of a distillery, was approached, and he agreed to contribute a truck and alcohol (in lieu of gasoline) to power the vehicle. Code-named Ezy, the Manila businessman was a thoughtful intellectual, and he hated the barbaric nature of Japanese rule. Anything Miss U needed, Ezy would provide it.

Several times each week, Elizalde's truck made the round trip from the Malate Convent garage and Juan Maluto's stalls in Cabanatuan town. There were no stumbling blocks. The Filipino drivers were officially licensed by Japanese authorities, and there were no restrictions on their moving about Luzon. On each trip, the truck was loaded with shoes, clothing, drugs, sweet potatoes, canned fruit, and mongo beans.

Periodically, groups of POWs from the camp, accompanied by Japanese guards, were allowed to drive bullcarts into town to purchase small amounts of goods from their ten to twenty cents per day pay. On the day before the underground's truck was to make its run, Miss U's contact in Cabanatuan town slipped word to the Americans about the kind of relief supplies that were coming.

Early in the morning, the Americans going to Cabanatuan town moved through the camp gate in a line of solid-wood-wheeled, low-slung bullcarts pulled by huge-shouldered, waddling carabao. Usually, the cart's only occupant was the driver. On reaching the Cabanatuan marketplace, the POWs shopped several stalls first before reaching Juan Maluto's bins, a tactic intended to divert Japanese suspicions from Miss U's main contact.

When the Americans began pawing Maluto's merchandise in search of something they could afford to buy, loud haggling erupted over the price the proprietor was asking, a scenario scripted for the benefit of the Japanese guards. Maluto always made it a point during the arguments to damn the Americans as "filthy pigs."

While the guards were ogling a few young Filipina women, who were deliberately flirting to distract the Japanese, the purchased items were loaded into the bullcarts. Then, making certain they were not being watched, Maluto and a few helpers rapidly slipped drugs, medicine, food, and clothing underneath the sacks of goods. These supplies had arrived only that morning from the Malate Convent. Back to camp went the carts, where they trundled past the bored guards at the gate. This primitive secret shuttle service between the camp and Cabanatuan town was known to the POWs as the "Carabao Clipper."

Among the items sneaked into the carts by Juan Maluto would be a bag marked with large red letters. On his arrival back in camp, a POW would take this bag directly to Lieutenant Colonel Ed Mack, one of Miss U's primary contacts. Inside the sack was a large amount of pesos for distribution to POWs in particular need.

Prisoners always needed money with which to make purchases in the Cabanatuan marketplace, in what passed as the camp commissary, and, on occasion, to bribe guards for a needed favor—perhaps a new toothbrush. Miss U and her conspirators hit on a scheme to keep a modest flow of money dribbling into the camp. Looter and Sassie Susie, carrying their product in baskets balanced on their heads, casually circulated among the Americans in the marketplace, selling bags of roasted peanuts to the POWs for one centavo (a few U.S. pennies) each. When the POWs returned to camp and opened their peanut sacks, they found inside as much as three hundred pesos, currency that had been tightly folded and inserted by Miss U's workers in Manila.*

Looter and Sassie Susie had narrow escapes from being unmasked as underground operatives. One afternoon the two women and a few friends were walking back to Cabanatuan town after selling peanuts and bananas to the barefoot Americans toiling in Farmer Jones's Garden. Actually, their mission had been slipping notes and messages to the POWs. A truck drew up alongside the Filipinas and a Japanese soldier leaned out of the cab and motioned for Looter to climb in with him. She dared not refuse or show fear.

Smiling broadly, Looter scrambled aboard and sat between the two Japanese. Her heart was pounding madly, and her palms were perspiring. She felt her covert activities had been discovered and she was being taken to a Kempei Tai station for grilling. She chatted amiably, however, and the truck finally halted in the center of Cabanatuan town.

"You get out now, missy," the smiling Japanese soldier said.

When she climbed down to the ground and the vehicle drove away, Looter's knees felt like jelly.

As the days and weeks inched past, underground activities in the marketplace became widely known among the population, and many citizens began working for Miss U or wanted to help in some manner. The exceptions were the handful of natives collaborating with the Japanese. The traitors were known to most residents in Cabanatuan. Soon, a strange malady struck the town: One by one, the collaborators mysteriously vanished, never to be seen again.

---

*One peso was equivalent to U.S. fifty cents.

8

Secret Radios and Boxcar Smugglers

Early on the morning of April 17, 1943, American technicians were monitoring Japanese radio signals from a concrete bunker at Dutch Harbor, a bleak, gray town in the Aleutians, a chain of volcanic islands that extends like a long finger more than nine hundred miles westward from the tip of the Alaskan Peninsula. High above the fogbound cliffs climbed seven three-hundred-foot radio masts.

At 6:36 A.M., one monitoring soldier tensed: He was picking up a cipher signal from Truk, a Japanese-held island in the Pacific, and bearing the code sign of Admiral Isoroku Yamamoto, commander in chief of the Imperial Japanese Navy and architect of the Pearl Harbor onslaught. Unbeknownst to the wretched prisoners at Cabanatuan, events soon to follow would give them their biggest morale boost.

The Dutch Harbor code-breakers studied the groups of intercepted figures and compared them with their secret key charts. By 11:00 A.M., they had decoded and translated the intercept. Dai Nippon's most revered admiral, fifty-nine-year-old Yamamoto, would be flying from the Japanese stronghold of Rabaul to Kahili airstrip on Bouganville, in the northern Solomons, on an inspection trip.

Details of Yamamoto's pending flight were flashed to Washington, where a decision was made to lay on Operation Vengeance: intercepting and shooting down the plane carrying Yamamoto. A crack U.S. Air Corps squadron, the 339th, based at Henderson Field on Guadalcanal in the lower Solomons, was selected for the mission. The squadron's twin-boomed P-38 Lightnings, carrying auxiliary fuel tanks, were the only fighters with sufficient range to make the 435-mile flight to Kahili.

The point of interception would be thirty-four miles short of Yamamoto's destination. The admiral was due to arrive at the airfield at precisely 9:45 A.M. on April 18.

At dawn that day, sixteen Lightnings, led by Major John W. Mitchell, lifted off from Henderson Field and set a beeline for the interception point. The mission's success would require a marvel of pinpoint navigation and timing. Mitchell took twelve of his planes up to twenty thousand feet to do battle on the top escort of Yamamoto's bomber, while Lieutenant Thomas G. Lanphier led the other Lightnings for a direct attack on the admiral's aircraft.

Nearing the hoped-for interception point, Lanphier and his wingman, Lieutenant Rex Barber, spotted Yamamoto's plane and began boring in on it. When within two miles of their flying target, Lanphier's flight was pounced on by six Zeke fighter planes that were escorting Yamamoto's bomber. Five P-38s dueled with the Zekes while Lanphier dove on the admiral's plane, which was skimming just above the jungle. Lanphier squeezed the machine-gun's trigger and sent a long burst into the Mitsubishi, which broke into flames, crashed, and exploded.

American security officers bottled up the blockbuster story. They didn't want the Japanese to know that their code had been broken; and they were concerned about the fate of Lieutenant Tom Lanphier's brother, Charles, who was a prisoner of war. Should the Japanese learn who had shot down Yamamoto's bomber, the POW brother no doubt would be subjected to the torments of the damned—before being executed. It was hoped that the Imperial warlords would conclude that Yamamoto had been a victim of bad luck when a P-38 patrol happened to stumble onto his Mitsubishi, not knowing who was aboard.

In New Guinea, General Douglas MacArthur, on hearing that Yamamoto had been ambushed, solemnly told aides that he could "almost hear the rising crescendo of sound from thousands of glistening white skeletons at the bottom of Pearl Harbor."[1]

As time passed, American commanders in the Pacific waited eagerly for some word from Tokyo concerning Yamamoto's fate. Had he truly been killed? There was only silence from Radio Tokyo. Finally, on May 24, five weeks after the aerial confrontation, Imperial Headquarters issued a communiqué: "Admiral Isoroku Yamamoto, while directing strategy on the front line in April, engaged in combat with the enemy and met gallant death in a warplane." A mammoth state funeral would be held for the Japanese hero, Radio Tokyo added, and the final rites would cost the equivalent of twenty-three thousand dollars.

That day in far-off Washington, President Franklin Roosevelt was holding a routine press conference in the Oval Office of the White House. Roosevelt, of course, already had been informed by U.S. Naval Intelligence of Yamamoto's demise within hours of the admiral's ambush. Now, a reporter told him that the Pearl Harbor attack architect had been shot down by American fighter planes.

In an incredulous tone, the President inquired: "Is he dead?"

Told that he was quite dead, Roosevelt feigned surprise and ejaculated: "Gosh!"[2]

A few hours later, U.S. commanders in the Pacific were given a jolt. The story, including the name of Lieutenant Tom Lanphier as the triggerman, was plastered across Australian newspapers. A grossly irresponsible reporter apparently had learned of Lanphier's identity from an unknown source. No doubt the gist of the Australian newspaper article reached Tokyo. However, as it turned out, the Japanese apparently did not realize that the man who shot down Dai Nippon's greatest hero had a brother in their clutches, for the POW Lanphier received only the normal mistreatment and abuse.[3]

While millions of weeping Japanese lined the streets of Tokyo to pay final tribute to Admiral Yamamoto as a horse-drawn vehicle carrying his ashes moved past on the way to the cemetery, two thousand miles to the south all prisoners at Cabanatuan were ordered to assemble. Trying to conceal his grief, Major Isuku Iwanaka, who had replaced Colonel Mori as camp commandant, eulogized Yamamoto and told of his "heroic death" in battle. Then Iwanaka issued a strict order: The POWs were "forbidden" to sing or smile for forty-eight hours as a symbol of their grief over the demise of the revered Japanese admiral.[4]

Actually, many of the Americans already knew about the Yamamoto ambush hours earlier. In recent months, trickery and Yankee ingenuity had resulted in several radios being hidden within the camp, and on these sets news was picked up from the outside world.

Most Japanese officers had radios, and when they went out of order, the instruments were taken to the powerhouse, where Americans were assigned to work. One POW had been a radio technician and could fix the broken sets within a few hours, or a day at the most. But he would tell the Japanese owners that the sets would require two or three weeks to repair, during which time the Americans listened to newscasts from the powerful San Francisco station. Fortunately for the Americans, the Japanese, in the words of one POW, knew "as much about radio repair as a bunch of idiots."

On other occasions when Japanese brought their malfunctioning sets to the powerhouse, they would be told that the owners would have to obtain parts from Manila. When the parts arrived, the Americans would tell them they were the wrong ones and keep the parts. So the Japanese sent for more parts. All of this took time. Meanwhile, the POWs were listening to the radios. What's more, they collected enough parts through this scheme to furnish a base for constructing new receiving sets for themselves.

There would be periods when the Japanese radios would work well, and the Americans in the powerhouse would have no access to broadcast news directly from the United States. So the POWs would speed up the generator and burn out a few of the Japanese sets. Soon, Japanese officers would storm into the powerhouse and order the American technician, "You fix!"

Inspecting the sets, the POW would shake his head sadly and inform the owners that the radios were so badly damaged that it would require at least a month to fix them. An hour later, the GIs were huddled around the repaired radios listening to San Francisco.

The powerhouse prisoners also had a clever ruse for sabotaging the camp staff's ability to listen to Radio Tokyo. During newscasts, the Americans would manipulate the camp current in such a way as to create ear-piercing static, leaving the Japanese listeners confused and furious.

No one knew exactly how many clandestine radios were in the camp. Each group kept secret its own set. When the Corregidor navy men had entered the camp, they brought with them an entire receiving set. Its components were carried by numerous POWs. One had a radio tube strapped to his inner leg; another, an amplifier under his armpit; a rheostat was slipped into a false sleeve; wire was taped around wrists; and condensers were carried in shoes. When they reached the camp, radio technicians sweated through long nights under blankets and by candlelight to assemble the pieces to create a workable set.

Along with food and water, news was the most important thing in the lives of the POWs. It sustained them. It gave them hope and encouraged them to hang in there despite the barbarities that were everyday occurrences. One of the chief dispensers of news was Chaplain Frank Tiffany, a tall, gentle giant in his midforties. Before he heard the call of God, Tiffany had labored for years as a farmhand in Canada and the northwest United States. At considerable hardship to his wife, small daughter, and himself, he attended a divinity school and was ordained a minister in the Presbyterian Church.

Chaplain Tiffany received and covertly distributed copies of The Cheer, the news sheets that Miss U and her confederates in Manila printed and sneaked into camp. As a result of the radio newscasts and The Cheer, the POWs kept track of the progress of the global war and debated endlessly over its implications with regard to the recapture of the POWs by American forces. They cursed the strikers in Detroit and ripped apart beetle-browed John L. Lewis, the union kingpin. The POWs even tried to figure out what was a "zoot suit," but were at a loss to do so.[5]

Another key underground contact inside the camp was hard-boiled Lieutenant Colonel Edward Mack, who had been in the regular army for many years. Mack was regarded as the unofficial camp mailman. Each month, hundreds of letters and notes were smuggled into camp by the underground, and Ed Mack traipsed around the sprawling compound delivering the mail. Often he would be stopped by an anxious American and asked, "Anything for me today, Colonel?" Hoping that he grasped Japanese psychology accurately, Mack carried the mail openly in cloth sacks, figuring that the guards would not be suspicious of any container in plain sight.

In addition to news received over the clandestine radios and Chaplain Tiffany's digests, the Carabao Clipper smuggled in the English language Manila Tribune, which was controlled by the Japanese lock, stock, and rising sun. All naval battles were depicted in the Tribune as stunning Japanese victories, although at Midway and in other clashes, the Imperial Fleet had suffered disasters and limped off to lick its wounds. In the fierce ground actions in the jungles of Guadalcanal and New Guinea, long stories portrayed American soldiers and marines as "inhuman gangsters and brutal animals" who tortured and killed all Japanese prisoners. Retreats by Adolf Hitler's legions in Russia and in North Africa were described as "strategic withdrawals."

Americans never learned to decipher the Japanese mentality. A classic example of oriental unpredictability occurred on Memorial Day 1943. Major Iwanaka, the camp commandant, had announced that only thirteen Americans would be allowed to conduct memorial services at the cemetery. However, when more than a thousand ragged prisoners showed up for the solemn ceremony, Iwanaka chose to ignore the flagrant flouting of his strict orders.

It was a strange situation that day. Scores of Japanese soldiers stood side by side with the Americans, respectfully bowing their heads as Catholic, Jewish, and Protestant chaplains recited prayers for the 2,644 POWs buried there. In the oddest episode of all, the Japanese general in charge of all POW camps in the Philippines sent a large wreath from Manila.

Not long after this cozy relationship on Memorial Day, a group of Americans was routinely entering the compound gate when their bullcart was halted and searched. A bag of messages from the underground to various POWs (identified only by code names) was discovered. The Japanese guards seemed to go berserk. They jerked the driver, Fred Threatt, off his perch and beat him savagely until he was unconscious. Then the guards dragged elderly Lieutenant Colonel Alfred C. Oliver, who had been the senior army chaplain in the Philippines; Colonel Edward Mack (Miss U's main contact); two other chaplains, Captain Frank Tiffany and Captain Robert Taylor; and three other POWs across the road to what had been a municipal jail.[6]

There the seven Americans were beaten and tortured periodically for forty-seven days. Chaplain Oliver was struck over the head with a rifle butt, breaking his neck. But none of the POWs disclosed the identity of Miss U or the people concealed behind the code names in the messages found in the bullcart.[7]

On occasion, Americans scored minor victories. A Japanese guard the POWs called Bullhead took a great interest in a tube of Burma Shave, a soapy concoction, which one man had in his possession. It apparently had arrived in a Christmas Red Cross package.

"Is good?" the curious guard asked.

"Very good to eat," the American replied. "I put it on my rice."

Bullhead promptly confiscated the tube and evidently squeezed a large batch on his rice, for he was back the next morning "mad as a hornet," in the words of a GI. Since the guards' food was also rationed, his supper had been ruined. Bullhead beat the POW with his fists.

After he had gone, the American grinned and told his comrades, "It was worth getting a black eye or two."[8]

Another GI triumph resulted from the unpredictability of the Japanese staff. One night, a POW was stricken with severe abdominal pains and was carried to the hospital. There Major Emil Reed diagnosed his ailment as appendicitis, and he sent word to a Japanese doctor in the camp that the man should be operated on immediately. In the past, if emergency surgery arose at a time that suited the whims of the Japanese, the patient would be put in a truck and taken to an army hospital in the region. But this time, the Japanese doctor replied, "So sorry, trucks no go tonight."

Americans had been brutally murdered or had died by the hundreds at Cabanatuan, but now the Japanese physician took an acute interest in the well-being of this lone American.

"You must operate here," he declared. Major Reed then launched a dissertation on the dangers of appendicitis and of the fact that he had neither the proper equipment nor the medicine with which to perform the surgery. The Japanese doctor was concerned and asked if there was anything he could do, even though his superiors had refused to allow trucks to go out that night.

"Well, we can give the patient relief and hope for the best by placing ice packs on his abdomen."

"So sorry, no ice. Will try find some."

Two days later, the patient recovered without surgery and returned to his barracks—much to the astonishment of Major Reed. The next day, Reed received a message from the Japanese doctor: "Come get ice."

Reed had failed to tell his opposite number that the man with appendicitis had recovered and been released. So a POW work detail was dispatched to bring back the three-hundred-pound cake of ice. For many days, the Americans on the hospital staff enjoyed cooling sips of ice water, a delicacy that they had once taken for granted but had not had since being captured.[9]

Meanwhile far to the south in mid-1943, General Douglas MacArthur brought in Colonel Courtney Whitney, Jr., to take charge of cloak-and-dagger operations in the Philippines and pave the way for MacArthur's eventual return. Whitney, who had been a pilot in World War I and practiced law in Manila for twenty years, headed the Philippine section of the super-secret Allied Intelligence Bureau (AIB). That organization was under the overall supervision of MacArthur's G-2 (intelligence) officer, Major General Charles Willoughby, who had been born Karl Weidenback in Germany and still spoke with a thick Teutonic accent.

Almost at once, Colonel Whitney and his small staff recognized a major problem in the Philippines: how to combat the constant flow of Japanese propaganda. Japan controlled all the media—radio, newspapers, magazines—and there were signs that the avalanche of anti-American propaganda was beginning to erode the morale of Filipino guerillas and civilians.

Whitney was especially concerned about the viewpoint of the nearly forty-five thousand Filipino POWs who had been released after undergoing what the Japanese called "reconstruction." Before being discharged, the Filipinos had to sign a pledge that they would do nothing to impede the establishment of the Japanese Greater East Asia Co-Prosperity Sphere. Most did sign—with fingers crossed or tongue in cheek. But perhaps scores of them had indeed been brainwashed into believing that the Americans were "exploiters," and, when MacArthur returned one day, these Filipinos might take up arms against his men.

Some five hundred Filipinos were currently being "reconstructed" at Cabanatuan. They had to sit through countless lectures on the glory of the Japanese Empire, and its magnificent war victories at sea and on the ground. They were told that they, the Filipinos, were the blood brothers of the Japanese and on their release, the natives should join in keeping the white devils out of the Philippines.

On August 10, Colonel Whitney submitted a detailed memorandum to Douglas MacArthur, outlining an antidote against the Japanese anti-American propaganda:

> Items scarce in the Philippines, such as cigarettes, matches, chewing gum, candy bars, sewing kits and pencils, would be individually packaged with the American and Philippine flags on one side and the phrase "I shall return" over General MacArthur's facsimile signature on the other side. These "victory packages" would be slipped into the Philippines via submarine and distributed throughout the islands.

MacArthur read the memorandum with apparent delight. At the bottom, he scrawled: "No objections. I shall return!"

Courtney Whitney would have his work cut out for him because Japanese anti-American propaganda had clearly made deep inroads. There were hundreds of native collaborators, whose motives were complex and varied. Some cozied up to the Japanese for personal gain, others because they feared the conquerors and believed that the American army would never return. There were those who preferred Oriental masters to Occidental ones. More than five thousand Filipinos joined the *Makapili*, a group sponsored by the Japanese and dedicated to keeping the white devils out of the Philippines. They were issued rifles and trained to fight American soldiers if MacArthur would try to return.

Eventually, millions of Colonel Whitney's "victory packages" flooded the islands. Nearly eighty dialects were spoken in the Philippines, but no translation of the English was needed. Every Filipino understood "I shall return!" It was a sacred personal pledge from Douglas MacArthur rather than from the United States government, which had abandoned the Philippines in her worst hour.

Many of the "victory packages" eventually were slipped into Cabanatuan camp, where they gave an enormous boost to POW morale and had a profound impact on the Filipinos. At Christmas 1943, the Japanese commandant, apparently believing that the Filipino POWs had been sufficiently "reconstructed," permitted two hundred and fifty of them to take short furloughs as a gesture of friendship, with the understanding that they were to return in ten days. Only twenty-five came back. The others picked up their families and fled into the mountains, where many of the men joined guerilla outfits.

Meanwhile in Manila, Miss U realized that shipping truckloads of food, drugs, and clothing to Cabanatuan camp was not enough. How to transport far larger volumes of supplies from Manila seemed to be an unsolvable problem. Then she hit upon an idea—and the Japanese would unknowingly cooperate in her scheme. Since Juan Maluto, the Cabanatuan marketplace entrepreneur, was in good standing with the conquerors, she asked him to rent a railroad boxcar from the Japanese, and he managed to connive one from them.

Periodically, Miss U received a courier-borne message from Maluto: "I am going to visit my mother." That was the signal that his boxcar soon would be departing from Manila for Cabanatuan. So several of the underground operatives would go to the Malate Convent, load their carts with supplies, and drive the two-wheeled vehicles to a railroad siding where Maluto's boxcar was waiting.

Miss U's workers belonged to several nationalities. Therefore, they all dressed like Filipinos so as not to unduly attract the attention of the Kempei Tai. They rapidly transferred the food, drugs, and clothing from the carts into the boxcar, and within hours, it would be rolling toward Cabanatuan.

The new shipment scheme worked smoothly as the boxcar traveled up and down the Japanese-controlled railroad, right past Japanese guards in the stations and at both terminals. Never was there any interference with this flow of crucially needed items. So effective was the operation that Miss U asked Maluto to rent a second boxcar. He hesitated, not wishing to press his good fortune. But finally he concocted a convoluted tale about why he required a second car, and within a week not one, but two, boxcars loaded with vegetables and goods were rolling between Manila and Cabanatuan.

9

An Audacious Escape

Seated at an oversized mahogany desk at his headquarters in Australia, General Douglas MacArthur, puffing on his trademark corncob pipe, listened silently as three American officers who had just escaped from a POW camp in the Philippines told of the deliberate pattern of atrocities that had been and were being inflicted upon American and Filipino prisoners by the Japanese army in the Philippines. MacArthur was shocked—and furious. Like other top commanders in the Pacific and in Washington, the supreme commander had thought that his men captured on Bataan and Corregidor were being treated correctly and humanely under the provisions of the Geneva Convention. It was August 1943.[1]

Relating their eyewitness stories to MacArthur were Air Corps Lieutenant William "Ed" Dyess of Albany, Texas; Navy Lieutenant Commander Melvyn H. McCoy of Indianapolis, and Army Major Stephen M. Mellnik. Dyess, who had been the leader of the 21st Pursuit Squadron, had been captured on Bataan; McCoy and Mellnik had fallen into Japanese hands on Corregidor. All three of the officers, together with seven other POWs, had pulled off a hair-raising escape from a camp on Mindanao.

The escape saga had its origin back in October 1942, when Colonel Mori, the Japanese commander at Cabanatuan, offered "one thousand literate laborers" the opportunity to volunteer for work at another unspecified locale. Among those choosing to go were ten POWs who, a few months later, would band together in the Philippines' first successful mass escape. Although all of the ten men did not know one another at the time, each was motivated by the same thought: Remaining at Cabanatuan would mean eventual certain death.

A day later, the one thousand "literate laborers" were marched to Cabanatuan town, piled into boxcars, and taken to Manila. After spending a night in Old Bilibid prison, the POWs were loaded onto what one American described as a "filthy old tub" for a ten-day voyage to Mindanao Island, six hundred miles to the south. A few lucky prisoners traveled on deck instead of down in the cramped, suffocating, stinking holds. Their good fortune was not triggered by a sudden burst of Japanese humaneness, but rather because it was impossible to squeeze one more prisoner in the holds.

A short distance out to sea, POW ringleaders began plotting mutiny. There were far more prisoners than there were Japanese guards. There was no doubt that the ship could be seized—providing extensive American casualties were disregarded. Commander Melvyn McCoy was consulted. An experienced seaman, McCoy was pessimistic. Even if the Japanese were overpowered, it was certain that a radio distress signal would be fired off first. Then, with the Americans in control of the vessel, it would be attacked and probably sunk, by Japanese warplanes. The mutiny scheme was abandoned.

Reaching the west coast of Mindanao on November 7, the prisoners were left in the sun for many hours, then they were marched along jungle trails twenty miles inland to a prison camp near Davao. Just past midnight, those who could still do so staggered through the gates.

The new home of the one thousand Americans long had been a harsh penal colony, nestled in what was regarded as an impenetrable jungle. It was where the prewar Philippine government had kept hardcore, long-term civilian prisoners. Most of the convicts had been moved to another island, but when the Cabanatuan group arrived, more than one hundred Filipino murderers still were being held.

Shortly after dawn, the new arrivals were formed up for review by Major Maeda, the camp commandant. Clearly, he was furious. Pointing to the large number of those in the ranks who were so ill they could barely stand, Maeda stormed about, shouting in pidgin English that he had requested prisoners who could perform hard labor, but instead, he had been sent a batch of walking corpses.

"You have been used to a soft, easy life since your capture," Major

Maeda told the Americans. "All that will be different here. Now you will learn about hard labor. Every prisoner will work until he is hospitalized!"

Maeda was a man of his word. Within a few months, eight hundred POWs, including two hundred who had gone partially or totally blind due to disease and diet deficiencies, were in a separate compound after being stricken with various illnesses.

In January 1943, Lieutenant Ed Dyess was handed a choice plum: chauffeur of the camp bullcart. His job was to haul poles and other items around the premises. In this capacity, he acquired a detailed knowledge of every nook and cranny of the sprawling camp. Japanese guards became used to seeing him and his carabao, so wherever Dyess popped up, no attention was paid to him. It was this job that instilled an escape plan in the minds of a few POWs.

The escape conspirators were spurred by the knowledge that Americans were still dying from disease and neglect, although at a slower pace than had been the case at Cabanatuan. It would be only a matter of time until they, too, succumbed to malaria, beriberi, or a shortage of food. If they were caught and executed, the plotters reasoned, it would simply mean a faster death than staying on and dying slowly from disease or cumulative malnutrition.

There was yet another compelling reason to reach Australia, one that overcame any doubts or fears they might have: an overwhelming urge to trumpet Japanese atrocities to the world, thereby improving the treatment of the thousands of prisoners who would have to be left behind in the Philippines.

One night in late February 1943, Ed Dyess, a natural-born leader, and Marine Captain Austin Shofner talked escape far into the night. It would be a daunting task. Australia was some fourteen hundred miles south of Mindanao. Much more information was needed, the two officers agreed. The would-be escapees would have to know the disposition of Japanese forces on Mindanao, the topographic features of that island, and the location of known guerilla bands.

Captain Shofner, of Shelbyville, Tennessee, by mutual consent of the schemers, became leader of the escape group. The former star tackle on the University of Tennessee football team, even though he had weighed only about 180 pounds, was recognized as a can-do type; to him, there was no such thing as an impossible task.

Shofner and Dyess realized that the means to get to Australia were limited, provided they escaped recapture on Mindanao. One method would be stealing a Japanese or Filipino boat along the coast. They toyed with the idea of sneaking up to a Japanese airfield near Davao City and seizing a plane, which Dyess or his sidekick pilot, Lieutenant Sam Grashio, would fly out.

Even getting away from the camp would be difficult: The entire region was full of swamps and jungle, portions of which were marked "unexplored." If the plotters were to reach Australia, they would have to form a team of men who were not only physically able to meet the ordeal, but also possessed needed skills.

Earlier, Captain Shofner had planned a breakout with two fellow marines, Lieutenant Jack Hawkins and Lieutenant Mike Dobervich. Hawkins, a graduate of Annapolis, was a cool customer, one who never lost his head in a tight situation. Dobervich, a Minnesotan, was known as "Beaver," a tribute to his eagerness, strength, and reliability. All three marines had seen combat. Shofner had been a company commander on Corregidor (where he was wounded), and Hawkins also had fought on the Rock. Dobervich had been captured on Bataan and suffered through the Death March.

Next, Lieutenant Leo Boelens was tapped. An air corps engineering officer and native of Basin, Wyoming, he was a genius at anything mechanical, a trait that could be crucial in the looming escape. If the schemers were to reach Australia, they would require a skilled navigator. Shofner suggested Lieutenant Commander Melvyn McCoy, who had graduated from Annapolis with the highest scholastic average in mathematics ever by a midshipman.

McCoy and three others also had been hatching escape plans of their own. So the four plotters joined with the six men in the Shofner-Dyess group. McCoy's companions were Coast Artillery Major Stephen M. Mellnik, and two army enlisted men, Sergeant Robert Spielman and Corporal Paul Marshall, both tough and resourceful. All four had been inmates at Cabanatuan.

Now the escape conspirators numbered ten. Two more were added: a pair of civilian Filipinos who were doing long terms in the penal colony for murder. Beningno de la Cruz was a handsome, intelligent man, a medical corpsman whose services might be crucial during the flight. Victorio Jumarong was exactly opposite to his fellow Filipino. He was inarticulate, crude, and semiliterate. But he had helped to clear the unmarked jungle trail over which the escapers would walk, so he would be a dependable guide—or so the plotters thought. Only one promise was made to the convicted murderers: If the escape were successful, the Americans would try to gain a pardon for the guides from Philippine President Manuel Quezon, who was in exile in the United States.[2]

If the plotters were going to survive in the inhospitable jungle, they would need supplies. So in the days ahead, by a variety of schemes and ruses, they collected canned and dried food, medicines, good shoes and leggings for each man, shelter halves, mosquito nets, knives, and bolos to hack their way though the tangled greenery. Leo Boelens, using his mechanical skills, created a workable sextant and a variety of other useful items in the machine shop.

All the plotters proved themselves to be adept burglars and thieves. Boelens stole binoculars, a hammer, a file, and a pair of pliers from the shop. Ed Dyess slipped into a hospital storeroom and swiped medicines, including quinine to fight malaria. Melvyn McCoy managed to get his hands on navigational tables. A protractor and dividers needed for navigation were "borrowed" from a navy POW who was not in the escape clique. Sam Grashio, who worked in the kitchen, stole a large quantity of matches. Compasses and watches were also "appropriated."

Now the daunting problem was how to get these supplies out of the camp. They could hardly be carried past the guards on the morning of the escape. One day, Ed Dyess drove his bullcart through the camp, surreptitiously collecting the stolen supplies hidden in numerous locations. After his cart was loaded, long poles were put on top, and Steve Mellnik sat on them, presumably to keep the poles from falling off. Guards ignored him when he passed through the gate with the escape supplies. Inside the thick jungle, Dyess and Mellnik swiftly concealed the booty for future retrieval.

Sunday, April 4, 1943, was the date set for the escape. A day earlier, the would-be escapees noticed that the guards were extra alert. Had the cache in the jungle been discovered? Had some POW "ratted" to the Japanese to curry favors? Then came frightful news: The Japanese had shot and killed a hospital orderly, who they said was trying to escape. So the guards were extra vigilant to prevent a mass breakout.

Two days after the shooting was the fateful day. By noon, the plotters either would be free men or face hideous torture and eventual death if recaptured. Each man hid his personal belongings, including extra garments, under his regular clothing, causing him to bulge in places. That morning, Captain Austin Shofner, who was in charge of the camp's plowing detail, strolled nonchalantly through the gate, ostensibly on his way to routinely change the grazing locations of the steers he used to do the plowing. Walking behind Shofner, presumably to assist him with the steers, were Lieutenants Sam Grashio, Jack Hawkins, and Mike Dobervich. All felt their hearts thumping furiously. Two guards ignored the four men.

In order not to attract undue attention, the second party of six men waited some twenty minutes before ambling toward the gate. In this group were Commander Melvyn McCoy, Major Steve Mellnik, Lieutenants Ed Dyess and Leo Boelens, Sergeant Bob Spielman, and Corporal Paul Marshall.

Moments before passing through the gate where two sentries with bayonet-tipped rifles were standing, a friend of Steve Mellnik, unaware of the escape plot, shouted that Mellnik's toothbrush was sticking out of his pocket. The six men felt cold fear stab through them. Then Mellnik's unknowing pal called out good-naturedly, "What're you planning to do, escape?"

Once the six men were out of sight of the gate, they ducked into a coconut grove and began to sneak toward the spot in the jungle where they had previously hidden their supplies. At one point, they had to cross a prison road that was always guarded by a Japanese sentry. Reaching the road, the six POWs formed into ranks and marched boldly into view. As they reached the sentry, Commander McCoy called for "eyes right," and as the others complied, he gave a snappy salute. Apparently flattered by this unexpected display of respect from a "work party," the Japanese smiled toothily and returned the salute. Not until the escapers were out of sight did they dare to breathe sighs of relief.

Shortly, the two POW groups joined around the supplies, soggy from rainfalls but most of the items still useful. Now there was a fearful and impatient wait. Where were the two Filipino guides? Had they informed the Japanese of the escape plot? For over an hour, the Americans fidgeted as the seconds ticked on . . . and on . . . and on.

Finally, there were rustling sounds in the underbrush. Japanese troops? Then Victorio Jumarong and Beningno de la Cruz burst into view. The guides explained that they had happened onto a group of friends whom they could not shake off.

With the convicted murderers in the lead, the escapers began marching along a muddy trail. The jungle heat was terrific, the silence broken only by the squawks of startled birds, or the occasional chatter of beady-eyed monkeys. Soon they were in a swamp with filthy brown water up to their knees. Head high, razorlike grass sliced into their skin. Each step had to be preceded by vigorous hacks with bolo blades.

Samuel Grashio remembered vividly the tough going: "Stream after stream had to be waded. Brambles tore at our clothes and our flesh. Mosquitos badgered us ceaselessly, and huge leeches fastened onto our arms and legs. The leeches could not be simply pulled off, rather they had to be touched with lighted cigarettes before falling to the ground. The wounds the leeches left behind often became infected."[3]

They trudged on for seemingly endless hours. What sort of trail was this that was so difficult to walk on? Or was it even a trail? Then the escapees grew alarmed when they spotted footprints in the mud. Closer inspection revealed that they were their own footprints. Victorio Jumarong, who had professed to knowing the trail intimately, obviously was unfamiliar with it. The escapers had been trekking in a wide circle.

Samuel Grashio recalled: "The impact (of this news) would be impossible to exaggerate. Our spirits simply collapsed. We were shattered, stunned. We had wasted many hours, and had cut a path near the camp, one that the Japanese could easily follow. We were struck by cold, sickening fear."[4]

Jumarong admitted that he was lost. So the group huddled, and by joint agreement, set out in a direction they thought would take them toward a railroad. Doggedly, they plunged onward, determined to put distance between themselves and the presumably pursuing Japanese. While hacking away at the heavy vegetation one Filipino struck a nest of yellow jackets. Furious swarms of the big bees stabbed into open flesh. There were loud yelps of pain. Each sting felt like a white-hot dagger had been inserted. Men plunged into the swamp water, remaining virtually submerged for nearly an hour until the savage insects flew away.

Soon a series of loud splashes echoed across the swamp. Japanese pursuers? The men froze, gripped by fear. All were relieved to see the ominous sounds had been caused by nearby crocodiles, hopefully ones with full bellies.

Reaching the Mindanao coast, the escapees stole a fishing craft that would do about five miles per hour. Clamoring aboard, they headed along the shoreline and continued throughout the night. With the first blush of dawn, they found themselves just astern of two Japanese coastal patrol vessels, both armed with three-inch guns. Again the escapees brazened it out. It was too late to turn back. The fishing craft deliberately followed the Japanese boats until they headed into a harbor. The escapees kept going.

Soon, the leaking old tub had to be abandoned, and the escapees got back on dry land and trekked into the jungle. Eventually, they reached the primitive village of Kapungagen, whose mayor, Eligio David, had been a prosperous businessman in Davao and fled when the Japanese approached. While resting and feasting for a few days, the refugees saw three men armed with BARs (Browning Automatic Rifles) suddenly appear. The newcomers were suspicious and quizzed the Americans at length. It became obvious that they thought the escapees were Germans or Italians, and therefore, allies of the Japanese.

These three men were scouts for Claro Laureta, who was guerilla chief in the region and a former member of the Philippine Constabulary. A day later, Laureta arrived in Kapungagen. He, too, was suspicious, but after lengthy questioning, the guerilla chief became convinced of the escapees' bona fides.

Claro Laureta agreed that the Americans should get to Australia to tell the world of the Japanese atrocities against POWs in the Philippines. But he scoffed at the idea that the men could reach the Land Down Under in a sailboat. He urged the Americans to abandon such a scheme and suggested that they go 120 miles to the north coast of Mindanao. There, he said, were large, well-organized groups of guerillas under the command of American officers. U.S. submarines occasionally appeared off northern Mindanao, and perhaps the escapees could catch a ride to Australia in one of the underwater craft.

Laureta said the escapees could make it to the north coast in about three weeks, even though the terrain was saturated with high mountains, thick jungles, and tribes of Manobos and Atas, both of which were headhunters.

Taking Laureta's advice, the Americans headed northward

through wild and rugged country marked "unexplored" on maps. Again they trekked through swamps, stinking jungles, along muddy, slippery paths, up one side of towering mountains and down the other. Finally, the exhausted band of refugees reached Misamis, a coastal town that was headquarters for guerillas in northwestern Mindanao.

In Misamis, the escapees contacted Wendell Fertig, the principal guerilla leader, who had bestowed upon himself the rank of brigadier general. Fertig, an American civilian engineer, had been a mining consultant in the Philippines for many years and escaped from Luzon shortly before Corregidor fell.

Wendell Fertig, whom some regarded to be as eccentric as he was cerebral, ran a first-class guerilla operation. Professional American soldiers drilled raw recruits, women auxiliaries made uniforms, bandages, and bullets, and technicians fashioned new pieces for ancient rifles. The entire province of Misamis Occidental was virtually one large guerilla force.

Fertig, who sported a wide-brimmed, Chinese coolie-type hat, rode around the province in a car driven by a guerilla chauffeur. Two swift powerboats had been "appropriated" from their wealthy owners to provide coastal transportation. From Misamis, guerilla couriers traveled by foot, by mule, and by boat, carrying Fertig's typewritten orders to guerilla leaders elsewhere on Mindanao.

For nearly three months, the ten American refugees from Cabanatuan and the Davao POW camp remained near Misamis while Fertig's communications men repeatedly radioed requests for a submarine pickup to MacArthur's headquarters in Brisbane, Australia. The clandestine transmitter had been built by a young Filipino guerilla from knowledge he had obtained in a prewar correspondence course.

Finally, in late June 1943, Australia sent word that the submarine *Thresher* was being dispatched to pick up Ed Dyess, Steve Mellnik, and Mel McCoy. Austin Shofner, leader of the escape group, and the other Americans would have to await the availability of other underwater craft.

Only a few days before the *Thresher* was due, a sizable force of Japanese soldiers, backed by aircraft and a cruiser, swarmed ashore near Misamis—at the precise locale for the submarine rendezvous. The Japanese had located Fertig's transmitter with radio direction finders and were hell-bent on capturing or killing the guerilla chief and his men. Unbeknownst to the Japanese raiders, they also might snare in their net the ten American escapees.

Many of Fertig's inexperienced guerillas, who had never heard a shot fired in anger, fled. Japanese shelling had knocked out the Misamis telephone system, and the radio transmitter had been hastily dismantled and moved to another location. Fertig and the escapees were in deep trouble. They were nearly encircled by the Japanese, and the guerilla chief was out of contact with his units.

Meanwhile, the *Thresher* was knifing through the ocean on its way to Misamis Occidental, which was swarming with Japanese. Fertig hurried out of the area to avoid capture and had no means to warn off the submarine. On the fourth day of the Japanese sweep, Fertig caught up with his radio transmitter, which had been reassembled. Only hours before the rendezvous was scheduled to take place, a coded message got through to Brisbane:

WARN SUB COMMANDER SITE FOR MEETING NORTH COAST IN HANDS ENEMY. SITE NOT FEASIBLE.

Word reached the *Thresher* on time, and a further exchange of messages set up a new rendezvous locale. Ed Dyess, Steve Mellnik, and Melvyn McCoy, guided by guerillas, scrambled through the jungles and over mountains for six days before reaching the new meeting place. Finally, weary and famished, the three Americans boarded the *Thresher* and soon were bound for Australia.

About a month later, Lieutenant Leo Boelens was bossing a Filipino work crew that was constructing a large airstrip, one nearly a mile long. It could accommodate the biggest U.S. bombers. One night, Boelens got word that the Japanese were patrolling the area, no doubt looking for the American, so he fled into the jungle. Two days later, he was told the Japanese had left, and he returned. Minutes later, he was pounced on by the Japanese, tortured cruelly, and executed. His remains were hurled into a shallow grave. After the patrol had left, Filipinos removed Boelens's mutilated body and gave him a Christian burial.

Leo Boelens was the only one of the Davao escapees who would not eventually reach the United States. Austin Shofner, Sam Grashio, Jack Hawkins, and Michael Dobervich were evacuated by submarines in the weeks ahead. Bob Spielman and Paul Marshall chose to remain with "General" Wendell Fertig and exact vengeance against the Japanese as guerillas.[5]

A month after reaching Australia and meeting with General MacArthur, Lieutenant Ed Dyess returned to the United States and wrote a detailed account of the Death March and the brutalities inflicted upon American and Filipino POWs at O'Donnell, Cabanatuan, and Davao. His unvarnished story avoided an aura of sensationalism and stuck to what he had actually witnessed himself or episodes told to him firsthand by those involved. Under wartime security, Dyess's report had to be submitted to the War Department. Secretary of War Henry Stimson, aware that he had hold of a political hot potato, rushed the account to President Franklin Roosevelt, who convened a conference of top military and government leaders to discuss the potential explosive situation created by Dyess's blockbuster story.

The agonizing question was: Would the release of Dyess's candid account trigger such an avalanche of outrage from the nations of the world that the Japanese would be forced to improve the treatment of POWs? Or would the release result in their adopting an even harder line, including refusing to accept Red Cross packages for the American and Filipino prisoners? There was a third facet to be considered. After millions of Americans on the home front learned of the atrocities inflicted on their fighting men, would they demand that the Allied global strategy of first bringing Adolf Hitler to his knees be scrapped, and an all-out assault on anything Japanese be substituted? After listening to arguments on all sides, President Roosevelt decided to suppress the Dyess report.

Acting on Roosevelt's directive, the War Department rushed an order to U.S. theater commanders to strictly abide by the decision to keep the Dyess account under cover. Douglas MacArthur, livid over the Japanese maltreatment of his men, fired back to Washington a signal that fell just short of insubordination, pointing out that the Australian government was conducting an investigation of the atrocities and that its results soon would be released to the world.

In early October 1943, the *Washington Times Herald* dropped a bombshell. Spread across its front page was a brief, reasonably accurate, though quite sketchy, account of the Japanese atrocities. Keeping a secret in the political hotbed that is Washington is akin to trying to hide the rising sun from a rooster. Clearly, someone in the know and outraged by Roosevelt's suppression had leaked bits and pieces of the Dyess story.

Meanwhile, Ed Dyess, who had been promoted to lieutenant colonel, begged General Henry Arnold, the air corps chief, to be permitted to go back to the Pacific as a combat pilot. Fearful of Dyess's fate should he again be captured by the Japanese, Arnold turned thumbs down on the request. But the general assigned Dyess to form his own P-38 squadron that, conceivably, one day would be unleashed against the Germans in Europe.

Colonel Dyess had been put in a deep freeze, presumably to isolate him from journalists. Only his immediate family in Texas and a few chums knew that he was stationed at March Field, California. One of those in the know was Dyess's fellow escapee, Captain Samuel Grashio, who also had been promoted. Like Dyess, Grashio had longed to live to see the day that he could tell the world of Japanese atrocities. As soon as he had arrived at Hamilton Field, California, on his return from Australia, Grashio was hustled before authorities and reminded repeatedly that he was not to discuss his life in prison camps with anyone. He had been effectively gagged.

A few days later, Grashio received orders to fly to Washington immediately and report to the Pentagon, the huge new war center erected on the banks of the Potomac River. Hardly had the young officer entered a room when a group of colonels impressed upon him yet again that he was to say absolutely nothing about his experiences in the Philippines.[6]

While Lieutenant Colonel Dyess was familiarizing himself with the swift, twin-boomed P-38 fighter planes, General MacArthur, in characteristic fashion, ignored Washington's edict on keeping the atrocities report quiet and took matters into his own hands. Mincing no words, the supreme commander in the Southwest Pacific issued a blunt warning to his opposite number, Field Marshal Hisaichi Terauchi. MacArthur declared that he would hold Terauchi and other Japanese commanders responsible if they failed to treat American and Filipino prisoners in a humane manner.

MacArthur's sledgehammer approach apparently struck a nerve in Tokyo. A short time later, the chief of the Japanese Prisoner of War Bureau sent a message to the commandants of all Japanese POW camps, urging them to exercise care "to avoid issuing twisted reports of our fair attitude (toward prisoners) which might give the Americans food for evil propaganda."

Meanwhile back in the United States, enormous pressure mounted for the Roosevelt administration to release full details of the Japanese atrocities in the Philippines.

Samuel Grashio recalled: "Ed Dyess's father, Richard, remarked loudly and often that those who favored repression did not understand Japanese psychology, and that his son knew that every POW in the Philippines would want the story told. Richard Dyess made scathing remarks about 'pencil pushing officers who would probably faint if they smelled gunpowder.' "[7]

Albert C. MacArthur, president of the American Bataan Club in the United States, was equally irate over what he called "the cover-up" in Washington. He charged that the same "bankrupt politicians" in Washington who had been responsible for America's unpreparedness were trying to persuade the American people "to forget their dereliction by suppressing what Ed Dyess had to say."

On January 28, 1944, a banner headline in the *New York Times* screamed:

5,200 AMERICANS, MANY MORE FILIPINOS DIE
OF STARVATION, TORTURE AFTER BATAAN

President Franklin Roosevelt and his military brass had had a change of heart and decided to release the full context of Ed Dyess's report. Across the land similar headlines and stories were splashed across front pages, and the airwaves were filled with accounts of the Death March and the POW hellholes.

Washington and the nation were shocked and angry. Taking to the floor of Congress, Senator Bennett Champ Clark of Missouri thundered that Japan "should be bombed out of existence," and he demanded that the Allies hang Emperor Hirohito as a major war criminal. Scores of other members of Congress expressed the same sentiments. Senator Richard B. Russell of Georgia described the Japanese soldiers as "brutish beings in human form."[8]

Earlier, on December 21, 1943, Lieutenant Colonel Ed Dyess was taking a routine training flight in a P-38 after lifting off from March Field. Near Burbank, California, the airplane developed an engine malfunction, struck a church steeple, and crashed. Dyess, now only twenty-six years of age, had survived Japanese bombs and bullets, the Death March, O'Donnell, Cabanatuan, Davao, jungles and swamps, but he did not live to see his account of calculated Japanese atrocities disclosed to the American people.[9]

10

Manila's Notorious Club Tsubaki

A favorite Manila haunt for Japanese officers and high civilian officials was Club Tsubaki. Located near the harbor, the night spot was owned by thirty-three-year-old Claire Fuentes, a vivacious brunette of Italian birth and Philippine citizenship. She let it be known that Club Tsubaki catered only to the Japanese, and even wealthy Filipinos were not welcome. Claire had stylish cards printed and addressed them to "the best people."

Club Tsubaki was packed each night with beer-swilling Japanese who lounged in low-slung rattan settees and portable armchairs. Clad in shimmering evening gowns with plunging necklines, the proprietress circulated among the guests, laughing, teasing, flirting. On any given night, she would spend most of her time at the table of the highest ranking or most important Japanese.

Actually, Claire Fuentes was not an Italian, but an American, whose real name was Dorothy Claire Phillips. She was a spy who used her popular club to collect information from the Japanese, and her "guerillas without guns" organization smuggled needed food and supplies into Cabanatuan camp. Club Tsubaki was headquarters for the covert operation.

Claire Phillips's first contact with the Philippines had been in spring 1941, when she played Manila as a singer with a touring American musical stock company. Her stage name then was "Claire de la Taste." After her Manila gig was concluded and she returned to the United States, she decided to make an extended visit to the Philippines. On September 20, 1941, she arrived in Manila. With her was Dian, her small daughter and the product of a hasty marriage that quickly had gone sour and ended in divorce.

After settling down in an apartment, Claire made a living by singing popular ballads in such posh establishments as the Manila Hotel ballroom and the ultramodern Alcazar Club. While warbling such lilting songs as "I Don't Want to Walk Without You" and "You Made Me Love You," she spotted a fine-looking American soldier on the dance floor. Finagling an introduction, she learned that he was Sergeant John Phillips, a radioman in the U.S. 31st Infantry Regiment. After a whirlwind courtship, the couple was married. Less than two months later, Sergeant Phillips and his regiment were fighting for their lives in the green hell known as Bataan.

In the wake of the American disaster on Bataan, Claire tried desperately to learn of John's fate. Then, in late August 1942, she received a telephone call from Father Heinz Buttenbruck, a German priest, who had a pass from his "allies," the Japanese, allowing him to roam Luzon freely while engaged in charitable work. Much of that "charitable work" involved his participation in a covert two-way courier service that smuggled letters between Manila and the Cabanatuan prison camp.

Father Buttenbruck, a husky, gray-haired man brimming with energy, periodically visited Cabanatuan camp. Since he might be searched on entering or leaving the enclosure, he could not carry written messages. But he had an incredible gift for recall, and he brought back to Manila in his head a large number of messages sent by POWs to loved ones. These messages he usually delivered by telephone from his encyclopedic mental storage bin.

Now, when Claire Phillips arrived in the study of the padre's rectory, she sensed by his compassionate nature that he had bad news. From an inside pocket of his cassock, Father Buttenbruck pulled out a list of recent deaths at Cabanatuan. In a low tone, he read, "Sergeant John V. Phillips . . . July 27, 1942 . . . causes, malaria and dysentery." She recognized his serial number, which ended with thirteen, a detail about which the couple had joked often in better times.[1]

Claire sensed the true cause of John's death—hunger and disease. So in the weeks ahead, she hatched a scheme to get back at the Japanese and to aid the POWs in Cabanatuan. She would organize an espionage ring. This would require freedom to move about without being arrested, so she would have to assume a new identity and obtain a pass.

With her olive skin, black hair, and flashing dark eyes, she decided to become an "Italian," since that would make her an ally of the Japanese. Although she did not speak a word of Italian, she realized that neither did most Japanese.

Claire contacted a young Spaniard, who had been a friend of her husband John before the outbreak of war. He was an accomplished linguist and worked as a translator at the Italian consulate in Manila. She bluntly put the question to him: "Can you obtain phony Italian identification papers for me?"

The Spaniard was shaken: If he performed such a deed and was caught by the Japanese, he probably would be beheaded. Finally, however, he agreed to try.[2]

Ten days later, the Spaniard was back. With him were the precious papers, made out to Claire Fuentes and showing that she had been born of Neapolitan parents, who had died several years earlier, and that she was a naturalized citizen of the Philippines. Apparently, the Spaniard had pilfered the forms at the Italian consulate and filled out the documents in authentic style as directed by Claire.

Claire's fraudulent credentials still had to be approved by Colonel Oshima Ohta, chief of the Japanese military police in Manila. With trembling knees and furiously pounding heart, Claire called on Ohta, who was suave and friendly. He explained that the occupiers did not expect Filipino citizens to cooperate with the "liberators," but would she promise not to do anything to help the enemy?

She rapidly mulled over that statement, then signed the papers, which the colonel stamped with his seal of approval. Claire, a devout Catholic, did not lie. In her mind, the "enemy" was the Japanese, and she most certainly would do absolutely nothing to "help" them.

As the days and then the weeks stole past, Claire was anguished by the fact that she and a few of her early recruits were unable to obtain useful intelligence from Japanese authorities, information she planned to relay to guerilla contacts in the mountains. Then she was struck by a wild scheme: If she could not go to the Japanese, why not arrange for them to come to her? So she decided to open a Manila nightclub, one near the waterfront where it would be easily accessible to Japanese officers arriving by ship.

Claire located a suitable building, but it would require a considerable amount of pesos to remodel the structure into an entertainment spot. No doubt she enjoyed much satisfaction in knowing that a wealthy Japanese businessman named Hochima, who had been an ardent fan of her singing at the elegant Alcazar Club prior to the war in the Philippines, put up the money. Hochima even came up with the name for the new establishment. *Tsubaki* is Japanese for camellia, a favorite flower in Dai Nippon and one that is hard to obtain. In Japan, the word *club* means exclusive.[3]

Drawing on her show business background, Claire put on rousing floor shows each night, complete with a five-piece band and featuring her five attractive, skimpily clad dancing girls. Their dances contained grotesque and sensuous movements and concluded with the graceful young women going into a frenzy described as a "joyous fiesta celebration."

The Japanese patrons, most of whom had had plenty to drink by floor-show time, watched goggle-eyed during the women's gyrations. The guests became even more attentive when the female performers mingled with them after the show. The dancers' nimbleness was of great help in eluding the drunken grabs at various parts of their anatomies.

All of the stage performers and other employees were ardent Philippine patriots, and they were valuable cogs in Claire's espionage operation. One of the dancers, Fely Corcurea, had several close relatives who had fought on Bataan, survived the Death March, and had not been heard from since. Fahny, a talented and clever black dancer, also had reason to hate the Japanese: Her father, a physician, was a prisoner in the civilian internment camp at Santo Tomás University in Manila. Fahny's two sisters, Anna and Lily, were also members of the Club Tsubaki dancing troupe.

Most of the Japanese patrons spoke smatterings of English and Tagalog. However, Claire realized that the guests talked mainly in Japanese when discussing military or secret matters, knowing that the Filipina dancers circulating among them after the floor shows did not grasp the language. Claire solved that nagging problem with the unknowing assistance of the conquerors, who had a standing offer of a free daily lesson to Philippine citizens wanting to learn the Japanese language.

Fely Corcurea had a natural talent for absorbing languages rapidly, so she was sent to the classes. Within a short space of time, the slim, sprightly Fely was able to speak and understand Japanese, and she also learned to read and write in hiragana and katakana alphabets. This skill permitted her to comprehend the notes that Japanese patrons often passed openly to one another while seated at tables with the Filipina dancers.

The information collected from inebriated Japanese officers each night would be of no value unless it reached sources that could transmit it to General Douglas MacArthur's headquarters in New Guinea, where the Americans and Australians were battling the Japanese. So Claire Fuentes established contact with Corporal John Boone, who had served in the 31st Infantry with her late husband, John. Boone had escaped during the Death March, taken to the hills north of Bataan, and organized a guerilla force that had now reached a total of fifty Americans and nearly a thousand Filipinos.

In keeping with the responsibility of a commander of such a sizable force, Boone "promoted" himself to major. His code name was Compadre. Each week, Claire's native runners, at great peril, slipped past Japanese military police in Manila and carried Claire's intelligence reports to Boone in the hills. She signed her information with her code name High Pockets, which came about because of her penchant for securing personal valuables and intelligence notes in her brassiere.

Early on, Boone had no means for relaying this information to an American headquarters. But High Pockets managed to secretly obtain a radio transmitter and receiver from a Filipino source in Manila, and piece by piece, so as not to attract Japanese attention, the set was transported to Boone's hideout by a series of Filipino couriers. Boone then sent High Pockets' information to an American guerilla command post on Mindanao, six hundred miles to the south, from where it was relayed to MacArthur in New Guinea.

Meanwhile, High Pockets had been establishing a lifeline between Club Tsubaki and the Cabanatuan camp. Weeks earlier, she had carpenters convert storage space at the club into a four-room apartment so she could be on the premises day and night. One morning, a courier brought her a note smuggled out of Cabanatuan and signed by Everlasting—code name for Chaplain Frank Tiffany. He wrote that POWs were dying daily from malaria, and he asked if she could send quinine.

High Pockets was distraught. There was no quinine on the market. Then, a day later, a notice appeared in the *Manila Tribune* that Emperor Hirohito, in his imperial benevolence, had sent the Philippine government a million quinine tablets for distribution to pharmacies. A specified ration was to be given to all Filipinos who applied.

High Pockets sent all of her employees, along with many others in her network, to pick up their quotas of quinine. Knowing that there would be no way for the Japanese to keep track of who was applying where, each Filipino hurried to four or five pharmacies to obtain the tablets. In just under a week, ten thousand quinine capsules had been collected. Several different couriers carried this crucially needed medicine to the marketplace in Cabanatuan town, from where the capsules were sneaked into the POW camp in carabao carts.

Some fifteen days later, High Pockets received a note from Chaplain Tiffany: "The quinine arrived. We can make use of all you can send. Much thanks. I hate to be begging all the time, but I do need shorts for my church services. I am ashamed to stand in front of the men looking so ragged. The boys say they'd sure like some candy . . . God bless you!"[4]

Within a short period of time, a courier brought a note to High Pockets in which Chaplain Tiffany picked out the ten neediest men he knew in the camp. Earlier, High Pockets had asked for such a compilation, because she knew that her network could not provide all the needs for all the POWs. At the head of Everlasting's list was the name Yeager, with the notation: "Bad tuberculosis. Might pull through if he had the will to live. Send him a box of candy. Write him cheery letter."

High Pockets summoned her dancing troupe, all bright, creative young women, and together they pooled ideas for writing the cheerful letter to Yeager. Then High Pockets said she was going to get a box of candy "even if I have to loot a Jap warehouse." In some manner, she obtained the hard-to-find confection, and it eventually reached Yeager, as did the upbeat letter.

Twelve days later, High Pockets received a note from Chaplain Tiffany: "Yeager received your candy and most cheerful letter. They made him very happy. Am sorry to report, however, that he died the next day."

Most Japanese army officers remained in Manila for only about a month, so when a new face showed up at the Tsubaki Club, High Pockets made it a point to pick his brains. One such newcomer was a young army captain who came alone each night.

"What's a big handsome man like you doing by yourself," she cooed.

He explained that he had just arrived from Japan a week earlier and knew none of the Filipina women.

"But you will make many friends after you have been here awhile," High Pockets suggested pointedly.

"No," he replied, his speech now slurred from heavy imbibing, "I'm leaving for Lingayen Gulf tomorrow."

High Pockets knew that Lingayen Gulf was where General Homma's invaders had come ashore in December 1941, and she had heard it speculated in the underground that MacArthur would land in that same locale when he returned.

"Lingayen Gulf!" High Pockets replied in mock astonishment. "Why should they send you up to that desolate, lonely place?"

"Well," the captain answered, gulping down another drink, "we came ashore easy, so we think the *Beikokujin* (Americans) might have same idea." Another heavy gulp. "So we fortify heavy, keep many soldiers there."

High Pockets allowed as how she didn't understand "all that war stuff."

Within forty-eight hours, the captain's remarks reached General MacArthur's G-2 in New Guinea.[5]

One day in mid-1943, High Pockets learned that an old friend, U.S. Navy Chief Petty Officer Charles Di Maio, was a POW at Cabanatuan. An outgoing, energetic man with an infectious grin and warm-hearted mannerisms, Di Maio had been an almost nightly customer at the Alcazar Club where Claire had been singing prior to the outbreak of war.

High Pockets wrote Di Maio through the Club Tsubaki-Cabanatuan pipeline, and two weeks later, he replied:

> When I got your letter I came to life again. You've done more for the boys' morale in here than you'll ever know. Now don't get mad, High Pockets, but I donated forty-three packages of tobacco (you sent) to the other boys . . . Some of them are flat on their backs they're so weak, and you should have seen the looks of gratitude when I handed them your tobacco sacks.
>   Take care of yourself, High Pockets. You deserve more gold medals than all of us in here together.[6]

Outgoing Charlie Di Maio promptly became one of High Pockets' contacts in the Cabanatuan camp, and she dubbed him with the code name Wop.

By fall 1943, living conditions were becoming far more difficult in Manila. American canned goods, clothing, and medicines 'had vanished, and now rice, lard, sugar, matches, and coconuts were not only limited, but strictly rationed by the Japanese. Still, there was enormous need for these commodities inside the Cabanatuan death camp. Manilans' new monthly food quotas were so small that they rarely lasted a family for a week. Most certainly, there was not enough food left over in High Pockets' underground network to ship to the POW enclosure.

Confronted with this desperate situation, High Pockets zeroed in on a frequent patron, a Japanese major, after she learned that he was in charge of a warehouse crammed with large amounts of rice. High Pockets and her beautiful dancer, Fely, double-teamed the unknowing target, exuding their charms and flattery.

When the major's mind was foggy from a night of imbibing, High Pockets pried from him the fact that he was unhappy with his low pay, and he hinted that he would be agreeable to financial offers. Running her fingers through the officer's hair and snuggling up close, High Pockets said she would be willing to pay him one hundred pesos for each sack of rice he could provide. He apparently was unaware that rice was selling on the black market for five hundred pesos per sack.

The major slammed his glass down on the table and stared angrily at Claire. She felt a cold chill streak up her back, knowing that the penalty for trying to bribe a Japanese officer was beheading.

"But my dear Major, you don't understand," she cooed. "This rice is for poor and sick Filipinos."

His features softened and he broke out in a wide grin.

Now eager to cooperate, the major said that when he saw a chance to take rice out of the warehouse, he would telephone High Pockets and say, "I very hot, come for a beer." This was the signal for the spymistress to send a few of her Filipinos into the alley behind the warehouse, where most of them would load the rice into wagons while the remainder served as lookouts.

In this manner, the underground warriors managed to slip thirty sacks out of the warehouse, but a few days later, Claire's deal with the major collapsed. He had been wheeling and dealing with other Manilans as well, for word reached Club Tsubaki that he was locked up and facing serious charges, none of them connected to High Pockets' operation. Soon, the thirty sacks of rice were sneaked into Cabanatuan, a sack or two at a time.

A few days after Operation Rice had run its course, High Pockets received an urgent request from Major John Boone, the guerilla chief in the hills: "Urgent. Find out what is in Jap ship in Manila harbor. Ship painted white with huge red cross."

Why was General MacArthur's headquarters interested in a Japanese Red Cross mercy ship? she pondered. She knew that the vessel had been in port for at least three days, for its skipper visited Club Tsubaki each night.

High Pockets sent for two teenaged Filipinos, who had jobs on the pier unloading ships, to serve as her eyes and ears. She asked them to slip aboard the Red Cross ship and break into one of the crates in the hold to see what was in the cargo. The snooping had to be done that same night. Both youths were terrified. If caught, a distinct possibility, they would be tortured to reveal their accomplices, then killed.

High Pockets tried to reassure them despite her own deep misgivings. The Red Cross ship's skipper and his officers would be in Club Tsubaki until well after midnight, taking in a special floor show and party she had arranged for them. All the two youths had to do was dodge a sentry on the vessel, she told them.

As soon as the ship's captain and his entourage entered the club, he told High Pockets that he would have to leave early, that his vessel had to sail at midnight. Claire's heart skipped a beat: The two Filipino boys would be trapped on the ship at that time. Unlike most Japanese patrons, the skipper drank very little, nursing one beer for two hours.

High Pockets ordered the floor show to begin at ten o'clock, rather than at the usual starting time of midnight. Wearing a powder-blue, tight-fitting, low-cut gown with an enticing slit on one side extending far up her thigh, Claire took a seat next to the skipper. While he was avidly watching the scantily clad female dancers, she managed to slip a "Mickey Finn" in his glass of beer. A few minutes later, the Japanese turned a ghastly greenish-white and slumped in his chair. Two waiters were called to half carry him to a booth where he stretched out and fell sound asleep.

High Pockets sent word to the junior officers at other tables that their boss was "quite tired," and that he wanted to remain with her to "rest." That pronouncement was greeted by raucous laughter and bawdy remarks.

The floor show continued until the performers, who were privy to the unfolding scenario, were nearly exhausted. Just past eleven-thirty, the junior officers began to depart. One of them whispered to High Pockets to send the skipper back as soon as possible, punctuating the request with an eyewink and a broad grin.

When the Japanese had cleared the club, a horse-drawn wagon was brought to the back door, and the skipper's inert frame was placed in it. High Pockets was fearful that he might die, and she didn't want his body to be found in her club. Furtively, the snoozing skipper was dumped along the dark docks near his Red Cross ship. Presumably, when awakened, he would surmise that he had tried to make it back to his vessel, but, for some reason, had keeled over.

Shortly after daybreak, the two excited Filipino dockhands arrived at the club. They had gotten aboard with no difficulty and had inspected the contents of several crates. One held out a handful of bullets, the type of "Red Cross" cargo being carried.

High Pockets scratched out a note to Major Boone and dispatched a teenaged girl to take the message, and the bullets, to the guerilla leader. Presumably, the large white ship with the oversized red crosses was bound for New Guinea to resupply Japanese forces there. American submarines, no doubt, would be lurking along the way to properly dispose of the disguised mercy ship.

As the days and weeks passed, High Pockets and her workers continued to smuggle food, medicine, and clothes into Cabanatuan while spying on the Japanese in Manila. Unknown to any of the conspirators, a giant dragnet of the dreaded Kempei Tai was closing in on them.

In early May 1944, one of High Pockets' couriers, a young Russian woman married to an American sailor imprisoned at Cabanatuan, was arrested by the Kempei Tai on a Manila street. On her were found several letters, signed with code names, which she had picked up earlier in Cabanatuan town for delivery in Manila. Strong men would have broken under the hideous tortures inflicted on the woman in the dungeons at old Fort Santiago. Finally, she cracked, revealing the true identities of some of Claire's organization.

One by one, many of High Pockets' key operatives were arrested and hurled into Fort Santiago. Friends urged Claire to take to the hills, but she declined, declaring that the Japanese had no incriminating evidence against her. However, she took prudent precautions, scouring her living quarters and removing all papers that might link her to espionage and to Cabanatuan camp.

She spent many sleepless nights. Only with the arrival of dawn did she close her eyes from sheer exhaustion. Then it came. Just past nine on the morning of May 22, she was eating breakfast in her quarters at Club Tsubaki when she heard the clump of heavy boots approaching her door. Moments later, four heavyset Japanese soldiers barged inside and leveled their weapons at her.

"You are Madame Tsubaki?" an officer asked.

She replied in the affirmative.

"Oh, no, you're not!" the man declared. "You are the notorious High Pockets!"

Claire was dragged out of the club and shoved into a car, whose driver pulled onto the road and drove to the Japanese Administration Building on San Luis Boulevard, only three blocks from Club Tsubaki. There rough hands hurled her into a locked room.

Early the next morning, Claire was blindfolded and hustled down a hall and into another room. There were two interrogators, it seemed to her. Clearly, they wanted their identities kept secret. One man spoke fluent, flawless English. Then she knew the reason for the blindfold. She recognized the voice as that of a reporter for a Japanese newspaper who had graduated from college in the United States. Claire had met him several times in recent months.

"Do you deny that you have written and received letters from the prisoners at Cabanatuan?" the voice demanded to know.

Since the Japanese obviously had intercepted some of the letters, she admitted that she had written "a few" of them and had received "a few" back. When Claire refused to detail how the letter smuggling worked, she was beaten with heavy blows that knocked her off the chair.

"Who is Wop? Who is Everlasting? Who is Compadre?" they screamed.

After moments of silence, the Japanese journalist read one of the letters she had written to Cabanatuan: "Dear Everlasting. I was glad to hear that you received cal and feel so much better. Will you please send out demijohn . . ."

They shouted at her, declaring that Cal and John Demi were actually the code names of two American POW brothers that she had been trying to help escape. It did no good for her to explain that cal was the abbreviation for calamanci, or lemons, and that a demijohn was a narrow-necked bottle of glass or stoneware enclosed in wicker-work.

"Liar!" they yelled and smashed Claire to the floor under a rain of heavy blows from their fists.

Despite repeated beatings and suffering the ancient Chinese water torture, High Pockets admitted only to sending to and receiving letters from Cabanatuan—facts that the Japanese had already known. So in July, she was transferred to Fort Santiago. There she was mugged and fingerprinted by an old "friend," a Captain Kobioshi, who had been a regular patron at Club Tsubaki. On one occasion, he had promised to give Claire the city of Portland, Oregon, once the Japanese flag flew over the White House in Washington.

Confronting High Pockets would be many bitter months of interrogations, beatings with boards and fists, relentless mental agony, and torture. On occasion, she would be forced to watch female and male prisoners being beheaded in an effort to make her confess.

11

Alamo Scouts and Rangers

With the approach of 1944, General Douglas MacArthur was conducting a reappraisal of his strategic plan for returning to the Philippines. For nearly a year and a half, his American and Australian troops had been leapfrogging up the spine of New Guinea in his hit-'em-where-they-ain't campaign of speed and surprise. However, the advance had covered only 240 miles—still 1,600 miles short of Leyte, in the central Philippines, where MacArthur intended to invade. At the current pace, it might take ten years to reach Corregidor, Bataan, and Manila. He decided that, to speed the advance, each leap would be lengthened.

MacArthur's eye was on the Vogelkop Peninsula at the western tip of New Guinea. Beyond that point lay the Moluccas, an ideal springboard for a mighty jump all the way to the Philippines. However, between his advanced forces and Leyte were a great number of Japanese troops on various islands. Just how many, nobody knew. The available intelligence was often fragmentary. Much of it came from dubious sources. To save lives, MacArthur needed accurate intelligence obtained by specially trained soldiers, whose task would be to infiltrate enemy territory and nail down facts about Japanese troop strengths and deployments. He also needed men who could live in the jungle for long periods on scant food and water, who could move silently, swiftly, and invisibly, stalking and killing Japanese or snatching prisoners for interrogation.

MacArthur called in Lieutenant General Walter Krueger, leader of the U.S. Sixth Army, and outlined his concept of this unique force. Then Krueger, in turn, summoned Colonel Frederick W. Bradshaw of

Jackson, Mississippi, who was a lawyer in peacetime. Bradshaw was shrewd, soft-spoken, and gifted in the intangible skill known as leadership. Krueger briefed the colonel on forming reconnaissance teams that would perform in the tradition of Davy Crockett and his frontiersmen. A Texan from San Antonio, Krueger remembered the epic fight put up by Crockett and his men against overwhelming hordes of Mexicans in 1836, so the name Alamo Scouts was coined.

Colonel Bradshaw selected as his second in command Major Gibson Niles, a native of Delmar, New York, who had performed on the varsity track and cross-country teams at West Point prior to his 1941 graduation. Gib Niles recalled the early days of the Alamo Scouts:

"There was no unit known as the 'Alamo Scouts.' Rather, there was the Alamo Scouts Training Center (ASTC). All assigned personnel were on temporary duty from their parent units. ASTC's primary mission was to train volunteers to be Alamo Scouts. Graduates of the rugged six-week training course were either selected for teams or returned to their parent units.

"We picked out godforsaken Fergusson Island, five miles off New Guinea, for our training center. Then we began calling for volunteers from army units already in the southwest Pacific. We wanted men with skills beyond their prowess as foot soldiers. We wanted men of individual initiative and competitive spirit. They had to be men temperamentally drawn by a game of high risks. They had to be crack marksmen, experts with many weapons, and also able and willing to kill with their own hands."[1]

Many of the early volunteers were eliminated; they were good soldiers but couldn't quite measure up to the rugged training and lofty standards demanded. The survivors in the competition consequently developed an esprit de corps of the kind desired—the Alamo Scouts knew they were the elite.

The Alamo Scouts functioned in a democratic manner seldom found in the U.S. Army. They were formed into small teams consisting of one officer and four or five men. Each team had a voice in selecting its own personnel. Each enlisted man was asked to name by private ballot the three officers, in the order of preference, whom he would be most willing to follow on a dangerous mission. Junior officers, in turn, were asked what men they desired to have with them.

Missions were selected by the G-2 (intelligence) officer of Krueger's Sixth Army. Maturity, experience, and availability at the ASTC were the primary considerations for choosing a specific team for a specific mission. Alamo Scouts were under operational control of the G-2 until their mission was accomplished, after which they returned to ASTC to await another task.[2]

Although new to the U.S. Army in concept, the Alamo Scouts wasted no time in springing into action. In New Guinea, they planned the kidnapping of General Hatazo Adachi, commander of the Japanese Eighteenth Army. Penetrating deep into Japanese territory, a team of Scouts hid near Adachi's headquarters and watched him and his bodyguards for several days. They had secured a floor plan of the house he occupied, including the direction each door opened. They mapped the route of the general's daily horseback ride along a jungle trail. However, the region was thick with Japanese troops and Adachi himself was constantly surrounded by guards.

Withdrawing to their own positions, the Alamo Scouts were eager to get the green light to try to snatch the Japanese general, this despite the heavy odds against success of the bold venture. When the scheme was put before General Krueger, he turned thumbs down. He agreed that the kidnapping would be a spectacular achievement and reap a great deal of propaganda value, but he held that no stunt was worth the life of a single Alamo Scout. The sixty-four-year-old Krueger doubted if the raiders would get back alive—but all of them were willing to try.

As MacArthur's drive up the coast of New Guinea rolled inexorably onward, the missions of the Alamo Scouts were greatly increased, especially after feedback from their perilous tasks reached higher army commanders. At Pegun Island, a team of Scouts under Lieutenant Robert S. Sumner of Portland, Oregon, was dispatched to rescue three downed American airmen. For five hours, they searched in vain for the men.

Robert Sumner recalled subsequent events: "As we were returning to our pickup point along the shore, a Jap patrol of platoon size spotted us. We signaled the PT boat offshore we were coming, and backed into the water with our weapons held ready. Then the Japs opened fire on us, and we shot back as best we could while nearly chest-deep in water. The machine guns on the PT boat joined in. Bullets were whistling past our heads from both directions."[3]

Showing the interservice teamwork that was the key to Mac-Arthur's success, the PT boat radioed an Australian Beaufighter flying offshore. It zoomed down, machine guns blazing, and scattered the Japanese. Meanwhile, Sumner and his men reached the PT boat, which proceeded to execute the maneuver known in the military as "hauling ass."

On a mission to Japanese-held Hollandia, a team of Alamo Scouts led by Lieutenant John M. Dove of Hollywood, California, was put ashore by PT boat and spent the day prowling the locale. When they were returning to their pickup point along the coast at night, Lieutenant Dove took his men through the heart of a small village where Japanese troops were sleeping in huts and along both sides of the road.

John Dove recalled why he had taken this hazardous route: "All of us were bone-tired after having climbed around the mountains for many hours. When we approached this village, I noticed that there were swamps with neck-high mud on each side. So we killed the two sentries the Japs had left to guard the trail and stole through the village as silently as we could."[4]

In late September 1944, Sixth Army intelligence learned from natives that a former Dutch governor, his entire family, and a large number of Javanese workers cultivating a huge plantation along the Maori River in New Guinea were being held as hostages by a Japanese force occupying the region. A team of Alamo Scouts slipped into the area on the following night, and an escaped Filipino prisoner who knew the site drew diagrams in the sand for the Americans. These rough etchings even showed the location of doors and windows in the huts where the Japanese slept. The Scouts were told the precise place the guards stacked their weapons each night, secure in the belief that no armed Americans could possibly reach them in their remote locale.

After reconnoitering the area along the Maori River, the Alamo Scouts returned to their base on Biak Island, where a decision was made to rescue the Dutch hostages and the Javanese plantation workers. Selected to lead the raid was Lieutenant Thomas J. Rounsaville of Atoka, Oklahoma, who had joined the Alamo Scouts from another rugged outfit, the U.S. 11th Airborne Division. Also coming from the 11th Airborne, Lieutenant William E. Nellist of Eureka, California, was selected as the assistant team leader. Eleven enlisted men, a Filipino interpreter, and three native guides rounded out the team that would have to deal with an estimated thirty Japanese soldiers guarding the hostages.

On the dark night of October 4, the Alamo Scouts team paddled toward shore in rafts that had been dropped over the sides of PT boats hovering near the mouth of the Maori River. The Scouts were heavily armed: Tommy guns, rifles, smoke and fragmentation grenades, and nasty looking trench knives. Crawling silently onto the beach and into the seclusion of thick vegetation, Tom Rounsaville and Bill Nellist sent guides along the shoreline and determined that there were no Japanese nearby. Now the Scouts began marching along a muddy, slippery trail that would lead them to the village objective three miles inland. It was an arduous trek, requiring more than six hours. In the eerie blackness, the Scouts paused.

Thomas Rounsaville recalled: "I promptly sent our guide, who had been an orderly for the Japs there and escaped from them, into the village. He was thoroughly acquainted with the locale and I wanted to get last-minute information on enemy dispositions. About an hour later, the guide returned and brought out a few Jap weapons with him. He said that Japs were positioned just as they had been when he escaped from them seven days before."[5]

Rapidly, a rescue plan was hatched. Lieutenant Nellist took four Scouts to a point where the Japanese were known to have two machine guns. When Nellist heard firing from the village, he and his men were to wipe out the pair of automatic weapons, then hurry to cover a trail over which the Japanese might rush in reinforcements.

Tom Rounsaville remembered: "At 4:10 A.M., we pitched grenades, then charged with knives, shouting bloody murder at the top of our lungs. Our attack came as a complete surprise. We killed fourteen Japs before they could get out of their huts. Four other Japs ran to a trench, where our boys knocked off two of them. The other two, wearing only shorts, fled into the jungle. Since time was important, we didn't bother to chase them."[6]

Twenty-two-year-old Corporal Andy Smith, a former civil service employee in St. Louis, was one of those who scoured each native hut to make sure no Japanese was in hiding. Smith recalled a curious incident: "In one of the huts I found a Jap phonograph, and there was a large stack of records next to it. Apparently the Japs had passed the time by playing music. I looked through the records and found one by Bing Crosby. I immediately played it, and it sounded real good."[7]

In the meantime, Lieutenant Nellist and his men quickly wiped out the Japanese machine gunners, and an interpreter and two guides dashed to the main enclosure to alert the Dutch and Javanese hostages to get ready to move out. Rapidly, the bewildered Dutch governor, the thirteen other members of his family, and scores of Javanese workers were rounded up. With Alamo Scouts in front and back, the long column began trudging over a narrow path toward shore. Shortly after dawn, Rounsaville, Nellist, their men, the hostages, guides, and interpreters were aboard two PT boats heading to Biak Island.

Not long after this bold mission, Sixth Army G-2 was told that a hundred missionaries were being held prisoners by a force of Japanese at Goya, an inland village in New Guinea. A rescue mission was laid on. An Alamo Scouts team led by Lieutenant Michael J. Sombar of Delaware, Wyoming, trudged for six miles along a jungle trail, often in knee-deep mud, to reach Goya. In less than twenty minutes, the Japanese force was wiped out and the missionaries freed. One nun threw her arms around Lieutenant Sombar's neck and exclaimed, "It's good to see an American again!"

On the trail leading back to the beach where two PT boats were waiting, a Japanese officer, who had been taken prisoner, refused to carry the pack of an elderly missionary who was exhausted. Speaking in flawless English, he protested that the Geneva Convention held that officers could not be forced to perform manual labor. A nearby Scout motioned toward three missionaries to get out of his line of fire and lifted his rifle. Quickly, the Japanese officer picked up the pack and lugged it to the beach.

None of the Alamo Scouts involved in these two daring rescue missions in Japanese territory had any way of knowing that the operations were, in essence, dress rehearsals for a much larger rescue of POWs that would be conducted a few months later at a camp in the Philippines known as Cabanatuan.

The success of the Alamo Scouts made a highly favorable impression on Douglas MacArthur and Walter Krueger. What was needed now to complement the surveillance and intelligence-collecting missions by the Alamo Scouts was a crack battalion trained to conduct hit-and-run raids deep behind Japanese lines. Since this force would range far and wide, they would be known as Rangers. Their origin was in April 1944, when thirty-three-year-old Lieutenant Colonel Henry A. Mucci, a Pearl Harbor survivor, arrived at Port Moresby, New Guinea, to take command of the U.S. 98th Field Artillery Battalion, an outfit trained for mountain fighting. Along with the men were a thousand mules to carry the artillery and shells. The unit had arrived in the Southwest Pacific in January 1943 and had not yet been in action.

General Krueger had planned to use the 98th Field Artillery in the New Guinea mountains, but no suitable assignment had been found. Morale plunged as the weeks passed. Then came another crusher: The battalion's mules were shipped to Burma, where Colonel Frank Merrill, an enterprising American officer, had formed Merrill's Marauders, a rugged group that was fighting deep behind Japanese lines in the mountains.

Henry Mucci, who wore a moustache and was of medium build, assembled the 98th Field Artillery, strode briskly across the field, and leaped upon a platform in front of his men. There he stood for a few moments, hands on hips, a .45-caliber pistol in a shoulder holster that would be his trademark. Finally, Mucci spoke: "I'm going to turn you men into Rangers," he declared. "From this point on, we will be known as the 6th Ranger Battalion."

Mucci told the men that they would be put through the most arduous six-week training course that diabolical minds could conceive, and those who survived the ordeal would be part of "the roughest, toughest outfit in the Pacific!" Mucci paused briefly, then declared: "If any of you think you can't hold up under all that, I'll send you to the hospital and you can spend the rest of the war washing nurses' panties!"[8]

"If you're old enough to fight and maybe die for your country, then you're old enough to drink beer," Mucci told his embryo Rangers. "I'll see to it that you get a regular beer ration."

Rousing cheers.

"However," the colonel warned, "If you've got a fat head the next morning and are unable to carry out your training, there'll be hell to pay!"

The 6th Ranger Battalion's strength would be about 570 men. The "batteries" of the 98th Field Artillery were changed to companies, each consisting of 65 men. Designed primarily for swift hit-and-run raids, the Rangers would have no heavy equipment, artillery, machine guns, or antitank guns. Bazookas, relatively light weapons, would be used to combat tanks and armored vehicles. With thirty-two Garand rifles, twelve carbines, four BARs (Browning Automatic Rifles), and ten Tommy guns, each 65-man unit would have firepower equivalent to that of the 190 men in a regular infantry company.

Early on, the former pack-mule artillerymen learned that Henry Mucci was not just a talker, but a doer. In low-key style, he led by example, the hallmark of successful combat leaders.

Soon after taking command, he told the battalion, "I'm going to give you a demonstration of the kind of hand-to-hand combat you're going to be taught. You'll see that the bigger they are, the harder they fall."

Then Mucci picked out husky Sergeant William R. Butler of Cleveland, Oklahoma, who stood six feet four inches. As the two men faced one another, the colonel told Butler to take out his trench knife. Butler did so.

"You see, I have no knife," Mucci called out to his soldiers. To them, this seemed to be an uneven matchup. Big Butler, who towered seven inches over the colonel and was armed with a nasty looking knife, would make mincemeat of the unarmed new commander. What the battalion did not know was that Mucci had undergone extensive training in hand-to-hand combat.

"Okay, sergeant, try to cut me up!" Mucci challenged.

Big Butler, a tough cookie, hesitated.

"Go ahead, cut me up!" the colonel urged.

Butler shrugged and lunged forward, his sharp blade glistening in the bright sun. Quick as a flash, Mucci leaped to one side, grabbed the sergeant by the wrist, and flipped him head over heels. Butler landed with a thud. Laughter broke out in the ranks.

"Any questions?" the colonel asked with a straight face.[9]

It soon became evident to the men of the embryo 6th Ranger Battalion that their lot would be a perilous one. Henry Mucci encouraged married men to transfer to another unit. Most of them chose to remain. In the days ahead, the colonel shipped out soldiers who, for a variety of reasons, he felt could not measure up. Grueling training in the sapping heat of New Guinea soon weeded out many more Ranger hopefuls.

One of the would-be Rangers was First Sergeant Charles H. Bosard, a five-foot-six, 140-pound bundle of energy, who had gained the respect of his comrades by his ability to lead by example. Like the other men, Bosard was near exhaustion at the end of each training day, yet he managed to keep a terse daily diary:

> May 9, 1944: Fired all of weapons while going over Misery Hill, across Torture Flats, and over obstacle course.
>
> May 11: Ran ten miles today with all weapons, ammo, and light field packs.
>
> May 26: We're all good swimmers now—250 yards carrying 50-pound pack.
>
> June 4: Out on amphibious training.

Henry Mucci was always in the thick of things. His men never knew where or when he would pop up. On twenty-five-mile hikes over rugged terrain, the colonel would be in their ranks. When bayonet practice was held, he would be there, thrusting and parrying. When men, cursing and panting, crawled for long distances in mock attacks on machine-gun nests, Mucci would have his nose in the mud with them.

There were rough hand-to-hand combat sessions (sometimes resulting in bloody noses and an occasional broken bone or two), and lengthy sessions on map-reading, handling rubber rafts in angry surfs, signal-blinking, radio operation, marksmanship, and killing silently and efficiently.

During the early days of arduous commando training, many of the would-be Rangers resented their demanding leader, Henry Mucci, who forever seemed to be shouting at them to try harder. "Little MacArthur!" they sneered. In the days ahead, however, the men gained enormous respect and admiration for Mucci, and they came to like the idea of being led by a gung-ho type. It soon became evident that Mucci, in turn, had developed a deep affection for his warriors.

Finally, the Big Day arrived. On June 19, 1944, the scrappy bulldog, First Sergeant Charley Bosard, scrawled in his diary:

"We are all *Rangers* now!"[10]

As with Bosard, each man in the 6th Rangers was bursting with pride—and eagerly anticipating the first mission. However, the days dragged into weeks, and no mission was forthcoming. Morale sagged. One Ranger declared: "Our role in this war is to sit on our asses and rot in a New Guinea jungle!"

None of the disappointed Rangers could know that their true destiny would be to conduct one of the global conflict's most electrifying missions involving a Japanese death camp.

12

Thumbs Down on a POW Rescue Scheme

Corporal William Becker III was only twenty years old, but months of almost constant running and hiding from Japanese patrols bent on his destruction had given him a maturity far beyond his years. Becker had been living like a hunted animal in the jungles of Luzon. There he operated an improvised meteorological station that he had helped to erect to provide General MacArthur's forces with weather conditions on the island.

There was nothing glamorous about Corporal Becker's job. Most of the time, he was extremely lonely and lived in fear. Like guerillas and undercover agents everywhere, he often wondered if he was risking his life for nothing. He began to doubt if anyone would ever use the weather data he was radioing to Australia each day—often while Japanese direction-finders in the region were trying to pinpoint his site before rushing in for the kill.

On August 6, 1944, an angry Bill Becker fired off a radio message reflecting the endless frustrations with which he was confronted. Out of whimsy, he addressed it to "General Douglas MacArthur." Becker no doubt thought that his message would get no further than some signal corps corporal:

> If this weather information is as important as I think it is and you say it is, then it deserves proper handling. It is getting just that at this end. If one radio set and good operators (in Australia) cannot be devoted to appointed frequency at appointed time, I just as well stop running and hiding. No contact all day August 4, no contact this morning. I volunteered to do a job and am doing it. Let us have some cooperation.
>
> —*Corporal William Becker III*

Indeed, a corporal in Australia did receive the indignant message, but he did not pigeonhole it as Becker had anticipated. Instead, he turned it over to Courtney Whitney, now a major general, who was in charge of guerilla and espionage operations in the Philippines. Whitney showed the signal to Douglas MacArthur, who read it while puffing on his corncob pipe.

The Supreme Commander of the Southwest Pacific decided to respond personally, and he assured Becker that the failure to establish radio contact with the guerilla was being investigated by his chief signal officer. MacArthur added:

> I understand the difficulties of your position, and everything possible will be done to assure prompt reception of your reports, which are of great value. But desire in the future (that you) endeavor to exercise patience and disciplined restraint expected of us soldiers and without which duty cannot be well done.
>
> —*MacArthur*[1]

Corporal Becker was one of the thousands of guerillas who had been highly active since Uncle Sam was driven out of the Philippines in the spring of 1942. The flame of armed resistance on Luzon had never ceased to burn brightly. Even while the doomed defenders of Corregidor had been firing their final feeble rounds, bands of guerillas were forming in the jungles and rugged mountains of Luzon, the largest and most heavily populated island in the Philippines.

In those early, chaotic days, the guerillas had little to recommend their chances for success. They were scattered around Luzon and unorganized. Guns were scarce. Ammunition was in short supply. To conserve bullets, some guerilla groups executed Filipino spies and traitors by beheading. Nevertheless, the guerillas were bound by patriotism and a fervent trust in General Douglas MacArthur. They believed his pledge, soon beamed to them steadily by a radio station in San Francisco, that "*I shall return!*"

Recalled Vicente Raval, a guerilla leader on Luzon: "We had total faith that MacArthur would come back. We never faltered in our hope."

At the same time, the Filipino guerillas totally mistrusted President Roosevelt and the Washington power structure, who, they were convinced, had conspired to sell out the Philippines.

Barbarities inflicted on the Filipinos, at the same time the invaders were calling on natives to "join us in the holy war against the white devils," reinforced the glue holding together guerilla groups. The conquerors also humiliated the Filipino civilians by orders to bow for five seconds to the Japanese soldiers they passed.

American Lieutenant Colonels Martin Moses and Arthur Noble, who had been with the Philippine 11th Division, had escaped from Bataan into the northern Luzon mountains, and within a few months they had more than six thousand Filipino guerillas under their command. At first, the ragtag band was armed mainly with machetes. Over the months, a steady stream of messages from Moses and Noble poured into General MacArthur's headquarters: "Four bridges blown up . . . Enemy telephone poles torn down . . . Food dumps burned . . . Much enemy arms and ammunition captured . . . Morale and behavior (of Filipino guerillas) excellent . . . Need more arms. Thousands eager to fight."

Eventually, Noble and Moses took one chance too many; they were captured by the Japanese, tortured and executed. Lieutenant Colonel Russell W. Volckmann and his executive officer, Major Daniel Blackburn, immediately took command, and the guerilla outfit continued to function without losing stride.

Russ Volckmann had been the intelligence officer and Blackburn the signals chief of the Philippine 11th Division. When Bataan had fallen, the division headquarters, located in a field, had several white flags hanging about in accordance with orders from higher up. Volckmann and Blackburn were whiling away the time by discussing the situation in the Philippines, waiting for the Japanese to arrive and take them prisoners.

Soon, an enemy company burst onto the scene and, despite the white flags, charged the headquarters, shooting wildly. It was a one-sided affair, for the Americans and Filipinos had already gotten rid of their weapons. Amid the heavy fusillades of bullets, chaos erupted. Volckmann and Blackburn slipped into a creek where they were concealed by heavy vegetation.

After the carnage concluded and the Japanese force departed, Volckmann and Blackburn crawled cautiously along the creek bank for a quarter mile, then headed northward to infiltrate Japanese positions and eventually reach the northern mountains of Luzon, where they began new careers as guerilla leaders.

For many months, Volckmann was chased around the rugged terrain by pursuing Japanese patrols, and he became legendary for his hair-breadth escapes. There was a saying among his sizable force of Filipino guerillas: "God walks with Russ Volckmann." To which Volckmann once responded: "I sure hope He doesn't stumble!"

In Nueva Ecija, where Cabanatuan camp was located, and other provinces in central Luzon, twenty-three-year-old Major Robert W. Lapham of Davenport, Iowa, commanded a guerilla force eventually numbering into the thousands. Unlike some guerilla leaders, Lapham was not personally ambitious, and he gave much of the credit for his successes to others. His second in command was U.S. Army Captain Harry M. McKenzie, who had been a civilian mining engineer in the Philippines for many years and had a Filipina wife and son.

Major Lapham was a charismatic leader. Though he smiled easily and spoke in a soft voice, this first impression was deceptive: Lapham was a fighter to the core and a man who commanded effortlessly through dint of character and behavior in the face of danger.

When Bataan had been on the verge of being overrun by Japanese forces and the Battling Bastards were being bombed and strafed mercilessly by clouds of enemy warplanes, Lapham, then an army lieutenant, and thirty-five other American soldiers had volunteered for a mission fraught with hazard. They were to infiltrate Japanese lines in northern Bataan, make their way northward through fifty miles of enemy-controlled territory to Clark Field, and blow up as many Japanese aircraft as they could. Odds were heavy that they would be killed or captured.

When only ten miles from bustling Clark Field, the largest air base in the Philippines, the American force on Bataan was surrendered by its commander, General Edward King. Consequently, the sabotage mission was scuttled, and Bob Lapham and the others decided not to capitulate but to split up and head for the hills to continue the fight.

Lapham made his way to Nueva Ecija Province where he began actively recruiting guerillas from the native population. There was no shortage of volunteers. Almost to a man, the Filipinos had a loved one or a close friend who had been subjected to Japanese atrocities on Luzon.

In keeping with the standard practice of American guerila leaders in the Philippines, Lieutenant Lapham promoted himself to major because of his far greater responsibilities and the large number of irregulars serving under him.

Major Lapham's two principal guerilla leaders in Nueva Ecija Province were twenty-six-year-old Captain Juan Pajota and Captain Eduardo Joson, who was one year younger. Both had fought on Bataan under General Wainwright as lieutenants in the Philippine 91st Infantry. During the withdrawal toward Bataan in late December 1941, Pajota and his platoon found the peninsula sealed off. So he and his men backtracked to Nueva Ecija to continue the fight as guerillas. Pajota was armed with a .45-caliber pistol; none of his men had weapons.

After Corregidor fell, Pajota launched an intensive recruitment campaign, and he found large numbers of eager volunteers, most of whom had friends or relatives in the Death March and were receiving brutal treatment at Camp O'Donnell. As the weeks passed, Pajota's men armed themselves—with bolos, ancient U.S. bolt-action rifles, and captured Japanese weapons.

After a meeting with Major Bob Lapham and Captain Harry McKenzie in the fall of 1942, it was agreed that Pajota's guerilla force would come under the overall command of Lapham. Pajota's designated territory was thirty miles square, extending from Cabanatuan thirty miles east to the Sierra Madre Mountains that ran along the coast of Luzon.

Some distance to the west of Cabanatuan camp, twenty-two-year-old Sergeant Ray Hunt, who had pulled off a daring escape during the Death March, organized a guerilla force in the towering Zambales Mountains. Like other American guerilla leaders, he had assigned himself a higher rank—in his case, captain—commensurate with his much heavier responsibilities. (Later these ranks would be made official by MacArthur's headquarters.) Hunt escaped death or capture numerous times in shoot-outs with Japanese soliders trying to crush his guerilla band.

Elsewhere in the Zambales, other Filipino irregulars were fighting under John Boone, a former corporal who was now a major. Boone had been in continuing contact with Miss U, the underground leader.

Another American guerilla chief in those rugged highlands was Lieutenant Colonel Bernard L. Anderson, who, as an air corps lieutenant, had escaped from Bataan. Anderson had a personal score to settle with the Japanese: His young fiancée was imprisoned in the Santo Tomás civilian internment camp in Manila.

One of the largest guerilla groups was the *Hukbalahap* (Peoples Army to Fight the Japanese), better known as the Huks. Its Filipino leader was Luis Taruc, a fire-eating Communist. By mid-1944, Taruc's force numbered some ten thousand men with three thousand rifles, although many of these men were "reserves," or part-time guerilllas. There was no doubt about how Taruc and his leaders felt about those they called "MacArthur's guerillas." They hated them almost as much as they did the Japanese.[2]

Ray C. Hunt, Jr., an American who had led his own three thousand-man guerilla force on Luzon, recalled Luis Taruc's group: "My experiences with the Huks were always unpleasant. Those I knew were much better assassins than soldiers. Tightly disciplined and led by fanatics, they murdered some Filipino landlords and drove others off to the comparative safety of Manila. They were not above plundering and torturing ordinary Filipinos, and they were treacherous enemies of all other guerillas (on Luzon)."[3]

When someone stood in Taruc's way, he dealt with him or her— efficiently and ruthlessly. A dynamic young woman, Felipa Culala, known as Dayang-Dayang, had organized her own guerilla band. She fought against the Japanese and tried to cooperate with the Communist-led Huks. Dayang-Dayang made one crucial mistake: She said openly in front of Luis Taruc and his lieutenants that she hoped the war would make her rich. Although widely regarded as a heroine, she was murdered by the Huks.[4]

As the months passed, Major Bob Lapham's guerilla force engaged in many hit-and-run clashes with Japanese patrols—and it had skirmishes with Luis Taruc's Huks. One day, in an effort to reach an amicable working agreement with the Huks against their common enemy, the Japanese, Lapham sent his executive officer, Harry McKenzie, and his adjutant, Lieutenant Jeremias Serrfica, to arrange a conference with Taruc and his top officers. In a confused situation, Lapham's two men either walked into a Huk ambush or else McKenzie got into a heated argument with Taruc and others. Whatever the case, McKenzie was shot in the chest and crumpled to the ground, blood spurting from the gaping hole.

Ray Hunt, who belonged to Lapham's organization, recalled: "McKenzie was lucky. The bullet did not hit a vital organ, he happened to get medical attention quickly, and the wound did not become infected. So he lived, but he never forgot or forgave. From that time forward, open war blazed between the Huks and Lapham's guerillas, always ending in gunfire."[5]

One of MacArthur's numerous female guerillas on Luzon was twenty-one-year-old Trinidad Diaz, who worked in a cement factory on the shores of a large lake, not far from the Cabanatuan POW camp. She had started her clandestine activity by collecting food and clothing for a nearby guerilla band, then began spying on the prison and passing the information along to the guerilla leader in Nueva Ecija Province.

Trinidad Diaz became infuriated over the brutalities being inflicted on the Ghosts of Bataan and Corregidor and her countrymen at the Cabanatuan camp. She sought revenge. So she persuaded six of the workers in the cement factory to join her. Together they killed five Japanese factory officials on the plant's wharf, dumped their bodies into wet cement (which soon hardened), and sent the guerilla leader the Japanese uniforms.

A short time later, Japanese investigators arrested Diaz; apparently she had been betrayed by a Filipino in the factory. She refused to admit any knowledge of the grisly fate of the five Japanese officials. For thirty-two days the young woman guerilla was tortured, but she remained silent. Then she was put to death.

By the spring of 1944, the "underground" war in the Philippines also became an "underwater" war as the U.S. Navy's largest submarines, capable of carrying fifty tons of supplies, made ready to shuttle in and out of Philippine waters, rendezvousing with the guerillas.

In Australia, Courtney Whitney, head of the AIB and now a Major General, would soon have more than a professional interest in the guerilla operations in the Philippines. His eldest son, Courtney, Jr., had left Yale University for the army and had reported for duty in Australia. On his arrival, General MacArthur arranged to have the younger Whitney assigned to his father's cloak-and-dagger organization.

Hearing that a small group was to be formed for the first major American arms-supply mission to Luzon guerillas, Lieutenant Whitney volunteered. The officer who would approve or deny his request was his father, Courtney Senior. It was an anguishing decision for the general, who was fully aware of the peril involved. Still, despite the danger, many volunteers were eager to strike a blow against the Japanese on Luzon, so whatever choice he made would be seen by some as tainted by favoritism. General Whitney took his dilemma to MacArthur.

"Let him go," the supreme commander advised.

"Sonny"—as young Whitney was nicknamed—and his comrades departed for Luzon by submarine in early 1944. Shortly after they cast off, Whitney's headquarters received an urgent warning from London: Certain sabotage materials manufactured in England had been found to be in danger of spontaneous combustion and should be destroyed immediately. The cable sent a surge of fear through General Whitney: because these defective explosives were at that moment on board the submarine heading toward Luzon with his son. But radio silence was in effect during daylight hours and no signal could be sent. The interminable wait for darkness was an agony for General Whitney.

When the submarine surfaced that night to recharge its batteries, word was received that the faulty explosives should be dumped overboard at once. But U.S. Navy Commander Charles "Chick" Parsons, the swashbuckling leader of the landing party who had lived in the Philippines for many years, refused to obey the order. The explosives would be needed by the guerillas on Luzon, and he intended to see that they got them.

Tension pervaded the sub during the remainder of its transit. The anxious, perspiring crew and passengers rode in almost total silence. Each slight noise set hearts thumping. Finally, the submarine reached a dark beach on eastern Luzon, where it was met by Filipino guerillas. Twenty-four hours later, some of the explosives were used to blow up a Japanese ammunition dump.

For many weeks, MacArthur's small fleet of submarines, whose bold skippers and crewmen were unsung heroes of the Pacific war, sneaked into the Philippines tens of thousands of weapons of all types—millions of rounds of ammunition, tons of explosives, vast quantities of radio equipment, and huge amounts of medical supplies. The path was being paved for MacArthur's impending return.

Not surprisingly in such a large and intricate supply operation, there were occasional slipups. Stock numbers on one box put ashore on Luzon indicated it contained Thompson submachine guns, ideal for the close-in jungle fighting and hit-and-run raids carried out by guerilla forces, but instead, the box held ancient U.S. Cavalry sabers. Disappointed but undaunted, the American guerilla leader who received them distributed the weapons among his men. Soon, Japanese commanders were receiving reports of truck convoys and outposts being attacked by wild-eyed, shouting Filipino "terrorists" wielding long, curved swords.

One submarine, the *Nautilus*, was met by Major Bob Lapham and Captain Juan Pajota, along with a force of guerillas, at Debut Bay, halfway up the coast of Luzon and about fifty miles east of the Cabanatuan prison camp. There the irregulars unloaded a cargo of automatic weapons, rifles, carbines, and hand grenades, together with several hundred thousand rounds of ammunition.

Now Bob Lapham was gripped by a fascinating scheme. If the *Nautilus* could navigate into Debut Bay almost to the shoreline and then return to Australia empty, why couldn't a small fleet of underwater craft be brought in to carry away American prisoners who would be freed from Cabanatuan? Already Lieutenant Colonel Bernard Anderson, leader of a large guerilla force west of the POW camp, had pleaded with MacArthur's headquarters to let him lead a raid to rescue the imprisoned Americans. Bob Lapham and Juan Pajota, whose domain included Cabanatuan, had also drawn up preliminary plans for freeing the POWs.

There was no doubt in the minds of these guerilla leaders that they had the power to wipe out the Japanese guards at Cabanatuan camp and free the estimated three thousand prisoners. But how would these feeble, emaciated, and sick POWs be able to cross fifty miles of the towering Sierra Madre Mountains on foot and reach Debut Bay, where, theoretically, thirty submarines would be waiting to take them aboard?

Anderson, Lapham, and Pajota tried several times to gain approval for this daring rescue scheme, but MacArthur's headquarters turned thumbs down. Even if enough Filipino civilians were recruited to carry the POWs in blanket slings, as was planned, pursuing Japanese troops certainly would catch up with the ragtag column and a monumental massacre could occur. Japanese fighter planes and bombers could also wreak havoc with the fleeing POWs and guerillas. The odds were far too chancy, MacArthur's headquarters concluded, to risk a rescue operation. Nor did the Southwest Pacific commander, who had been waging warfare on a shoestring, have thirty submarines to spare. And, perhaps most importantly, MacArthur was planning to return to the Philippines within the next few weeks and all of his naval forces would be needed in that mammoth invasion.

With the arrival of fall 1944, Manila was gripped by tension and electric anticipation. Numerous indications pointed to the fact that Douglas MacArthur was about ready to fulfill his pledge to return to the Philippines. Hundreds of thousands of special stamps Courtney Whitney had ordered struck for a Guerilla Postal Service reached the islands and were being used by partisans in the rural regions as regular postage on letters sent through the legitimate post office system. Many of these letters arrived at the Manila post office, where Filipino workers, affecting not to notice the bogus stamps, routinely processed the envelopes.

The words "I Shall Return!" were crudely painted on walls and on buildings in Cabanatuan town, Tarlac, Manila, and elsewhere. Postal workers risked their lives by rubber-stamping the phrase on mail, even on letters for delivery to Japanese military facilities. Dawn breaking over Manila would sometimes find a large billboard with "I Shall Return" painted on it overnight.

Sheets of paper bearing nothing but MacArthur's slogan turned up in Japanese army files. The phrase was found on large stickers pasted on the backs of Japanese military busses and troop trains, at the entrance to theaters and at railroad stations, even in brothels.

Off the southern Philippine island of Mindanao on September 7, the young skipper of an American submarine had a large Japanese freighter, the *Shinyo Maru*, in the crosshairs of his periscope. The vessel had no markings on it, so presumably it was being used to shuttle war materials between Japan and the Philippines. Minutes later, the order to "Fire!" rang through the sub, and two torpedoes burrowed through the water, striking the *Shinyo Maru* broadside.

There was a mighty explosion; the *Shinyo Maru* keeled over, then plunged to the bottom. Not until after the war was it known that going down with it were 675 American prisoners of war who had been captured on Bataan and Corregidor and were being shipped from Cabanatuan camp and elsewhere in the Philippines to Japan to work as coal

Navy Lieutenant John D. Bulkeley when he escaped to Australia after rescuing General Douglas MacArthur from Corregidor. Later Bulkeley received the Congressional Medal of Honor. (Courtesy of Alice Bulkeley)

Banzai! Japanese soldiers celebrate the capture of Mount Limay during Bataan fighting. (U.S. Army)

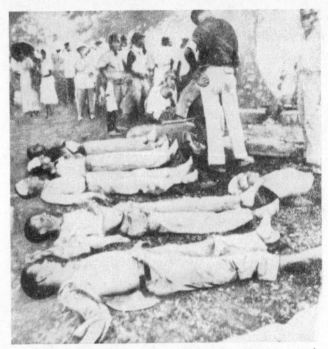

Murdered Americans along the Death March route. (Captured photo, U.S. Army)

Toting feeble comrades in blankets, Death March survivors approach the front gate of Camp O'Donnell. (Captured photo, U.S. Army)

Miss U, Margaret Utinsky, the underground leader, packs a pistol while fighting as a guerilla lieutenant. (National Archives)

Japanese conquerors post rules and regulations for Philippine civilians in a city on Luzon. (National Archives)

The Alamo Scouts team back from rescuing sixty-six Dutch and Javanese civilian prisoners from the Japanese. Rear row, left to right: Francis Laquier, Harold Hard, Franklin Fox. Front, left to right: Lieutenant Tom Rounsaville, Alfred Alfonso. Later, all were involved in the Cabanatuan mission. (Courtesy of William Nellist)

A favorite hangout for Japanese military brass, and the center for High Pockets's (Claire Phillips's) underground network. (National Archives)

Carabao carts hauling materials inside the Cabanatuan camp. This conveyance was also used by the POWs and underground to smuggle in food, medicine, money, letters, and printed news digests. (U.S. Army)

Captain Austin C. Shofner, USMC. One of ten in the POW camp to escape to Australia. (Courtesy of Austin Shofner)

Lieutenant Samuel C. Grashio. He escaped from the POW camp to Australia. (Courtesy of Samuel Grashio)

Fely, one of Club Tsubaki's entertainers, was an expert at extracting military information from Japanese officers, such as Captain Arita (*right*). (National Archives)

Eight American guerilla leaders on Luzon shortly after being decorated by General MacArthur with the Distinguished Service Cross. From the left: Harry McKenzie, Robert Lapham, Edwin Ramsey, Manuel A. Roxas (first postwar president of the Philippines), Bernard Anderson, Ray Hunt, John Boone, and Alvin Farretta. (Courtesy of Ray Hunt)

Captain Robert W. Prince (*top left*) led the Ranger attack on the Cabanatuan POW camp. Lieutenant Colonel Harry A. Mucci (*bottom left*) commanded the overall operation. Staff Sergeant Theodore Richardson shot the lock off the front gate. (Courtesy of Robert W. Prince)

6th Rangers get partial concealment from tall grass as they close in on the Cabanatuan camp. (U.S. Army)

Part of the Alamo Scouts team after their return from Cabanatuan. Standing from left: Gilbert Cox, Wilbur Wismer, Andy Smith. Kneeling from left: Galen Kittleson, Lieutenant William Nellist. (Courtesy of William Nellist)

A few of the Filipino guerillas in the Cabanatuan mission.

Ranger Private First Class Vernon Abbott carries a POW, Staff Sergeant Charles Mortimer, to an ambulance after a U.S. vehicle convoy went out to meet the returning column. (U.S. Army)

Private First Class Robert Lautman (*left*), who went on the Cabanatuan mission as a photographer, talks with a freed American sergeant. (U.S. Army)

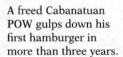

A freed Cabanatuan POW gulps down his first hamburger in more than three years.

Colonel James Duckworth, senior officer at Cabanatuan, is interviewed by reporters on his return. Duckworth broke his arm during the rescue operation. (U.S. Army)

Mission accomplished. Rangers fall into an exhausted sleep on their return from Cabanatuan. Filipino onlookers thought that they were dead. (Courtesy of Robert W. Prince)

Alamo Scouts team leaders after being decorated by General Walter Krueger. From left, Lieutenants William Nellist, Thomas Rounsaville, Robert Sumner, and John Dove. (Courtesy of Thomas Rounsaville)

POW Cecil "Red" Easley carried one feeble comrade and led another nearly blind one out through the Cabanatuan gate. (Courtesy of Cecil Easley)

General MacArthur chats with an old friend, Chaplain Alfred C. Oliver, shortly after Oliver and other POWs returned safely from Cabanatuan. (U.S. Army)

President Franklin Roosevelt chats with Rangers and Alamo Scouts who took part in the Cabanatuan mission during their visit to the White House in March 1945. (Courtesy of Robert W. Prince)

miners, stevedores, and in war factories. Eighty-five other POWs managed to reach shore and were rescued by Filipino guerillas.

Two weeks after the POW tragedy at sea, four-star Admiral William F. "Bull" Halsey, the two-fisted, hard-cussing epitome of a salty old sea dog, was on the bridge of his U.S. Fifth Fleet flagship, the mighty battleship *New Jersey*. Through his binoculars he could see the hazy outlines of the mountains in the central Philippine islands. Halsey was in a position to strike Manila and other key targets on Luzon for the first time since America had been driven from the Philippines more than two years earlier.

On the night before he would unleash his carrier-borne warplanes against the Japanese-held capital, Halsey called in his Filipino steward. Pointing to a map of the city, the admiral said, "I want you to know what we're going to do, because many of you have relatives in Manila. All of us pray that none of them will be injured."

The chief steward, Benedicto Tulao, who had been with Halsey for two years, solemnly asked the admiral, "Those are Japanese installations there, sir?"

"Yes."

"Bomb hell out of them!"[6]

13

Eagles Soar Over Cabanatuan

September 21, 1944, dawned hot and sticky. At Cabanatuan camp, Sergeant William C. Seckinger of Lilly, Pennsylvania, was standing under an improvised shower in the hospital section when he heard the roar of aircraft engines. Looking into the clear blue sky, he saw two planes, one right on the tail of the other, diving toward the camp. Suddenly, there was a burst of machine-gun fire. Seckinger pondered fleetingly if he should dive for cover. Then the first airplane smashed into a nearby hill and the pursuer pulled up and flew away.

Then it struck Seckinger: He had witnessed a dogfight. He had recognized the Zero before it struck the ground. But the victorious craft looked "strange."[1]

A Japanese patrol was sent to inspect the wreckage, and it brought back the remains of a Japanese pilot. Word sped through the camp. There was great elation. Some Allied plane had done the job. But whose aircraft was it? Some POWs conjectured that it was one of the "Flying Tigers," a crack American volunteer outfit once based in China under the command of Major General Claire Chennault. Others thought the mystery plane belonged to the Royal Air Force of Great Britain.

Sergeant Seckinger and numerous other prisoners had seen the insignia, a white star with a white bar to either side, but they did not recognize it, because the U.S. Air Corps had adopted the insignia after Bataan and Corregidor. A short time later, waves of airplanes flew directly over Cabanatuan camp, causing deep curiosity and subdued elation among the POWs. They recognized that these definitely were not Japanese planes. Someone in camp had received a deck of cards in the

Red Cross supplies, and on each card was a picture of a different type of American warplane and its name. Now excitement reached a fever pitch: A glance at the cards disclosed that these were U.S. Navy Hellcats.

William Seckinger's memory of this sky spectacular was vivid: "It was as though our pilots had put on the air show strictly for our benefit, and it raised our morale as nothing else could have done. The Japs gave us orders to stay in the buildings when the planes flew over. Under no circumstances were we to wave or make demonstrations to low-flying planes. But the indomitable spirit of the men would not be beaten down. We were out waving our arms frantically and showing pieces of white cloth to attract attention and let those pilots know that we were American prisoners."[2]

Earlier that day, swarms of Hellcats had lifted off from Admiral Bull Halsey's U.S. Fifth Fleet aircraft carriers 40 miles east of Luzon and just over 145 miles from Manila and other targets in the central part of the island. In less than an hour, the first flights were approaching Clark and Nichols airfields and other targets on Luzon. It was these formations that Sergeant Seckinger and his POW comrades had seen.

Halsey's pilots, eager to be striking heavy blows against the Philippines' conquerors, caught the Japanese with their flaps down. At Clark Field, a Japanese colonel squinted into the early morning sun, pointed a finger at Halsey's approaching planes, and exulted to an aide: "See our splendid war eagles! How swiftly they fly! How gracefully they maneuver!" Moments later, explosions rocked the ground and the colonel fled for cover.[3]

Wave after wave of carrier-based American warplanes swept over Manila, Clark Field, Subic Bay, Nichols Field, and elsewhere that day. So overpowering—and unexpected—was the assault that only a handful of Zeros got into the air to challenge the intruders. The next day, Halsey's planes were out in force again over southern and central Luzon.

After the relentless pounding of Japanese targets for two days, Rear Admiral Robert B. "Mick" Carney, Halsey's longtime chief of staff, totaled up the damage: 405 Japanese warplanes destroyed or damaged, 103 ships and boats sunk or damaged, Clark and Nichols Fields demolished, Manila harbor littered with wrecks. Fifteen U.S. planes did not return to their carriers.

In Bull Halsey's name, Mick Carney sent a signal to all ships in the Fifth Fleet:

> The recent exceptional performance (over Luzon) yielded gratifying gate receipts because of the brilliant performance put on by my group of stars before the best audience in the Asiatic theater. Although the capacity audience hissed very loudly, little was thrown at the players. As long as the audience has *a spot to hiss in*, we will stay on the road.[4]

William Seckinger recalled the Japanese attitude at Cabanatuan in the wake of Halsey's air onslaught: "In the early days, the Japs found that most of us would not try to escape. Not because the opportunities were not there, but because we were weak and sick. Their vigilance, therefore, had somewhat relaxed. Now it increased twofold in fear that we were going to make a mass breakout.

"We felt like rats in a trap. Secretly, many of us had prepared to defend ourselves, devising weapons of all descriptions, from knives to clubs. I had twenty rounds of .45-caliber ammunition that had been smuggled in [by the underground], and I was on the lookout for a gun. We were hoping that there would be a chance to kill some Japs."[5]

At the conclusion of the two-day American air assault, morale at Cabanatuan soared. Deliverance seemed to be just over the horizon. A slogan raced through the camp: "Thanksgiving Turkey in Albuquerque!" That was the optimistic view. Most of the other POWs thought that they would be back home by Christmas. Clandestine radios were tuned to powerful stations in Allied countries. But no word came of American landings in the Philippines. Bit by bit, morale began to ebb.

It was about eleven o'clock in the morning of September 28, when Miss U—Margaret Utinsky, the underground leader—immaculate in her crisp, white nurse's uniform, was caring for an ill woman in the Manila hospital where she worked as a cover for her covert activities. Suddenly, Miss U heard the heavy tramp of boots coming up the corridor. Moments later, she looked up and stiffened: In the door, carrying rifles with fixed bayonets, were eight Japanese soldiers.

"You will come!" an officer wearing a samurai sword barked at Miss U. She was escorted out of the hospital with the Japanese on all sides, and taken to Fort Santiago, the ancient bastion perched alongside the Pasig River in Manila. Miss U knew that she was at best a suspect considered worthy of "interrogation" by the Japanese, for Fort Santiago was where they took the most dangerous "enemies of the emperor."

Within hours, Miss U found herself seated in a room across a table from a Japanese officer. Next to him was a young Japanese interpreter. Only later would the American woman learn that the interpreter had been born in the United States and had lived in San Francisco with his family for twenty years. With war in the Pacific on the horizon, the son had gone to Japan to fight for the homeland of his ancestors.

A barrage of questions was hurled at Miss U. Where were you born? When? What was your real name? She insisted that she was a Lithuanian, born in Kovno, and her name was Rosena Utinsky.

Between questions, the two men talked to one another in Japanese. Miss U could not understand a word they were saying, but she sensed from the tone of their voices that they were disagreeing over her guilt or innocence of some unspecified crime against the Japanese emperor. For hours, she deftly fended off the questions.

Suddenly, the officer jumped from his chair, purple with rage, and struck a mighty blow with his fist against the woman's face, knocking her to the floor. Blood streamed from her mouth, and she felt (correctly) that her jaw had been broken. She spat out two broken teeth onto the floor.

With no show of emotion, the officer told her to get back onto the chair, and the grilling resumed. Miss U's head was spinning madly, her face pained her enormously, and her vision was blurred.

"Where is your father?"

"He died when I was a little girl."

"What was your mother's name?"

She invented one.

"If you are Lithuanian, then why don't you speak that language?"

"My aunt took me to live in Canada when I was very small, and we always spoke English because she was English."

The grilling continued mercilessly all day. Then Miss U was thrown into a foul and slimy dungeon—a holdover from centuries past—and the door clanged shut behind her. That night, six other women shared the unlighted cell. Only a bucket served as sanitary facilities. In the morning, two Filipino prisoners, naked except for G-strings, removed the bucket, emptied its contents, then brought it back to the cell. They were Catholic priests. Because the people seemed to venerate priests, the cleric prisoners were always given tasks involving the greatest humiliations.

All through the long night, Miss U, aching in every inch of her body, wracked her mind: Who or what had betrayed her? After daybreak, she was again taken to be interrogated. A large stack of papers were on the desk of the Japanese officer. On top was a document she recognized: It was her application for duty as a Red Cross volunteer. She had signed it in October 1941 while war clouds were hanging over Manila. Now she had her answer: Someone in the Filipino Red Cross medical unit, with which she had gone to Bataan two years earlier, had been the Judas. She was positive the betrayer had been a Filipino doctor with whom she had once clashed because of his seeming Japanese loyalties.

For two nights, Miss U slept on the cold stone floor without even a newspaper for cover. Her feet were bare; they had taken her shoes. Her hair was matted and uncombed; they had removed her hairpins. Dried blood flakes clung to her lips. She had not washed in three days. However, she felt fortunate: Some of the other women in her eight-foot-by nine-foot cell had not washed, combed their hair, or changed their clothes in three months. Undernourished, the cellmates had eaten only *lugao*, a foul smelling rice boiled in water until it tasted like laundry starch.

On the fifth day of her interrogation, the Japanese officer tossed a paper at her and demanded to know if that was her handwriting on it. She studied the sheet, then admitted that it was indeed her writing. The document was the telltale Red Cross application, on which she had given her nationality as American. She explained that she had lied because she feared the Red Cross would not let her work if they knew she was a foreigner.

Now the Japanese officer and his interpreter—(the former California resident)—had grown frustrated and furious. This obstinate woman would admit nothing.

"Lies! All lies!" they yelled at her, slapping her face repeatedly while demanding to know why she had been making trips between Manila and Cabanatuan. Then the rough stuff began.

Miss U was forced to kneel for hours on the edge of a split piece of bamboo that was a sharp as a knife. The keen-edged bamboo cut deeper and deeper into her knees. Muscles in her hips and thighs cramped and ached. Blood ran down her legs. All the while, the Japanese screamed questions and slapped her face. Miss U refused to admit to being an American, nor would she even cry out in her anguish.

That night, curled up on the stone floor of her cell, Miss U was in enormous pain. The next day, the torture began again. Her hands were tied behind her back, and a rope hanging from the ceiling was tied to the rope around her wrists. She was jerked several feet off the ground and hung there for hours while her tormentors yelled questions and struck her with heavy blows from a thick strap. Fists smashed into her face repeatedly, and the burning coals of lighted cigarettes were ground into her belly.

For thirty-two days, Miss U was subjected to daily torture. She admitted nothing. Had she "confessed," as her Japanese tormentors demanded endlessly, it not only would have meant her own beheading, but the underground apparatus she had built up for two years would have been decimated with wholesale arrests and executions. Colonel Ed Mack, various chaplains, and other key contacts in the Cabanatuan hellhole would suffer similar fates.

Meanwhile, word of Miss U's arrest and confinement in dreaded Fort Santiago spread throughout her underground apparatus and inside of the Cabanatuan POW camp. By coincidence, she had been hauled out of the same hospital where one of her agents, American Ernest Johnson (Brave Heart) was a patient. Johnson sent word of the arrest to Sparkplug (the wealthy former Spanish naval officer, Ramón Amosategui), who bribed a Filipino in Manila city hall to destroy the record of Miss U's marriage certificate, which listed her as an American. Then Sparkplug called at the home of Mrs. Robert Yearsley, an American who had escaped internment at Santo Tomás because she was blind. Strangely, the Japanese permitted her husband to remain free to care for her. The couple's son, Robin, was a POW at Cabanatuan.

Many months earlier, the sightless Mrs. Yearsley and Miss U had hatched a scheme to get money to Robin and for him to send messages to his parents. When Miss U was preparing a shipment to Cabanatuan, she would telephone Mrs. Yearsley and ask for a certain cake recipe. This was the signal for Mrs. Yearsley to send a young Filipino to her with money for Robin. When Miss U received letters from the son, she would telephone his mother and say that she had baked a cake.

Now, Sparkplug told Mrs. Yearsley that the underground leader was in custody, and she sent her Filipino courier rushing to Cabanatuan by train. There he contacted Miss U's undercover operatives, who smuggled word in to Colonel Ed Mack. Convinced that the elaborate underground network was on the verge of being destroyed, Mack and other involved POWs scurried about burying incriminating evidence—pesos, notes, anything that might point to the covert operation that had been operating for two years under the noses of the Japanese.[6]

On the thirty-second day of her incarceration and torture, Miss U was once more taken from her gloomy dungeon. But this time, her guard led her to another room. There were different Japanese officers seated behind a long table. A new interpreter asked if she was willing to sign a document pledging never to take any action against the Japanese government. Startled, she crossed her fingers and replied yes.

"Then," said one Japanese, smiling broadly, "We have good news for you. You are going to be freed."

Through eyes hazy from her long ordeal, Miss U scanned the document, one sentence of which read: "Since I have been in Fort Santiago, I have received courteous treatment from all officers and sentries and been provided with good food." Laboring to keep her hand from shaking, she signed the paper.

Thirty minutes later, Miss U was escorted out of the front gate, and she began staggering along a sidewalk, hopefully in the direction of Auntie, her apartment. Her once immaculate white nurse's uniform was wrinkled and crusted with mud and dirt. Her hair, uncombed for thirty-two days, was matted and filthy. Dizzy and befuddled, she collapsed in a patch of weeds and lay there, semiconscious, for an undetermined period of time.

Finally, a young Filipino riding a bicycle with a sidecar spotted Miss U. Fully aware that she was an American and that he could be jailed or tortured for giving aid, the youth helped her into the sidecar and drove her to her apartment. There Maria, her longtime devoted Filipina maid, took one look at her and burst into tears.

Miss U was an ugly sight. Large sores and infected wounds covered much of her body. After Maria assisted in giving her a bath, Miss U had to be taken to the hospital. There, a Filipino doctor told her that her gangrenous leg would have to be amputated. She protested vigorously, willing to take her chances that the leg would miraculously heal itself.

For six weeks, she lay in a hospital bed, but at the end of that period, the "miracle" had been granted: She left the medical center with both legs.

Within days, Miss U was back directing the smuggling of food, clothing, medicine, and money into Cabanatuan camp. But soon there were haunting signs that the Japanese net was again closing in on her. The Apostolic Delegate of Manila was aware of Miss U's underground, and he knew that Father Lalor and the other Irish priests at the Malate Convent were important cogs in her organization. One night, a Filipino youth knocked urgently on the door of Miss U's apartment. While working for the Japanese at Fort Santiago, he had been spying for the Apostolic Delegate. By happenstance, the young man had seen a list containing the names of Father Lalor and his fellow priests at the convent—and an unidentified woman known simply as Miss U.

Confirmation that Miss U was in grave danger came just before dawn when a Filipino arrived with a message from Father Lalor. Through his own sources, he had learned that the Kempei Tai planned to arrest her that morning. Just two hours after Miss U fled Manila and headed for the mountains to hook up with Major John Boone's guerillas, a squad of Japanese soldiers burst into her apartment—only to find that their prey had vanished.

While Miss U had been suffering the torments of the damned in a Japanese dungeon, sixty miles to the north Cabanatuan POWs were steadily being brought out to be shipped to Dai Nippon or to other locales to work in war-related endeavors. Captain Juan Pajota, whose guerillas had been shadowing the prison almost constantly for many months, reported that only two thousand POWs remained, down from a population high of some twelve thousand men shortly after the fall of Bataan and Corregidor. Some ten thousand prisoners had died or been shipped to Japan or other locales.

Pajota climbed on his horse and rode, along with a few bodyguards, to the isolated headquarters of Major Bob Lapham, the guerilla chief in Nueva Ecija Province, to discuss the situation at Cabanatuan camp. Lapham and Pajota agreed that this was the ideal time to attack the stockade and liberate the POWs, because the Japanese focus in the Philippines no doubt would be in the bloody fight that would take place when MacArthur landed on Leyte and the looming American invasion of Luzon.

After exchanging several messages with Lieutenant Colonel Bernard Anderson, the guerilla leader to the west, Lapham radioed MacArthur's headquarters and again asked for permission to launch an effort to bring out the Cabanatuan inmates. Again, the request was rejected.

While these other events were unfolding, on October 10, 1944, tall, powerfully built General Tomoyuki Yamashita strode into the modern office building overlooking the Pasig River in east Manila that served as headquarters for the Japanese Fourteenth Army, the unit charged with the defense of the Philippines. Capable tough, and flamboyant, Yamashita was a folk hero in Dai Nippon, the Japanese counterpart to General George C. Patton in the United States.

Known as the "Tiger of Malaya" for his dramatic capture of the "impregnable" British fortress of Singapore early in the war, Yamashita took command of the Fourteenth Army and began energetically preparing a hot reception for the eventual return of Douglas MacArthur, whom he regarded as arrogant. If MacArthur was foolish enough to try to invade the Philippines, Yamashita told the Japanese press, "I will confront him with the only words I spoke to the British commander during the negotiations for the surrender of Singapore: 'All I want to hear from you is yes or no.' "

General Yamashita was convinced that MacArthur, if he came, would try to invade the logical target, Luzon, where nearly all military installations and most of the large cities and industry were located. MacArthur had other ideas. He knew that Yamashita would be laying in wait for him on Luzon, so he would invade Leyte, a large primitive island some three hundred miles to the south. MacArthur's A-Day would be October 21.[7]

Spearheading America's return to the Philippines would be Lieutenant Colonel Henry Mucci's 6th Ranger Battalion, which he had honed into an elite fighting machine in the forbidding jungles of New Guinea. His men were eager for action: It had been nearly two years since their outfit (then known as the 98th Field Artillery Battalion) had departed the United States to do battle in the Pacific. So far, the Rangers had not heard a hostile shot.

Sixth Army commander Walter Krueger had assigned Mucci's Rangers a crucial mission. On A-Day minus 3, they were to seize three tiny islands—Dinagat, Suluan, and Homonhon—perched at the entrance to Leyte Gulf in order to clear the way for the main invasion. Guerilla reports and air reconnaissance had indicated that the Japanese had installations on the islands, probably search radar whose electronic feelers could flash word to Manila that a big American battle fleet and convoy was approaching.

On the same day that General Yamashita had taken over defense of the Philippines with orders from Tokyo to hold the islands at all costs, the sea armada that would bring Douglas MacArthur and his men back to the Philippines weighed anchor in the wide, blue bays of Hollandia, in New Guinea, and Manus and began sailing northward. There were 738 ships in Vice Admiral Thomas C. Kincaid's Seventh Fleet, which was under MacArthur's direct control.

Just before 8:00 A.M. on A-Day minus 3, the cruiser *Denver*, lying sixty-five hundred yards offshore, pounded Suluan with its big guns, there by earning the honor of shooting the first rounds in the liberation of the Philippines. Shortly afterward, five hundred Rangers under Major Robert W. Garrett, a tough soldier leading tough men, stormed ashore. Minutes later, General Yamashita's headquarters in Manila received an urgent signal from a Japanese radio station on Suluan: "The enemy is landing! Long live the Emperor!"

Then the station went dead. Garrett's Rangers had blown up the facility and killed its Japanese staff and guards. Heading rapidly overland, the Rangers were raked by a concealed machine gun. Private First Class Darwin C. Zufall was killed, giving him the unwelcome distinction of being the first armed American soldier to give his life in the return to the Philippines. The same burst of fire also wounded Private First Class Donald J. Cannon.

Garrett's Rangers then charged a lighthouse where thirty-two Japanese soldiers were cut down in a brief but fierce firefight. Suluan was secured.[8]

As dusk approached, two more Ranger companies, plus a company of the U.S. 21st Infantry Regiment, landed on Dinagat against minor opposition. On the prowl for souvenirs, Lieutenant Joseph Therrien pried open a trunk locker belonging to a Japanese lieutenant killed in the fighting and found a neatly folded American flag. Shortly after dawn, the Stars and Stripes were hoisted on a crude pole by Sergeant Francis Anderson while other Rangers stood in a circle and saluted. It was the first American flag to fly freely over Philippine soil since the Corregidor debacle in May 1942.[9]

For the next seventy-two hours, Henry Mucci's Rangers swarmed over the three jungle-covered islets they had invaded and killed in excess of seven hundred Japanese who fought until the bitter end.[10]

Alerted by the radio station on Suluan and by air reconnaissance that a powerful American sea force was charging toward Leyte Gulf, Lieutenant General Sosaku Suzuki was confident that MacArthur's highly publicized return to the Philippines would result in a monumental disaster for the invaders. Suzuki, commander of the 35th Division on Leyte, was almost euphoric as he told his staff: "My only worry is that the American leader (MacArthur) might attempt to surrender only the troops in this operation. We must demand the capitulation of his entire forces, those in New Guinea and other places as well as on Leyte."[11]

Shortly after dawn on A-Day, Douglas MacArthur stood on the bridge of the cruiser *Nashville*, anchored in Leyte Gulf. His thoughts flashed back to mid-March 1942. Then, as a result of a presidential order, MacArthur had escaped from Corregidor in John Bulkeley's battered PT-41. A proud man, MacArthur had been defeated and humiliated. Since then, his heart always had been with the Battling Bastards of Bataan and the garrison of men and nurses on Corregidor that he had to leave behind. As far as he was concerned, those had been America's blackest days since Valley Forge. Now, thirty months later, he was returning at the head of a veteran army that would eventually number three hundred thousand men to keep a sacred pledge. As aides clustered around MacArthur, he used his corncob pipe to point over the glassy green water of the Gulf of Leyte at the greatest fleet ever assembled in that part of the world.[12]

At 9:30 A.M., after a heavy bombardment from warships offshore, Walter Krueger's assault troops hit the beaches near the town of Tacloban. Aboard his flagship, Krueger could not believe his good fortune. Opposition had been minimal. He had no way of knowing that the Japanese commander, General Suzuki, had pulled back from the beaches and established a defense in depth, with strongholds in the hills.

When the third wave went ashore, Douglas MacArthur went with it and stood erect in the landing craft. There was a sudden crunching noise as the barge grounded in shoal water fifty yards from the shore. A ramp was lowered and MacArthur, displaying a dexterity that belied his sixty-five years, walked down the ramp and began wading through the surf. Water was up to his knees, and the sun glinted off the mass of gold braid on his trademark cap. In the bushes behind the beach, in foxholes and propped in trees, Japanese snipers were plentiful.[13]

Reaching dry coral sand, MacArthur moved to one side of the entourage that had waded in with him and onto a low mound. Standing almost motionless, he gazed about the terrain pockmarked by hundreds of exploding shells and slowly lighted his pipe. In the trees, a Japanese automatic weapon suddenly opened fire. MacArthur did not even duck.

Heavy firing broke out inland, and MacArthur walked off in that direction. He reached a squad of 24th Infantry Division men who were wide-eyed on seeing a four-star general with the invasion assault troops. Spotting four or five newly dead Japanese, the general walked over and turned the corpses with his foot to see their insignia.

With a look of satisfaction, he remarked to his companion, Carlos Romulo, Resident Commissioner of the Philippines, "Sixteenth Division. They're the ones who did the dirty work on Bataan!"

Bataan and Corregidor. Corregidor and Bataan. Douglas MacArthur's mind would never ease until he had rescued the American and Filipino survivors and eradicated a stain on Uncle Sam's honor by driving the Japanese from the islands.

MacArthur strolled to a spot where signalmen had set up a portable broadcast unit that would carry the message he was about to deliver by radio to thousands of Philippine homes, as well as to the rest of the world.

Four hundred miles northwest of the Leyte invasion beaches that morning, Major Emil Reed and a knot of other POWs had their ears glued to a patchwork radio that had been built from pieces smuggled into Cabanatuan camp. The volume was turned low. In a doorway, one prisoner kept an eye open for any approaching guards. Reed and his companions were electrified by what they were hearing: General Doug-las MacArthur speaking directly from Leyte. Suddenly, "home" was eleven thousand miles closer to the POWs.[14]

To the Filipino civilians, the guerillas in the hills, the underground, and the prisoners of war, MacArthur's first words were the fulfillment of a promise: "I have returned! By the grace of Almighty God, our forces stand again on Philippine soil—soil consecrated in the blood of our two peoples . . . "

In the broadcast background, the Cabanatuan POWs could hear the dim chatter of Japanese machine-gun fire from behind the Leyte beaches.

MacArthur continued: "Rally to me. Let the indomitable spirit of Corregidor and Bataan lead on . . . . Let no heart be faint. Let every arm be steeled. . . . "[15]

14

Hell Ships and Vanishing Guards

Ten days after the invasion, the fight for Leyte had turned into a brutal, bloody slugging match. American foot soldiers were hacking westward in the direction of the key Japanese supply ports, Ormoc and Palompon, on the west coast of the primitive island. Because of the mountainous, thickly jungled terrain, crisscrossed by steep gorges, there was no continuous front line. Often the "front" was a three-foot-wide path over which the GIs, loaded with heavy gear, trudged along in single file. Always sudden death lurked at every turn, on every path.

Meanwhile, General Douglas MacArthur was preparing to launch another of his lightning surprise operations. The U.S. 77th Infantry Division, commanded by Major General Andrew E. Bruce, would storm ashore three miles south of Ormoc, on western Leyte, then drive north and east to link up with units pushing westward from Leyte Gulf. MacArthur hoped to catch General Suzuki's formidable force in a vice between the U.S. forces converging from the east and the west.

In preparation for Bruce's landing, Alamo Scouts Lieutenant Robert Sumner and six of his men slipped ashore from a PT boat in the Ormoc region just before midnight on November 6, 1944. The team's mission was to infiltrate deep behind Japanese lines to radio back to Sixth Army headquarters information on Japanese strengths, deployments, and movements, as well as to keep Ormoc under observation. It was through Ormoc and Palompon that General Yamashita was rushing reinforcements, ammunition, and supplies from Luzon to the hard-pressed Japanese force on Leyte.

Far inland from the beach, Lieutenant Sumner and his men set up

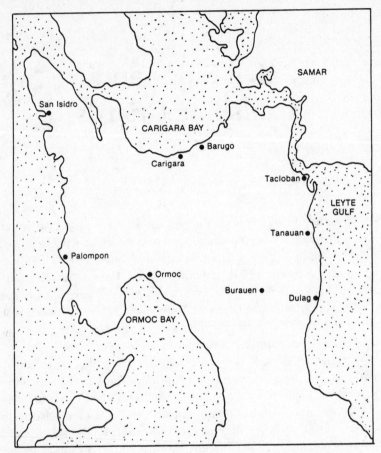

Northern Leyte

shop in the midst of Japanese activity. A major Japanese headquarters and airfield were but four miles away, at Valencia. The team had no way of knowing that it was engaged in the longest sustained Alamo Scouts mission of the war.

Sumner set up sea watches, road watches, and intelligence-gathering nets. Information radioed back on Japanese shipping in and out of Ormoc resulted in American warplanes pounding these vessels. Then came a near-catastrophe: The Scouts' radio refused to function.

Robert Sumner remembered a strange event that occurred: "Just then a Japanese plane flew over and dropped a canister not far from us. Presumably it was intended for some Japs. A couple of our Scouts went out to recover it, however, and brought it back. We didn't know what the cargo was until opening the canister—it was a radio. Our skilled guys realized that we could replace our own transmitter/receiver that was temporarily down with parts from this Jap set. The next day our Jap pilot 'friend' came back and dropped some spare parts, which we appreciated."[1]

Just before dawn on December 7—one month and a day since Bob Sumner's Scout team had stolen ashore—Andy Bruce's 77th Infantry Division was in transports eight miles off the western coast of Leyte. Known as the Statue of Liberty Division because nearly all of its original members were from New York City, Brooklyn, or Jersey City, the GIs called themselves the Old Buzzards. Many were family men, and at induction, their average age had been thirty-two, eight years older than the typical American foot soldier.

Armed with the detailed intelligence collected by the Alamo Scouts, the Old Buzzards charged onto the beach and pushed rapidly inland, opposed by scattered bands of Japanese who fought until killed. Three days later, Bruce's men captured the port of Ormoc.

Now, General Bruce was preparing to attack the other port, Palompon, about twelve miles west of Ormoc. However, his maps and charts of Leyte were extremely old and inaccurate. So several of Sumner's Scouts, who were still holed up inland, sneaked through Japanese positions to provide Bruce with crucial information collected in conjunction with local guerillas. This intelligence concerned current landing-beach data, as well as the strengths and locations of Japanese forces in the Palompon region. A few days later, Palompon was seized by the 77th Infantry Division, thereby denying General Yamashita the final port into which he could pour troops, guns, ammunition, and food.

Robert Sumner remembered: "Finally, after six weeks, we infiltrated Japanese *and* American lines and reached our Alamo Scouts Training Center, now in eastern Leyte, on December 23. All the other Scouts were there. It was the first time we had been together since the previous August in New Guinea, and we all ate our Christmas dinner two days later."[2]

While the no-holds-barred fighting was raging on Leyte, the Imperial High Command in Tokyo issued orders for all American POWs in the Philippines to be shipped to Japan as rapidly as possible. Those who could not walk were to be left behind, presumably to be dealt with at a later date. In Manila on December 12, some sixteen-hundred prisoners from Cabanatuan, Old Bilibid, and other lockups on Luzon were packed like sardines into the dark, suffocating holds of the unmarked *Oryoku Maru*, a sixteen-thousand-ton converted ocean liner that would become known as Hell Ship No. 1.

Among those on the *Oryoku Maru* was twenty-four-year-old Lieutenant Henry J. Stempin of Milwaukee, Wisconsin, who had been a company commander in the 57th Infantry (Philippine Scouts). Back in his hometown, Stempin had not made it to his Marquette University graduation ceremony on June 30, 1941. While his classmates marched up to the stage to get their diplomas, Stempin, a brand new "shavetail" (second lieutenant), was sailing to the Philippines.

Henry Stempin recalled the Hell Ship: "There began one of the worst periods of my three and a half years in captivity. The Japs closed the hatches, depriving us of air. There was no water or food. Temperatures rose to what must have been 120 degrees, and our thirst became overwhelming."[3]

In violation of the Geneva Convention, the Japanese failed to mark the *Oryoku Maru* as a POW ship.

Stempin remembered: "Before our ship could even set sail, it was attacked by a swarm of American warplanes, whose pilots, of course, had no idea their countrymen were aboard. Men who had endured the Death March and brutalities for many months panicked. They tried to claw and scratch their way up the ship's walls to reach the hatches. Before our airplanes flew away, perhaps a hundred of the POWs had died, suffocated, or been trampled to death."[4]

During the hours of darkness, the *Oryoku Maru* slipped out of Manila Bay and steamed north along the western coast of Luzon. Shortly after dawn, the POWs felt a streak of renewed fear: the telltale sounds of powerful airplane engines. Clearly, American planes were overhead, back to finish to job. Moments later, there were bomb explosions and the angry chatter of machine guns. Again, panic in the coal-black holds. The prisoners scrambled madly over one another in an effort to get out of their dungeons. A few Japanese soldiers opened the hatches and fired rifles and pistols point-blank into the shouting, jostling mass of sweaty, half-crazed mass of humanity. Then there was a heavy crunching noise: The ship had gone aground only three hundred yards from shore.

According to Henry Stempin: "A large number of POWs were dead, but the hatches were opened, and those of us who had not been killed or critically wounded had to swim to shore while the Japanese were blasting away at our bobbing heads with machine guns."[5]

On shore, the surviving thirteen hundred POWs were rounded up and shifted to the *Enoura Maru*—Hell Ship No. 2. Once more the POWs headed for Japan. They were given almost no food, and water was rationed by the spoonful. Off Formosa on January 8, 1945, the unmarked *Enoura Maru* was pounced on by American fighter-bombers. The ship was ripped apart by bombs, and an estimated five hundred POWs perished. Now Lieutenant Henry Stempin and the dwindling number of survivors were transferred to Hell Ship No. 3, the *Brazil Maru*.

As the *Brazil Maru* zigzagged northward in the direction of Japan, the lightly dressed prisoners, who had been wearing only tattered tropical clothing, were confronted by a horrible new enemy—intense cold. That condition forced the POWs to strip the clothes off the dead for their own use, and to pile the bodies near the hatches to block the freezing air.

That brutal ocean trek remained deeply etched in Henry Stempin's being: "Not only were we freezing, but our thirst was overwhelming. Sewage overflowed from the two buckets that were used for latrines. The stench was overpowering. People became crazed and were cutting each other up, trying to suck blood, and were drinking their own urine."[6]

When the "walking dead" finally were brought ashore at Moji, in northern Kyoshu on January 20, 1945, even the Japanese officers receiving them seemed to be genuinely shocked at their pitiful condition. Lieutenant Stempin estimated that his weight had dropped from its normal 165 pounds to about 90 pounds. Within days, the Americans were performing hard labor deep in dingy coal mines and in shipyards or were building bridges and unloading ships—backbreaking work for even healthy men.[7]

Meanwhile at the Emperor's Palace in the heart of Tokyo, Prime Minister Kuniaki Koiso was trying to explain to Hirohito what had gone wrong on Leyte. Three months earlier, a confident Koiso, who had just replaced the disgraced General Tojo (who had resigned in the wave of a steady flow of American victories), had called on the emperor to assure him that if MacArthur struck the Philippines, the Imperial armed forces would gain their greatest victory since the Battle of Ten-nozan in 1582. Now the customarily mild-mannered Hirohito was angry. How would he explain to the people the impending fall of Leyte? A flustered Koiso mumbled that his pledge would still be fulfilled if MacArthur were to try to invade Luzon.[8]

Douglas MacArthur indeed had his eye on Luzon. But first, he would have to invade Mindoro, the large, wild, mountainous island separated from Luzon on the north by the seven-mile-wide Verde Island Passage. Mindoro's northern point, Cape Calavite, lay only ninety miles from Manila. N-Day was set for December 15, 1944.

Based on intelligence collected by a team of Alamo Scouts and other sources, MacArthur was banking on the belief that General Yamashita would leave Mindoro lightly defended and concentrate his armed forces on Luzon for the final showdown in the Philippines. This intelligence proved to be remarkably accurate. On all of Mindoro there was only a hodge-podge Japanese force of some 1,000 men. They were about to face 11,878 American invasion troops, mainly thirty-four-year-old Colonel George M. Jones's crack 503rd Parachute Infantry Regiment, and the 19th Regiment of Major General Frederick A. Irving's 24th Infantry Division.

As expected, the Mindoro invasion force was confronted by token opposition, and by N-Day plus 2, American and Australian engineers had put four southern airfields into operating order and U.S. warplanes were flown in. It had been a nearly text-book-perfect operation. The final springboard to Bataan and Corregidor and Manila was secure.

Nine days later, on December 26, General MacArthur issued an upbeat communiqué: "The Leyte campaign can now be regarded as closed except for minor mopping-up operations." General Krueger's Sixth Army was pulled back to prepare for the decisive invasion of Luzon, and the job of mopping up was turned over to Lieutenant General Robert L. Eichelberger's newly formed U.S. Eighth Army.

MacArthur's term, "mopping up," infuriated Eichelberger's foot sloggers. The "moppers" knew that General Suzuki's force, although backed into the wild mountains in northwestern Leyte with no hope of escape, numbered an estimated twenty-seven thousand. All of the Japanese soldiers were willing, even eager, to die for the emperor.

On the same day that MacArthur trumpeted the conquest of Leyte, General Tomoyuki Yamashita was a portrait of confidence while being interviewed by newspaper reporters from Tokyo at his Manila headquarters. Leaning back in a swivel chair, the general declared: "The loss of one or two islands does not matter. The Philippines have an extensive area, and we can fight freely to our heart's content."[9]

That night, Radio Tokyo, quoting Yamashita, embellished on his remarks: "The battle of Luzon, in which three hundred thousand Americans are doomed to die, is about to begin."

On January 6, 1945, while Douglas MacArthur was preparing his forces for the leap to Luzon, puzzling events were taking place at Cabanatuan camp. Early in the morning, as the living skeletons looked on in disbelief, all the Japanese guards formed up and marched out through the gate. Major Emil Reed, the medical officer from Texas, remembered: "The Japs told us that we were to consider the camp nothing but a hospital. The five hundred–plus POWs were made up of sick or disabled men. I was one of ten medical officers, along with forty medical enlisted men, remaining in camp."[10]

Nearly all the prisoners were fearful. Why had the guards suddenly departed? Was this a Japanese trick to entice the POWs to launch a mass escape, at which time they would be ambushed and slaughtered? Would their corpses be buried under the rice fields, never to be discovered? If MacArthur's forces were to invade Luzon, the POWs feared, they would never live to welcome them.

Despite the worries that gnawed at their innards, within an hour of the guard contingent marching off, the POWs, walked, hobbled, and even crawled to the Japanese part of the camp to steal food or supplies that may have been left behind. They found that in their haste to depart, the guards had indeed, left a great deal.

Feeble as they were, the prisoners piled their loot into a pair of bullcarts and returned to their area with many cases of milk (which most had not even seen in nearly three years), large amounts of rice, sugar, beans, corn, and other fresh vegetables. Like ravaged beasts, the POWs began gorging themselves with food. The men could not resist the uncontrollable urge to eat as much as desired. Soon most of the prisoners became violently ill and regurgitated the food.

Despite the prohibitive odds against a successful mass escape, prolonged discussions were held to explore that possibility. It was evident that it would be a hopeless endeavor. Most were ill. Numerous men were without one or both legs. Many had gangrene. Perhaps half of the POWs were too feeble to walk long distances. For now, the escape scheme was abandoned.

As a safeguard against attacks by "friendly" aircraft whose pilots might mistake Cabanatuan as a Japanese camp, the POWs created a huge sign that was stretched out in the open where it could readily be seen from the air. It read: *SEND TOBACCO*.

On January 6, the same day that the Japanese guards left Cabanatuan, Admiral Tom Kincaid's massive invasion fleet was plowing northward in the China Sea along the west coast of Luzon. Destination: Lingayen Gulf. All the while, the ships were running a gauntlet of Japanese torpedo planes and *kamikazes* (suicide aircraft), which were inflicting a heavy toll. S-Day was set for January 9, 1945.

Leading the fleet was the heavy bombardment group commanded by Rear Admiral Jesse B. Oldendorf. His big warships were to kick off the invasion by shelling Japanese beach defenses and the big guns thought to be emplaced along Lingayen Gulf.

Two weeks before S-Day, Lieutenant Colonel Russell Volckmann, the guerilla leader in northern Luzon, and his men had recovered documents from a crashed Japanese plane that spilled a closely guarded secret: General Yamashita had pulled back his troops and shore batteries to avoid torrential bombardments and would concentrate his formidable force on Luzon in the mountains to the east of Lingayen Gulf.

Volckmann had radioed MacArthur's headquarters: "There will be no, repeat no, opposition on the (Lingayen) beaches." But, apparently, the urgent message had been pigeonholed somewhere in the headquarters maze.

Commanding the ground assault would be Walter Krueger, the Sixth Army leader. No American, including MacArthur, was as intimately acquainted with the military features of Luzon as was Krueger. In 1908, not long after his graduation from West Point, then Lieutenant Krueger, a serious-faced young man with hair parted dead in the center, was assigned to the Philippines and made a topographical inspector. At the head of a party of engineers, young Krueger rode and tramped up and down the central plain of Luzon, including jaunts through the village of Cabanatuan, then a collection of native shacks. Never in his wildest dreams had Walter Krueger fancied that thirty-six years later, he would be leading a powerful army through this region.

While most officers clawed and scratched to obtain higher rank, General Krueger disliked the lofty impersonality forced on him by his job as Sixth Army commander.

"Hell," the sixty-four-year-old officer told reporters a few weeks earlier, "I'd rather have a regiment." Then he added: "I don't do much (as an army commander) except think a lot, scold a little, pat a man on the back now and then—and try to keep a perspective."

Despite his advanced years, Krueger could outwalk men many years his junior. Like MacArthur, his physical stamina amazed his troops. Once, on Leyte, a GI watching Krueger scramble up the side of a rugged cliff called out to a comrade, "Look at that old bastard go! He must be part mountain goat!"

Two of Krueger's corps would make the assault, storming ashore at points seventeen miles apart along Lingayen Gulf. Major General Oscar W. Griswold's XIV Corps, consisting of the 37th Infantry Division (once the Ohio National Guard) and the 40th Infantry Division (National Guardsmen from California, Nevada, and Utah), would hit the western beach near the town of Lingayen. Major General Inis P. "Bull" Swift's I Corps, including the 6th Infantry Division (originally regular army units) and the 43rd Infantry Division (National Guardsmen from New England), would come ashore on the eastern beach near San Fabian.

Attached to General Krueger's headquarters was newly promoted Marine Major Austin Shofner, who had been one of the ten Americans involved in the hair-raising escape from the Mindanao POW camp. Shofner had reached the United States in time to arrive at his Tennessee home on Christmas Eve 1943. A few days later, he pleaded with the Marine Corps commandant to allow him to return to the Pacific in a combat role. As a battalion commander in the 5th Marines in the bloody invasion of Peleliu on September 15, 1944, Shofner was wounded. Again he insisted on getting back into action as soon as he had recovered. Now his function was to be advisor to Krueger on guerilla operations.[11]

Just after dawn on S-Day, the stillness along Lingayen Gulf was shattered when Admiral Oldendorf's big guns roared. Hundreds of shells exploded along the shoreline and onto nonexistent ·Japanese coastal batteries. Burdened with weapons and heavy combat gear, Walter Krueger's foot soldiers, nervous and tense, climbed over the railings of their transports, made the hazardous descent down slippery rope ladders, and dropped with a thud into gently bobbing landing craft. Except for a handful of panicky Japanese stragglers who fired a few rifle shots before fleeing into the jungle, there was no opposition on the beaches.

"I don't like it," exclaimed one battle-hardened soldier of the 37th Infantry Division as he rested briefly after his outfit occupied the little town of Binmaley. "It ain't like the Japs to simply haul ass!"

Five hours after the first GI splashed ashore at Lingayen Gulf, Douglas MacArthur waded onto the beach. His shoes were still dripping water when he urged Walter Krueger to send mechanized forces in a lightning dash southward to Manila. "I know every wrinkle of the topography, and you can do it," exclaimed the Supreme Commander.

Consequently, Krueger ordered Oscar Griswold's XIV Corps to plunge southward and for Bull Swift's I Corps to protect Griswold's flank by attacking toward the east and northeast.

Colonel Henry Mucci's 6th Ranger Battalion had made the convoy trek in four large LCIs (landing craft, infantry), but it was S-Day plus 1 before the men were ferried ashore. By this time, the assault troops had penetrated far inland, so Mucci and his men marched southward for three-quarters of a mile and dug in to await orders. That night, the Japanese air force left its calling card, a bomb that exploded harmlessly in an empty field next to the Ranger bivouac area. After dawn, the battalion marched southward and set up camp near Walter Krueger's Sixth Army headquarters near Calasio.

For days, the wily Japanese melted away ahead of Griswold's Manila-bound columns, which were snaking fitfully down a handful of dirt roads and paths, hemmed in on both sides by thick jungles. "The 'front' here is thirty feet wide and thirty miles long," was the standard GI joke.

So far, there had been little Japanese opposition, and Griswold's corps had suffered only twenty-five casualties. Near the town of Tarlac, the armored spearheads rolled past a large cluster of nipa shacks, dust-covered and deserted. None of the young GIs even gave the abandoned site a second look, unaware that this was Camp O'Donnell, where thousands of American and Filipino servicemen captured on Bataan had perished under brutal conditions.

Hardly had the Americans landed at Lingayen Gulf than General Yamashita declared Manila an open city, just as MacArthur had done in December 1941, when the circumstances had been reversed.

"I do not intend to preside over the destruction of Manila," the Tiger of Malaya told his staff. Besides, he did not consider the capital as having military significance.

Yamashita established his new headquarters in Baguio, a prewar summer resort perched five thousand feet up in the mountains, 125 miles north of Manila. Then he issued orders for his formidable force in southern Luzon to pull back to the mountains around Baguio, where, he was convinced, he could resist American efforts to dig him out—perhaps for years.

Now, a haunting new specter reared its ugly head for the 511 POWs remaining at Cabanatuan. Thousands of Japanese troops withdrawing northward from the Manila region were traveling on the road leading past the prison camp. While in transit, these units, which often included a few tanks, stayed in the camp for a day or two before pressing onward.

William Seckinger recalled: "These Japs' behavior was bewildering. They seemed to regard us POWs as something to stay clear of. If they wanted food, which they easily could have taken from us, they *asked* for it. It was fantastic that they, the same kind of Japs who had starved and beaten and murdered Americans through two years and nine months of living hell, were now trying to ingratiate themselves with us.

"Our commander, Major Emil Reed, a very bold man, was concerned that trouble would develop, that one of our boys might go wild and kill a couple of Japs and we would all be murdered. So Major Reed, who was skin and bones like the rest of us, went through the camp rounding up Japanese and telling them to get the hell over to their own area and leave us alone."[12]

Three days after the Lingayen landings, the POWs in Cabanatuan grew bolder in light of the disinterest shown in them by the transient Japanese soldiers. Now that the prisoners had filled their stomachs with the vegetables and milk brought in from the Japanese area a week earlier, their focus turned to fresh meat, a carabao that was grazing across the road that separated the Americans' side from the Japanese area.

A captain convened a council of war, and it was decided that ten or twelve of the less feeble POWs would conduct a midnight raid against the targeted carabao.

"If the Japs halt us, try to bluff them," the captain said.

Among those in the raiding party was Private First Class Cecil "Red" Easley of Houston, Texas, who bore scars on his forehead from bomb fragments when the Japanese had struck Clark Field in December 1941. At the designated time, the POW group marched toward the front gate. The men were jittery, not knowing if they would be shot for trying to escape.

Cecil Easley remembered: "We were carrying empty litters on which to bring back the parts of the carabao. When we reached the gate, the two Jap guards just stared at us, apparently not knowing how to react to this unexpected situation. As we passed them, the captain gave them a sharp salute and we kept moving, not daring to look back.

"We went to the corral and pounced on not one, but two carabao, then butchered them with improvised knives. Carrying the portions on our litters, we returned through the gate. Just then, one of the Japs shouted, 'Halt!' This is it, we all thought. Instead, the man went up to our captain and evenly *asked* if he could have a little of the meat, as he was starving. The captain, a big-hearted fellow, gave him a large chunk, and we went on into the camp. When we got to the kitchen, all of us said a prayer."[13]

Providence had smiled on the prisoners: The steaks provided by the hefty carabao resulted in many of them gaining weight and stamina, assets that would prove to be invaluable in saving their lives during events that would soon involve Cabanatuan.

Meanwhile, sixty-five miles northwest of the prison camp, Lieutenant Colonel Henry Mucci and his 6th Ranger Battalion were frustrated and angry. In what may have been the most significant invasion of the Pacific war, the crack outfit had not been given a battle assignment. Instead, much to the Rangers' chagrin, they were serving as guards for Walter Krueger's Sixth Army headquarters.

Then on January 16—S-Day plus 7—there came a promise of action. Mucci was ordered to send a team of Rangers to conduct a reconnaissance of Santiago Island, a tiny dot in Lingayen Gulf. Through scattered intelligence reports, General Krueger felt there might be as many as thirty-five hundred Japanese troops on Santiago, and he was uneasy to have such a potent force in the Sixth Army's rear.

Colonel Mucci selected Captain Arthur "Bull" Simons, the powerfully built leader of B Company, to head the reconnaissance force of three other officers, nine enlisted men, and a Filipino interpreter. Just before ten o'clock that night, Simons and his men boarded a PT boat and set a course for Santiago Island.

A few hundred yards off shore from the objective, the Rangers scrambled into inflated rubber rafts and began paddling to the island. When they had nearly reached the beach, Simons noticed that the land contours did not match those of Santiago. A navigational error had dropped off the intruders at the tiny island of Saiper. So the Rangers had to row arduously for more than two additional hours to reach Santiago. There they sneaked silently ashore and learned from natives that the Japanese garrison had pulled out twenty-four hours earlier.[14]

When Captain Simons reported back to Sixth Army headquarters, General Krueger decided that Santiago would be an ideal spot for setting up a radar facility to warn of the approach of Japanese warplanes. So Henry Mucci was ordered to send two Ranger companies to secure Santiago and provide a perimeter defense for the radar erection project. More or less arbitrarily, Mucci chose E Company and Simons's B Company for the mission.

Simons and his Ranger force climbed into large landing craft and headed for Santiago. None of them had any way of knowing that, due to the luck of the draw, they would not participate in a looming prisoner rescue operation that would be one of the war's most electrifying events.

The Rangers brought ashore with them two bulldozers, a couple of Jeeps, and three trucks—items that dazzled the isolated natives of Santiago. While work was progressing on the radar erection, the Rangers fanned out to beat the bushes in search of lurking Japanese. None was found. Three days after landing, the radar was operational.

In the meantime, Lieutenant Leo V. Strausbaugh replaced Bull Simons as commander of the Santiago force. Simons had been called back to the mainland for a special assignment.

Leo Strausbaugh remembered the peculiar situation: "The U.S. Army turned over to me a rather large sum of money in Philippine pesos to be used to pay the natives for their labor and to get the economy going on Santiago. We organized the natives into work units and had them build shacks or anything else we could think of that represented labor. We kept paying them until the money was gone. Two weeks after arriving, our force returned to the mainland."[15]

Shortly after daybreak on January 26—S-Day plus 17—American mechanized reconnaissance units rolled into Guimba, a small town in Nueva Ecija Province about twenty-five miles directly northwest of the Cabanatuan prison camp.

William Seckinger recalled: "The Americans were drawing closer and closer. Barrios housing Japanese soldiers only a few miles from us were being dive-bombed. We could hear the crump of the exploding bombs, and sometimes could see smoke from fires that had been set. Then two light airplanes (which we learned later were Piper Cubs used for observation by the U.S. Army) circled our camp for about an hour. We went wild with excitement. American flags that had been hidden were brought out and waved. One plane dove and dropped what apparently was a note, but some Japs came running out of a building and grabbed it."[16]

Now that friendly forces were approaching, a new surge of fear gripped the Cabanatuan men. Would the Japanese suddenly charge back into camp and massacre the prisoners out of vengeance? If MacArthur's troops and the Japanese soldiers defending the region clashed violently, would the POWs be decimated in a cross fire? What if MacArthur's officers were not aware that Cabanatuan held POWs? Would they pulverize the camp with an artillery bombardment and air strikes, thinking that it was a Japanese army facility? Many prayed for a miracle.

15

A Perilous Mission

At Sixth Army headquarters near Calasio, south of Lingayen Gulf on January 26, 1945, Colonel Horton White, Walter Krueger's intelligence chief, leaned back in his chair and listened intently to a briefing by Major Bob Lapham, the American guerilla chief. On learning of MacArthur's landing on Luzon, Lapham had ridden a horse for thirty miles through Japanese territory from his base in Nueva Ecija Province until he came in contact with Sixth Army spearheads.

After telling American officers that he had crucial information about POWs, he was rushed to see Colonel White. Lapham told the colonel that, based on his own observation and information provided by his Filipino guerillas, there were about five hundred POWs, mainly Americans, languishing in Cabanatuan camp and in danger of being murdered by vengeance-seeking Japanese soldiers.[1]

Horton White, a large, pleasant, courteous man, rose from his chair and strolled to a wallmap of Luzon. Running a finger across the surface, he found Sixth Army's most forward position, at Guimba, twenty-five miles west of the prison camp. In reply to White's question, Lapham said there were approximately nine thousand Japanese soldiers in the general vicinity of the stockade, most of whom were either withdrawing northward toward the mountains around Baguio or were moving into defensive positions to meet Walter Krueger's oncoming invaders.

Bob Lapham said that the Japanese vehicle and tank traffic along the road directly in front of the prison camp was heavy, and that Japanese units were using the camp as a stopover on their trek into the

161

northern mountains. At any given time, there were between one hundred and three hundred enemy troops in the Cabanatuan compound. Lapham, who had been bedeviling the Japanese in Nueva Ecija Province for more than two and a half years and had a hefty price on his head, added that a strong enemy force was bivouacked along the Cabu River, less than a mile northeast of the POW camp, and that perhaps as many as five thousand Japanese soldiers were in and around the town of Cabanatuan, four and a half miles southwest of the stockade.

Then Lapham hit Horton White with alarming news: Unless these five hundred–plus POWs could be rescued, there was very real danger that the Japanese would murder them when Sixth Army spearheads approached the camp.

Deeply concerned about the ultimate fate of the Ghosts of Bataan and Corregidor, Colonel White and his assistant, Major Frank Rowale, rushed to see General Krueger. After giving the Sixth Army commander a terse rundown on the Cabanatuan POW situation, White strongly recommended that a crash operation be mounted to rescue the prisoners before the Japanese had a chance to kill them. Krueger listened thoughtfully, asked a few questions, then gave the mission the green light.

Just before noon the next day, Lieutenant Colonel Henry Mucci, the peppery leader of the 6th Ranger Battalion whose men were guarding Sixth Army headquarters, strode briskly into White's hut in response to an urgent summons. Soon the two men were joined by Major Bob Lapham and three Alamo Scouts lieutenants, John Dove, Bill Nellist, and Tom Rounsaville.

Working together, the officers rapidly created an operational plan to snatch the POWs from under the noses of the Japanese. In concept, the rescue scheme was simple. Paced by two teams of Alamo Scouts that would leave Guimba twenty-four hours in advance to reconnoiter the camp, a force of more than a hundred Rangers would march a circuitous route of about thirty miles (all of it through Japanese-controlled territory), sneak up to the stockade under cover of darkness, kill some 250 Japanese soldiers inside the stockade, collect 511 feeble, bewildered, ill, and, in some cases, immobile prisoners, and shepherd them back to American lines.

However, the reality was fraught with peril. Mucci's Rangers and the Alamo Scouts would have to dodge Japanese units and patrols all the way to the camp. Unlike the natural concealment provided infiltrators by the thick jungles of New Guinea and Leyte, the Rangers' route would be largely across featureless terrain, mainly dry rice paddies, where they might be spotted by enemy warplanes and ground soldiers. If the raiders avoided visual detection, they could be betrayed by barking dogs, large numbers of which were in every barrio. Or a Filipino traitor, seeking to curry favor with or gain a payoff from the Japanese, could tip off the enemy and the infiltrators would be ambushed and decimated.

Finally, there would be the daunting problem of Japanese trucks, many of them loaded with soldiers, and tanks traveling on the road leading past the stockade. Tanks were of much concern to foot soldiers, especially in the case of the looming raid in which the Americans would have only a few bazookas and rifle grenades to deal with the tracked monsters.

Horton White, Henry Mucci, and the other officers agreed that Rangers would hit the compound at 7:30 P.M. on January 29, only some fifty-four hours away. That designated time would permit the Rangers about an hour of darkness to slither and creep across the flat, open ground to the stockade, where they would lie in wait for the signal to crash the front and the rear gates.[2]

Although attacking under the cover of night was essential, the timing raised yet another disquieting specter: What would the moon be doing that night? If it shone in all its brilliance, which Sixth Army weather forecasters predicted, the Rangers might be detected long before they reached the stockade. In that event, it would be highly unlikely that the rescue force would even reach the gates, much less crash their way inside the compound. If the moon chose to hide behind clouds at H-Hour, the night might be so black that the Rangers and Alamo Scouts would be unable to discern their comrades from the Japanese, and chaos might ensue, making it impossible to free the POWs.

After a three-hour discussion, Colonel White asked, "Any questions, gentlemen?"

There were none. If anyone present felt as though he was taking his men on a suicide mission, he kept his concerns to himself.

Jeeping back to his nearby command post, Henry Mucci tersely expressed the views of those who would take part in the Cabanatuan raid, telling his driver: "We'll succeed in this mission because of our grueling training and soldierly qualities." Then, grinning wryly, he added: "And by luck and the grace of God!"[3]

Leaving the conference, guerilla Major Bob Lapham was disheartened and frustrated. After engaging in countless hit-and-run raids against the Japanese, he was told that he could not go on the most significant rescue mission of the war. His knowledge of Japanese troop positions and installations in Nueva Ecija Province made him far more valuable to Sixth Army intelligence. So Lapham set up his headquarters at Guimba, from where he could direct the activities of his guerilla forces.

In keeping with the standard practice of American guerilla leaders in the Philippines, Lieutenant Lapham had promoted himself to major. He had also elevated his two main Filipino leaders, Lieutenants Juan Pajota and Eduardo Joson, both of whom had fought on Luzon under General Wainwright, to captains.

At midafternoon on January 27, less than an hour after his conference with Colonel White, Henry Mucci called in his Charley Company commander, twenty-five-year-old Captain Robert W. Prince. Wearing his trademark shoulder holster and puffing on a pipe, Mucci came right to the point.

"Bob, we're going to conduct a raid twenty-five miles behind Jap lines to free our Bataan and Corregidor boys at Cabanatuan prison camp," he said. "Charley Company and a platoon from Fox Company will carry out the mission. You will be in command."[4]

Mucci added that Prince also would plan the operation, and the colonel would go along and be in charge of the overall mission, coordinating the Rangers, Alamo Scouts, and the Filipino guerillas.

Captain Prince of Seattle, Washington, hoped that he did not betray his surprise over the news. Tall and of medium build, the soft-spoken officer was hardly Hollywood's version of a two-fisted leader of rough and tough Rangers. In fact, he had occasionally asked himself why he had volunteered for the gung-ho outfit. Always, he came up with the answer: because of the challenge and because he had great confidence in Henry Mucci's leadership qualities.

Prince had graduated from Stanford University in the spring of 1941 and was commissioned a second lieutenant of artillery from his ROTC course. His ROTC colleagues had been called to active duty almost immediately, but an impacted wisdom tooth had delayed Prince's army entrance for four weeks, a happenstance that eventually may have saved his life.

Unbeknownst to Captain Prince when informed that he was to lead the Cabanatuan raid, one of his closest pals had died at the same camp from hunger and disease many months earlier. Back in the summer of 1940, Prince and Reid Shertleff, a student at the University of Utah, had spent six weeks as tentmates at Fort Ord, California, where they were taking cadet training as part of the ROTC program. They had hit it off at once, and in the months ahead, continued to develop their friendship.

After graduating from Utah University in June 1941, Reid Shertleff, still self-conscious over the shiny gold bar on each shoulder, was inducted into the army and promptly shipped to the Philippines, where he fought on Bataan and survived the Death March and Camp O'Donnell, only to die after being transferred to the hellhole of Cabanatuan. Had it not been for Bob Prince's dental troubles, the Stanford graduate also might have been sent to the Philippines and shared his friend Reid's fate at Cabanatuan.

Now on Luzon, Captain Prince withheld from his boss, Henry Mucci, the fact that he, Prince, was in relatively poor physical condition, which would make the grueling ordeal especially difficult. After his Charley Company had landed on Dinagat in the Gulf of Leyte in October 1944 to scour the island for enemy troops, Prince and his men had remained for twenty-eight days. While there, the captain's feet became infected with what the GIs called jungle rot or crud. This malady caused him little pain, but he had done no hiking for three months. Now these two tender feet would have to carry Prince for some sixty-five to seventy miles on the march to Cabanatuan camp and back.

Lieutenant John Murphy, who would lead the Fox Company platoon under Prince, was a portrait of a typical rugged Ranger. Born in Springfield, Massachusetts, Murphy had been a star quarterback at Notre Dame University, where he also participated in other bruising sports. Returning home after graduation, Murphy was bitten by the political bug and ran for the Massachusetts state senate. However, he was defeated, and a short time later, he entered the army. Now he was one of the most admired and respected officers in the 6th Ranger Battalion.

As soon as word of the Cabanatuan mission spread through the

Ranger camp, a family fuss erupted. Those who had not been selected to go pleaded with Colonel Mucci to take them along. Major Robert "Woody" Garrett, the battalion executive officer who had led five hundred Rangers ashore at tiny Suluan Island in Leyte Gulf, came up with a novel twist. He insisted that Mucci was far too valuable to the Rangers to risk his life in an extremely hazardous mission, so Mucci should stay behind and let Garrett lead the operation. The proposal fell on deaf ears.[5]

Shortly before dusk that day, January 27, Mucci assembled the men chosen for the mission.

"This will be a tough but rewarding task," Mucci declared. "We'll be behind enemy lines the entire time. The guerillas tell us there'll be about 250 Japs in the camp. We'll jump them at night. Get inside quick and knife 'em up! I don't want any of our boys from Bataan and Corregidor killed. Bring out every prisoner. Bring 'em out even if every Ranger has to carry a man or two on his back!"

Henry Mucci, a tough hombre, then spoke in an emotional tone: "Men, I want all of you to go to church. Get down on your knees and pray. Swear to God that you'll die if need be rather than to let harm come to our POWs!"[6]

Robert Prince recalled: "Colonel Mucci told me, and I in turn told my men, that this was purely a volunteer mission and anyone who wished could decline to go and no one would ever question his courage or dedication. No one backed out. In fact, everyone was eager—this was the plum of all assignments in the Pacific. There was one major problem: Every Ranger in the battalion wanted to go, and only 121 could go."[7]

At the conclusion of Mucci's briefing, the Rangers were told that there would be church services (both Catholic and Protestant) in thirty minutes. Corporal James B. Herrick of Long Beach, California, was among those streaming toward the ramshackle huts that served as improvised chapels. Every Ranger going on the mission attended—and presumably swore to die if need be to protect the POWs, as Mucci had suggested.

James Herrick recalled: "Some Rangers who hardly ever attended a church service would point a finger and say, 'There goes so and so. If he is going, so am I.' It was amusing to me to see them go to church because they knew the danger involved in the mission."[8]

Meanwhile at Guimba, the forward position of American spear-heads, two teams of Alamo Scouts were rapidly preparing to leave for Cabanatuan camp. All thirteen men were veterans of numerous dangerous reconnaissance missions behind Japanese lines in New Guinea and on Leyte, but those operations paled in significance compared to the crucial task that now had been entrusted to them.

Led by Lieutenant Tom Rounsaville and Lieutenant Bill Nellist, the Alamo Scouts would have to infiltrate Japanese territory, reconnoiter the stockade, and report their findings back to Colonel Mucci when he and his Rangers arrived near the prison camp. Rounsaville and Nellist had been in charge of the Scout teams that had rescued some one hundred Dutch and Javanese nationals from the Japanese along New Guinea's Maori River back in September 1944, so that experience had taught them valuable lessons that would be put to use in the mission at Cabanatuan camp.

Bill Nellist's team included Staff Sergeant Thomas Siason and Private First Class Sabas Asis, both Filipino-Americans; Corporals Wilmer Wismer and Andy Smith; and Privates First Class Gilbert Cox and Galen Kittleson. Rounsaville's group was composed of Sergeant Harold Hard, a graduate of Michigan State University; Technical Sergeant Alfred Alfonso, a Hawaiian-Filipino; Private First Class Rufo Vaguilar, a Filipino-American; Private First Class Francis Laquier, an American Indian; and Private First Class Franklin Fox, an Ohioan.

At 7:00 P.M., with darkness falling, Tom Rounsaville and Bill Nellist shook hands with their good friend and fellow Alamo Scout, Lieutenant John Dove, who would accompany the Rangers as liaison officer.

"I'll see you fellows in twenty-four hours," Dove declared.[9]

Single file, the Alamo Scouts marched eastward out of Guimba. Wearing green fatigues and soft hats, they were armed to the teeth. Each man carried a .45 pistol and extra magazines, three hand grenades, a rifle, bandoleers of extra bullets, and a nasty looking trench knife. A few had lightweight carbines in lieu of rifles, and one Scout lugged a Tommy gun, which was particularly effective for close-in fighting. When it was time to storm the Cabanatuan stockade, they would join with the Rangers. The Alamo Scouts would have their work cut out for them. Should they fail, or be ambushed and decimated, the entire delicately timed rescue mission could go awry.

Meanwhile back at Sixth Army headquarters, Colonel Mucci was conferring with officers of the U.S. 547th Night Fighter Squadron, whose sixteen P-61s were based near Lingayen Gulf. Led by Lieutenant Colonel William C. O'Dell, the squadron had extensive experience in providing night air cover for PT boats landing reconnaissance units behind Japanese lines.

These P-61s would play a crucial role in the rescue mission. One of the swift craft would buzz Cabanatuan camp at low-level to distract the Japanese soldiers at the same time the Rangers were slithering across dry rice paddies to the stockade. Other P-61s would patrol the dark skies of central Luzon to seek out and destroy Japanese troop-carrying vehicles and tanks that might head for the POW camp once the shooting began.

Known as the Black Widows because they were deadly, operated mainly at night, and were painted black, the P-61s would also be on call to rush to the Rangers' aid in the event they collided with Japanese tanks or armored vehicles. Along with speed and maneuverability, the Black Widows, which carried crews of three, had sophisticated radar in their noses, permitting them to detect enemy planes in flight at night. The sleek craft were armed with four .50-caliber machine guns and four 20-millimeter cannon. All of this awesome firepower could be controlled by the pilot and brought to bear on a single target. Any Japanese airplane, tank, or vehicle caught in the Black Widow's web had as much chance of surviving as, in the words of one P-61 pilot, "a snowball in hell."[10]

That night of January 27, every Ranger going on the raid intently studied air reconnaissance photographs of Cabanatuan camp. Numerous details of the prison layout were provided by Bob Lapham's guerillas, who had been spying on the stockade for many months. Guerillas also would serve as guides, provide flank protection during the Rangers' long and arduous march to prevent ambushes, and send back up-to-date information on Japanese troop movements in Nueva Ecija Province.

Long before daylight on January 28, the Ranger camp began to stir as those going on the Cabanatuan operation prepared to depart on the first leg of their trek, a sixty-mile ride to Guimba. Just past 5:00 A.M., there were shouts of "Load 'em up!" and Mucci's men scrambled into seven GI trucks. Paced by the colonel in a jeep, the tiny convoy sped away.

16

Cross-Country Dominos

Late in the stifling morning of January 28, the tiny convoy carrying Henry Mucci and his band of Rangers halted in a grove of trees a mile outside Guimba. Leaping down from the trucks, the raiders were gripped by a mixture of tension and excitement: Each man knew that he was about to embark on one of the war's most spectacular and perilous operations. Never in history had the United States Army been called on to rescue such a large number of POWs from so deep in enemy territory.

Among those dismounting was Captain James C. Fisher of Arlington, Vermont, the 6th Ranger Battalion surgeon. A stocky, crew-cut, pleasant man in his late twenties, he was the son of famed novelist Dorothy Canfield Fisher, and he was one of the battalion's most popular figures. Always amiable with an infectious smile, the combat doctor insisted that the Ranger enlisted men not call him Captain Fisher, but rather Jimmy. Uncomfortable with addressing a commissioned officer only by his first name, they settled for "Captain Jimmy."

As a boy, Fisher lived with his parents in France, and he traveled about Europe extensively. His schooling was in France, and when the Fishers returned to their native Vermont to live, Jimmy's schoolmates had a hard time understanding him because of his heavy French accent.

James Canfield Fisher had an impressive medical pedigree. An honors graduate of Harvard Medical School, he took his internship at Boston City Hospital and remained on the staff there for more than two years until called to active duty by the army. It would have seemed logical for the army to assign Jimmy Fisher to the European Theater of Operations, where he could put both his surgical skills and his extensive knowledge of the languages spoken in those countries to better use. Instead, the doctor was shipped to the 98th Field Artillery Battalion bound for the Pacific.

While the pack-mule outfit, which became the Rangers, languished in New Guinea in the backwash of the war for month after tedious month, Fisher not only tended to the physical needs of the men in his battalion, mainly the treatment of tropical diseases, but he found time to administer to the civilian population, most of whom had not known that there was such a thing as a medical doctor. Several New Guinea infants were given the first and middle names Jimmy Canfield after the caring American physician who brought them into the world.

Also going along were Lieutenant John W. Lueddeke and his four-man team of Photo Unit F of the 832nd Signal Service Battalion. All of these men had volunteered for the rescue mission, and they were combat trained. One, Sergeant Frank J. Goetzheimer, proudly wore the coveted wings he had earned as a paratrooper.[1]

These combat photographers had seen more action than anyone in the Ranger battalion. They and others in the 832nd Signal Service had the mission of recording on film the war in the Southwest Pacific. Since MacArthur began his leapfrog offensive up the spine of rugged New Guinea, the battle cameramen had splashed ashore with amphibious assault waves, leaped into combat with paratroopers, and gone along on bomber raids. Each photographer was armed with a pistol, but his most coveted possession and the one he carefully nursed was his camera.

Among those checking and rechecking their weapons were long-time close pals, Corporal Francis R. Schilli of Weingarten, Missouri, and Corporal Roy F. Sweezy. Schilli had been raised on a farm in a devout Catholic family, and he not only knew all of his own faith's teachings and rituals, but also many of those in Protestant religions. Roy Sweezy was also a farm boy, from Michigan.

Sweezy and Schilli had much in common other than their rural heritages. Both were quiet, almost introverted at times. In an outfit of men who were often hard drinkers and hard cussers, where the number one discussion subject was usually women, Sweezy and Schilli were known to blush when a risqué joke was told in their presence. However, each was a Ranger to the core—physically strong, tough, dedicated.

While his somber Rangers were preparing to go, Henry Mucci was deeply concerned that the fog of war might result in General Krueger's troops mistaking the returning columns of Rangers and liberated POWs for Japanese troops and open fire. So the colonel sent couriers rushing to the command posts (CPs) of the 6th Infantry Division, the 20th Infantry Regiment, and the 1st Infantry Regiment to coordinate recognition signals. It was decided that when the Rangers would near their own lines on the return march, they would fire two green flares to identify themselves.

Meanwhile, Sergeant James M. Irvine set up a powerful radio set in the backseat of a command car, which would remain outside Guimba to provide a communications link between the Rangers and Sixth Army advanced headquarters. Mucci's men would pack a pair of radios, although strict broadcast silence would be observed except in the event of an emergency. If the raiders were to run into big trouble going or coming, the Rangers would contact by radio the P-61 Black Widows based near Lingayen Gulf.

Just past 2:00 P.M., the Rangers, with Colonel Mucci in the lead, marched eastward from Guimba. Destination: Cabanatuan prison camp. Estimated time of arrival: twelve hours later. Distance to be covered on the march: about thirty miles. Typically, the Rangers would travel light and fast. They did not lug packs or wear steel helmets. Each man carried a canteen of water and two days' streamlined rations. Either they would return in two days or they might not return at all. No insignia of rank was worn on their green fatigues and cloth hats. If ambushed along the way, Mucci didn't want the Japanese picking off key officers and noncoms.

The Rangers were walking arsenals: BARs (Browning Automatic Rifles), Tommy guns, pistols, bazookas and rockets, hand grenades, trench knives, rifles and extra bandoleers of ammunition. Although the Geneva Convention forbid medical personnel from carrying weapons, Captain Jimmy Fisher, who had long been aware that the Japanese army ignored international law, had a pistol stashed in his pocket. His medics were also armed.

Guided by two Filipino guerillas, the Ranger column marched for two miles along a road, then turned south and proceeded over flat rice paddies for three miles to the Licab River. Fording the shallow stream, Mucci and his men, their boots dripping water, continued for about a half mile to the barrio of Lobong, which was the command post of the Filipino guerilla chief, Captain Eduardo Joson.

As arranged previously by Major Bob Lapham, Joson and eighty of his guerillas joined Mucci's men for the next leg of the march. Left behind by Joson were twenty of his heavily armed men; they were to guard his headquarters from attacks by Communist Luis Tarlac's Huks, the large guerilla group that had alternately been warring on the Japanese and on other Filipino guerilla bands.

Now there were more than two hundred men in the marching force. Soon they were engulfed by darkness. Tension grew thicker. Strange sounds in the rice paddies and bamboo thickets were magnified. Eyes tried to pierce the blackness. Ears strained to pick up telltale clues of danger.

When about nine miles into Japanese territory, the Rangers took a short break in head-high cogan grass about three hundred yards short of the National Highway, which ran from Manila northward through Cabanatuan town and on to San Jose. This main thoroughfare was heavily traveled by Japanese truck convoys and armored units pulling back from southern Luzon to the mountains around Baguio, where General Tomoyuki Yamashita planned to hold out indefinitely.

Sprawled on the ground, the Rangers heard an alarming sound— the clanking of Japanese tanks. As Mucci's men poked their heads above the tall grass, they saw the silhouettes of ten tanks rumbling past on the road. After what seemed to be ages, the last iron monster faded from sight. The Rangers issued collective sighs of relief.

Henry Mucci, presuming that enemy truck convoys would be using the road, quietly circulated among his men and instructed them to crawl forward and leapfrog over the highway, one or two at a time. Should a single Ranger or guerilla be caught in truck headlights, the Japanese could be tipped off that a raiding party was deep behind their lines.

Down on all fours, the raiders began crawling forward. As they neared the road, a pale moon broke out from behind a cloud, flooding the countryside with its rays. Moments later, the Rangers felt their hearts skip a beat—a Japanese tank was parked on or near a small bridge. This discovery caused Mucci to reconsider the leapfrog tactic, because the tankers no doubt had a clear view of the road in both directions.

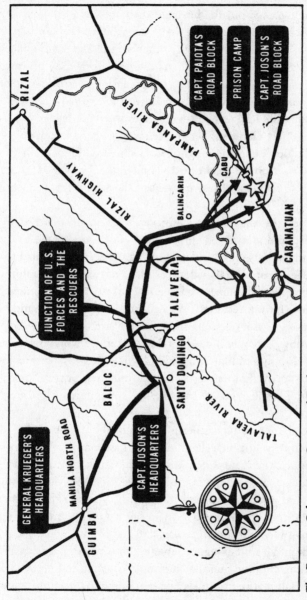

The Route to Cabanatuan Camp and Back

Captain Bob Prince brought out his map and, by the heavenly illumination, picked out the bridge. Under the span, the map showed, ran a deep east-west ravine. So the Charley Company commander suggested that the raiders reach the other side of the road by slithering through the ravine under the Japanese tank, crawling onward for a hundred yards or so, then making a mad dash to a large clump of trees about a quarter-mile away. Mucci agreed to the new scheme. Alone and in pairs, the Rangers began edging toward the bridge.[2]

James Herrick remembered: "As I wriggled closer, not only did the tank's silhouette become much clearer, but I could actually hear the Japs talking. Soon, I was directly under the bridge. My heart was pounding so furiously I was convinced the Japs a few feet above me would hear it."[3]

For perhaps sixty anxious minutes, the Rangers and Filipino guerillas creeped and crawled through the ravine under the bridge and reached the woods without detection. Minutes later, Mucci had them on their feet again, and they double-timed across open country for two miles. Then the column slowed to a fast walk.

James Herrick recalled: "We walked single file and played dominos, meaning that if one man thought he heard or saw something and dropped down, we all fell like dominos. Then we would be up and off again. After hours of marching and playing dominos, we became very tired and sleepy. Sometimes when we put men out as flank guards during brief breaks, we had to wake up these guards when we started out again."[4]

Several miles after slithering through the ravine under the National Highway, the marchers reached a second major north/south thoroughfare, the Rizal Road. Mucci sent scouts forward, and they reported back that the Japanese traffic was light. So the two hundred Rangers and guerillas crawled through the grass to the road and, in twos and threes, leapfrogged to the other side, then ran for a mile before halting for a short rest. It was 4:30 A.M.

Daylight was breaking on January 29, when the nearly exhausted Rangers and Filipino guerillas arrived at their initial destination, the barrio of Balincarin, five miles north of Cabanatuan camp. Mucci and his men had been marching, running, and playing dominos and hide-and-go-seek for nearly twelve hours, and they had covered twenty-five miles in the darkness.

In the meantime, the two teams of Alamo Scouts led by Tom Rounsaville and Bill Nellist had reached the vicinity of the Cabanatuan camp. Except for dodging a few Japanese patrols and the enemy traffic on the National Highway and Rizal Road, their long trek had been uneventful. However, they arrived extremely weary and footsore. Carabao tracks in the rice paddies had hardened in the dry weather and broiling sun, so it had been much like walking on cobblestones for thirty miles.

As previously planned, Bill Nellist and Tom Rounsaville met Colonel Mucci in Balincarin, and they greeted their old friend and fellow Scout, Lieutenant John Dove, Mucci's liaison officer on the mission.

"How'd things go?" Rounsaville asked.

Known for his dry wit, Dove replied, "We left behind miles and miles of dogs with hoarse voices from constant barking!"[5]

Rounsaville and Nellist had bad news for Henry Mucci and Bob Prince. The terrain around the camp was flat and featureless, so there had not been time for the Alamo Scout teams to get close enough to secure sufficient information on how many Japanese troops and tanks were inside the enclosure. From Filipino guerillas, the Scouts had learned that Japanese traffic had been heavy on the road leading past the camp.

There was another dreadful disclosure. Lieutenant Carlos Tombo, intelligence chief of Captain Juan Pajota's guerila force, confirmed to Nellist and Rounsaville that six to eight hundred Japanese combat troops were bivouacked along the Cabu River, a few hundred yards northeast of the POW enclosure, and that perhaps as many as five thousand Japanese troops were deployed around Cabanatuan town, apparently preparing to do battle with General Walter Krueger's oncoming Sixth Army.

Meanwhile, Captain Juan Pajota had ridden into Balincarin on a mule and conferred at length with Colonel Mucci. Pajota, who had been a lieutenant in the Philippine 91st Division, was trained in electronic communications and in infantry tactics, skills that had served him and his guerilla band well during two and a half years of hit-and-run raids in Nueva Ecija Province.

Captain Pajota confirmed the findings of the Alamo Scouts and his own intelligence chief, Carlos Tombo, and added that perhaps an entire Japanese division was moving northward along the road in front of the prison camp. Since the Japanese traveled mainly at night to avoid marauding American warplanes, it would be highly likely that the Rangers would collide with this far greater force should they attempt to attack the stockade that night.

Based on the information he had received since reaching Balincarin, Mucci decided to postpone the raid for twenty-four hours to give the passing Japanese division time to clear Cabanatuan camp. Shortly after making that decision, Mucci and his Rangers left Balincarin and marched southward for two and a half miles to the barrio of Plateros. Although secrecy was the password for the entire rescue mission, the Bamboo Telegraph informed the 306 citizens of Plateros that a large group of Americans was headed for their barrio and would arrive within hours.

Villagers in Plateros went wild with excitement. This was the most fascinating news that they had ever received. Girls and young women hurried to don their fanciest duds, then danced and leaped from one hut to another, calling out, "The Americans are coming! The Americans are coming!" None had ever seen an American.

Just as dusk was gathering, Henry Mucci led his dust-caked and perspiration-stained Rangers into Plateros, a collection of nipa huts. Earlier orders had been given for the infiltrators to be especially quiet, as the barrio was only a mile and a half from Cabanatuan camp. Suddenly, the head of the Ranger column was ambushed—not by armed Japanese but by thrilled, animated Filipina teenaged girls and young women. The giggling members of the reception committee were clad in white dresses and carried leis made of freshly picked flowers, which they draped around the necks of Colonel Mucci and several others. Behind the female reception committee were the other residents, all of them equally excited.

Henry Mucci remembered: "They asked if they could sing songs. I told them they could but they would have to do so softly, for we were twenty-five miles behind Japanese lines and only a stone's throw from the prison camp."[6]

A few score Philippine voices joined in a subdued, but stirring, if off-key, rendition of "God Bless America."

James Herrick remembered: "It sure was beautiful, and all of us felt choked up over this rousing reception. But all of us knew the Japs were only a short distance away."[7]

The reception of the Filipina beauties and the choral rendition of

"God Bless America" was only the start of a festive gala planned by the residents of Plateros. Although short on food themselves, the natives had slaughtered a prized cow to provide suitable food for the evening meal. Above the laughter and joyous chatter could be heard the braying of burros, the clucking of chickens, and the squealing of pigs, all of whom apparently felt that it was necessary to join in the welcome for the Americans.

Henry Mucci remembered an unexpected development: "Suddenly, the mayor of another town in the area showed up in the barrio. I was pretty suspicious of him because he had been mayor all through the Jap occupation. He brought us a bottle of prewar whiskey. It was Scotch, and it was good. We passed it around, so that a lot of the Rangers could get a little sip. Then I had the mayor put under armed guard until the rescue operation was ended."[8]

One of the Filipino guerillas mingling with the Rangers in the barrio was eighteen-year-old Private Godofredo Monsod, Jr., who was grimly dedicated to exacting vengeance on the Japanese. His father, Godofredo Senior, had been chief of the Japanese-sponsored Philippine Constabulary in Cabanatuan. Actually, the elder Monsod, who had been a major in a Philippine division that fought on Bataan, was pro-American, as were his top lieutenants and most of his men.

On numerous occasions, Chief Monsod had led members of his Constabulary into the Zambales Mountains with orders from the Japanese to track down and wipe out guerilla bands. A few days later, Monsod and his men would return to Cabanatuan and relate a harrowing story of a flaming gun battle with the guerillas, resulting in numerous casualties in the ranks of the Constabulary. Indeed, there had been "casualties"—patriotic Filipinos who had joined the guerillas. The gun-battle reports had been phoney to mask the disappearance of Chief Monsod's supposedly pro-Japanese constables.

A few months before the Rangers were assigned the rescue mission, Chief Monsod had been arrested by the notorious Japanese secret police, the Kempei Tai. Apparently, a Filipino traitor had snitched on Monsod as being zealously pro-American and he was hurled into a dungeon at Fort Santiago in Manila. After being relentlessly tortured for many days, Monsod was beheaded. Since no one else in the Cabanatuan Constabulary was arrested, it was clear Godofredo had remained silent.

Now, teenager Monsod was eager to get a crack at the Japanese, but he was armed only with a bolo, a long single-edged knife. So a few Rangers rustled up a rifle and a pistol for the youth to take into action.

Shortly after the crack of dawn on January 30, the Rangers were treated to a breakfast of coffee, eggs, and fruits, all of which had been scraped up by the villagers. Then, just before 9:30 A.M., Colonel Mucci gave his officers final instructions. Captain Juan Pajota and Captain Eduardo Joson, the two guerilla chiefs in Nueva Ecija Province, were given critical roles. Pajota was to take ninety-one armed men four hundred yards northeast of the POW camp, set up a roadblock, and prevent the Japanese force bivouacked along the Cabu River from rushing to the prison once the fireworks began. One hundred and fifty of Pajota's unarmed irregulars were to assemble twenty-five carts and carabao at the Pampanga River, a mile and a half to the north of the POW enclosure, and help to escort the freed prisoners on the way back to American lines.

Captain Joson's seventy-five armed guerillas would set up a similar roadblock eight hundred yards southwest of the camp and halt any Japanese force trying to break through from Cabanatuan town. Since the largest enemy concentrations were in that vicinity, a Ranger bazooka team, led by Staff Sergeant James O. White of Sullivan, Indiana, was assigned to Joson.

Each guerilla band had twenty-five land mines, which would be sprinkled along the road in front of both ambush sites. Joson and Pajota also were given one bazooka each, which their own men were to handle after receiving twenty-minute crash courses from the Rangers.

Colonel Mucci stressed to Pajota and Joson that they were to hold at all costs. Privately, Mucci and Bob Prince harbored nagging doubts about the Filipinos' ability to achieve that goal. All of the guerillas had tangled with the Japanese in hit-and-run raids many times, but would they stand their ground against an organized assault, possibly supported by tanks hell-bent on crashing through to the POW camp? Should one or both roadblocks crumble, the Japanese in the region could inflict a debacle upon the Rangers, the Alamo Scouts, and the POWs.

Late that afternoon, the Rangers were given a final briefing. They would sneak up to a low knoll seven hundred yards from the front gate and await darkness. Then they would begin wriggling over dry rice paddies to the stockade. It was hoped that the Japanese would be distracted from their approach by the P-61 Black Widow that would buzz the camp at treetop level. At the same time, Lieutenant Carlos Tombo and his guerillas, along with a few Rangers, would cut the telephone lines leading out of the camp to prevent the Japanese commander from spreading the alarm. John Murphy's platoon would slip around to the rear gate and, at 7:30 P.M., touch off the raid by firing into Japanese barracks.

Then the Rangers, along with several Alamo Scouts, would charge through the front and rear gates, kill the Japanese, and bring out the POWs. As soon as all the prisoners had cleared the stockade, Prince would fire a red flare, the signal for the Rangers to withdraw and form a rear guard for the POW column already bound for the Pampanga. On reaching the river, the captain would shoot a second red flare, indicating that it was time for Pajota's and Joson's guerilla bands to pull back to Plateros.

Lieutenant John Lueddeke, leader of the Unit F photographic combat team, and his cameramen were mildly disappointed to learn that the POW camp would be assaulted at night. They had looked forward to snapping some of the most dramatic pictures of the war in the Pacific. But it would be disastrous to have flashbulbs popping in the blackness while the Rangers were snaking across open ground toward the POW camp or while the hand-to-hand fighting would be raging inside the enclosure.

"We felt like an eager soldier who had carried his rifle for long distances into one of the war's most crucial battles, then never got a chance to fire it," Sergeant Frank Goetzheimer recalled.

Meanwhile, that afternoon at Cabanatuan camp, Sergeant Bill Seckinger was standing in the open, shielding his eyes with one hand as he gazed into the bright blue, sunshine-drenched sky. American warplanes were out in force, and the Japanese soldiers in the camp were getting increasingly jittery.

Seckinger recalled: "Our planes were strafing roads and bombing bamboo thickets all around us. We wondered if there was any significance to this intensified air activity. Tension among us was at the breaking point. Any minute, we feared, the Japs might open fire and kill all of us."[9]

Elsewhere in the prison camp, Private George R. Steiner of Loomis, California, was also outside his barracks as a pair of P-38s roared across the enclosure only two hundred feet up. In the past, Steiner had noticed, the Japanese soldiers in the compound were especially fearful of the swift, twin-boomed P-38s, aptly known as Lightnings.

Steiner recalled: "When these two P-38s buzzed the camp, a lot of the Japs dashed out of their huts and leaped into foxholes, which were half full of rainwater. Then they quickly scrambled out of the foxholes, hurried inside, put on rain gear, ran back outside, and jumped into the same holes."[10]

In another hut, Private Robert J. Body of Detroit, Michigan, and two other POWs were huddled, conversing in low tones, while planning an escape even though the penalty if they were caught would be death. They felt that American lines were only thirty miles or so to the west and that they would have a fifty-fifty chance of getting there.

Body remembered: "We were desperate. We had been guests of the Imperial Japanese Government for two years and eight months, so we felt we could no longer impose on their hospitality. Now was the time, if ever there would be, we decided. We planned to break out at eight o'clock that night. Of course, we had no way of knowing that the Rangers were just outside the camp."[11]

A few minutes past 5:00 P.M., while Bob Body and his two comrades were preparing to make a break for it in three hours, Henry Mucci's Rangers and guerillas were filing southward out of Plateros. Concealed by head-high cogan grass, they marched for a half mile and waded across the Pampanga River. There the force split, according to plan.

Captain Eduardo Joson and his guerillas and Captain Juan Pajota and his men headed cross-country to the sites for their roadblocks. Mucci and his Rangers continued southward. Word was passed back for talking to cease. The Rangers were now within a mile of the camp, and the slightest noise might give away their presence. An occasional twig snapping underfoot sounded like a cannon shot to the tense raiders. Soon the men got down on their bellies and began creeping and crawling over barren flatland for a half mile to the knoll only seven hundred yards from the front gate. A purple twilight was gathering.

Henry Mucci recalled a random thought that struck him: "The Pampanga River to our rear was about three hundred yards wide and waist-deep in spots and had a fair current. We had forded it with no trouble. Now I prayed there wouldn't be rain before we had to cross it again going in the opposite direction, because it was the kind of river that could rise a couple of feet in a very short time, and we would have to cross it with our sick and weakened POWs."[12]

Sprawled on the ground, the tense Rangers waited for night to pull its veil over them. Most were gripped by a sense of uneasiness. They were twenty-five miles deep into Japanese territory. Had they been detected or betrayed along the march route? If so, there would be no one to come to their aid. It appeared normal in the prison camp to their front, but were the wily Japanese lying in wait, ready to loosen withering blasts of fire into the Rangers while they were snaking toward the compound in the open rice paddies?

17

Creeping Up on
a Dark Stockade

January 30, 1945, 5:50 P.M.

Among the Rangers sprawled on the knoll and waiting for Captain Bob Prince to give the signal to head for the stockade was Staff Sergeant Theodore Richardson of Dallas, Texas, who would be the first man to bolt inside the enclosure if the raid went according to plan. Tall and husky, Richardson checked and rechecked his Tommy gun, the weapon he would use to bash off the massive lock on the wood and barbed-wire front gate.

At the same moment less than a half mile away inside the camp, Major Emil Reed, the 26th Cavalry surgeon, was standing near the gate through which Richardson would charge. In a bizarre twist of fate, the Ranger and the POW were not only from the same city, but they had close family ties. Major Reed's wife and Richardson's sister-in-law were friends back in Dallas, both belonged to the same Sunday school class, and they often talked with one another on the telephone.

5:55 P.M.

Captain Bob Prince peeked at the luminous face of his wristwatch. Five minutes to go. Like the others, his adrenaline was pumping. His mind was awhirl as it whisked through the assault plan. Had every detail been nailed down? Prince had no time to think about his feet, which had been tender for three months and now were troubling him after the thirty-mile march, much of it over the cobblestone-like carabao tracks in the dry, concrete-hard rice paddies.

6:00 P.M.

Night descended on Luzon. Bob Prince again scanned his timepiece, then waved his men forward. His signal was passed down the skirmish line, and men got on their bellies and began inching forward. They would have a half mile of dry rice paddies to cover before reaching assigned positions around the stockade.

Lieutenant William J. O'Connell of Boston, and thirty of his men, including Sergeant Richardson, were snaking their way toward the twenty-foot-wide front gate. They would literally be gate-crashers once the shooting erupted. Lieutenant Melville B. Schmidt of New Orleans, and his platoon, slithered ahead on the heels of O'Connell's men. Schmidt and his Rangers would have the task of opening the POW section, killing the Japanese there, and directing the prisoners to the main gate. John Murphy's platoon would slip around to the rear gate and, precisely at 7:30 P.M., fire into the Japanese barracks. That shooting would be the signal for the assault to be launched.

Bob Prince, along with Captain Jimmy Fisher, the battalion doctor, and his medics, would head for a ditch alongside the road that ran past the front gate. From that position, Prince would be able to react to any unforeseen emergency during the raid and make certain that all POWs were out of the camp and on the way to safety.

One of those wriggling across the rice paddies was Staff Sergeant August T. Stern, Jr., of Baltimore, Maryland. The going was strenuous, even for the superbly conditioned Rangers. Stern and the others had to cradle their rifles, Tommy guns, and BARs in their arms and they edged forward with noses only inches from the dirt. Soon their green fatigues were drenched with perspiration from the exertion and extreme tension.

August T. Stern, Jr., recalled: "I'd glance up on occasion and could see the Jap guards in the watchtowers. I said a prayer: 'Please, God, don't let them see us.' "[1]

6:10 P.M.

Inside the camp, Robert Body and his two comrades were tossing a few vegetables they had stolen into a tattered knapsack. Body and his fellow POWs were growing steadily more tense. In less than two hours, they would launch their jailbreak.

The Layout of Cabanatuan Camp

LEGEND

NO. 1 . . . . TANK SHED.
NO. 2 . . . . REAR GUARD QUARTERS.
NO. 3 . . . . PILL BOX.
NO. 4 . . . . ENEMY TRANSIENT QUARTERS.
NO. 5 . . . . ENEMY OFFICERS' QUARTERS.
NO. 6 . . . . ENEMY ENLISTED MEN'S QUARTERS.
NO. 7 . . . . MAIN GATE & GUARD HOUSE.
NO. 8 . . . . GUARD TOWER.
■×■ PILL BOXES.
×××× BARBED WIRE FENCES.
⇦ SUPPORT ELEMENTS.

SCALE 1:3,000

4½ MILES TO CABANATUAN

ASSAULT ELEMENT

MAIN GATE

NO. 7

0.9 MILES TO CABU

NO. 3

NO. 8

ALL ALLIED PRISONERS WERE CONCENTRATED IN THIS ENCLOSURE.

NO. 5

NO. 6

NO. 1

NO. 4

NO. 2

SUPPORT ELEMENT

6:20 P.M.

Captain Juan Pajota and his guerillas arrived at the site a few hundred yards northeast of the prison camp where they would confront the Japanese force of some eight hundred men bivouacked along the Cabu River. The Filipinos were heavily armed with weapons that had been smuggled in by Douglas MacArthur's submarines during the past year.

Pajota sent scouts some three hundred yards ahead of his roadblock, and they crept so close to the river that they could hear Japanese soldiers chattering. These scouts reported that the enemy had posted no sentries on the wooden bridge across the Cabu. So three or four guerillas sneaked onto the span and placed a time bomb on the far (Japanese) side. It was set to go off at about 8:00 P.M. when, Pajota concluded, the enemy force trying to break through to Cabanatuan camp most likely would be on the bridge.

6:35 P.M.

Piloted by Lieutenant Kenneth Schrieber, a P-61 Black Widow had been circling central Luzon for the past twenty minutes. Then Schrieber banked the swift aircraft, greatly lowered its altitude, and called out to his two crewmen, "Hold your hats, fellows, here we go!"

At treetop level, the Black Widow buzzed the POW enclosure at nearly four hundred miles per hour, then pulled up and headed for its base. It was hoped that the planned gimmick would distract the Japanese in the camp from the fact that more than a hundred Rangers were slithering across the dark, flat fields toward the compound.[2]

6:50 P.M.

As the Rangers inched ahead, all seemed normal in the camp. A light breeze was blowing, and except for the muted sound of men moving over the rough ground, it was eerily silent. Now the raiders were only a hundred yards from the stockade. Suddenly, a strange sound from within the compound split the night—*gong! gong! gong!*

The Rangers froze. Stomachs knotted. Mouths went dry. Had they been detected? Was the curious gong sound a signal to open a torrent of fire against the sprawled Rangers? At any moment, they expected brilliant searchlights to sweep the landscape.

For what seemed to be an eternity, the Rangers remained like statues. Actually, it had been ten minutes. When the Japanese failed to take any action, the intruders resumed wriggling forward. Only much later would they learn that the gong sound had emanated from a ship's bell that a navy POW had improvised and had a habit of sounding the watch at periodic intervals.

Inside the camp, POW Cecil "Red" Easley was deeply worried; in recent days, nearly all of the inmates felt that the Japanese would embark on a murderous rampage against them. So the gong sound added to their gnawing concerns. Easley heard a barracks comrade grunt: "That goddamned old sailor and his bleeping gong are going to get us all killed! Why doesn't someone shut the bastard up?"[3]

7:10 P.M.

Captain Bob Prince and most of his Charley Company slipped into the ditch in front of the stockade. Nearby were Captain Jimmy Fisher, the battalion surgeon, and two of his medics, Staff Sergeant John W. Nelson of Minneapolis, and Corporal Robert L. Ramsey of Kansas City, Missouri. Concealed only by darkness, the Rangers felt as if they could reach out and touch the Japanese guards only twenty yards away at the front gate.

Some Rangers could see the glowing coals of cigarettes being smoked by guards in the watchtowers. Others could discern Japanese soldiers lounging in their underwear in their still-lit barracks; these were transient troops who were to hit the road at dawn to continue their trek to the northern Luzon mountains. No doubt the 250 or so Japanese within the compound felt secure in the belief that the nearest armed American soldier was twenty-five miles away.

It was so quiet that some Rangers felt their breathing would give them away. Now, countless crickets thought the time was ripe to commence raucous chirpings, which, to the men cursing under their breaths, sounded like strident blasts from loudspeakers.

7:20 P.M.

Since Lieutenant John Murphy and his men had the longest distance to negotiate, they were just now within fifteen yards of the back gate.

They had crawled up a drainage ditch for the final lap, and now they rested their rifles on the outer ring of barbed wire, aimed at the barracks holding the transient Japanese soldiers. By arm motions that could barely be discerned in the darkness, Murphy had three of his men—Staff Sergeant Cleatus G. Norton of Hendersonville, North Carolina; Staff Sergeant Richard A. Moore of Santa Clara, California, and Technical Sergeant Melvin H. Gilbert of Maplewood, Oregon—crawl about ten yards to the far side of the gate. As they were inching along the fenceline, a Japanese soldier in the tower only a few feet above them called out what seemed to be the equivalent of "*Halt!*"

Since the moon was peeking through the clouds, the guard may have spotted the three Rangers' dim forms, or else he sensed movement of some kind. Disaster loomed. The entire raid was in jeopardy, for the assault was to begin when Murphy's men cut loose with their weapons. If the Japanese started firing at the three sergeants, it could upset the timetable, because the other Rangers might think the shots were the signal to attack.

Sergeants Norton, Moore, and Gilbert lay motionless. Hearts thumped furiously. They could sense the guard's eyes boring into them. He was only ten yards away. Moments later, the Japanese soldier began calling out, apparently summoning help. Every few seconds he shouted, but no one came to his aid.[4]

7:40 P.M.

Inside the enclosure, Private George Barber, a British soldier captured at Singapore who had escaped and was recaptured in the Philippines, was lugging a sack of potatoes to the guardhouse. There were about fifteen Japanese soldiers sitting around and talking. Barber made a good target for their barbs. With great gusto, they asked him if he thought he would get out of Cabanatuan camp before he died of old age.[5]

POW leaders tried to mask their deep concerns over the distinct possibility that the Japanese might slaughter the prisoners as MacArthur's troops drew closer. Major Ralph Hubbard thought about his wife and young son in Oklahoma City. Navy Lieutenant George W. Green reflected on how ridiculous he must look with his naval officer's cap and tattered, filthy burlap pants.

7:42 P.M.

In the ditch near the front gate, Captain Bob Prince was growing antsy. H-Hour had passed twelve minutes earlier, but there had not been a peep from Lieutenant Murphy and his men on the far side of the compound. What had gone wrong? Prince had no way of knowing that the three sergeants' brush with disaster had kept Murphy from opening fire on schedule.

7:44 P.M.

Suddenly, the silent night was split by a murderous crescendo of gunfire that echoed for miles across the flatland as John Murphy and his platoon poured heavy fusillades of bullets into the barracks where the transient Japanese troops were relaxing in their underwear. Once the blasting began, Sergeants Norton, Gilbert, and Moore raised their weapons and riddled the guard above them at point-blank range.

Cleatus Norton remembered: "The Jap never knew what hit him. All of our Tommy gun and rifle bullets hit him at once, and he fell from the tower."[6]

In one of the rickety huts inside the fence, Private Edward S. Gordon of the 4th Marines was nibbling a piece of bread he had made from rice flour. When the ear-splitting racket erupted, Gordon heard a thud and limped outside. The dead body of the Japanese sentry that the three Ranger sergeants had peppered with bullets was crumpled at his feet.

7:45 P.M.

Amid the crescendo of gunfire, Sergeant Ted Richardson scrambled from the ditch and dashed to the eight-foot-high front gate. With the butt of his Tommy gun, he began pounding on the oversized padlock. It refused to give. So the sergeant whipped out his .45-caliber pistol and started to aim it at the recalcitrant lock. At that moment, a Japanese soldier a bare ten yards inside the gate fired his rifle, missing Richardson, but knocking the pistol from his hand.

Lugging a BAR, Private First Class Leland A. Provencher of Litchfield, Minnesota, charged across the road on Richardson's heels. Now Provencher instinctively raised his automatic weapon and squeezed off a burst, knocking over backward the Japanese soldier who had shot at his comrade.

Richardson calmly picked up his pistol and fired several rounds into the lock, causing it to shatter. Provencher and Richardson threw open the heavy, twenty-foot-wide gate, and charged inside, followed by a crush of men belonging to Lieutenant Bill O'Connell's platoon.[7]

Ted Richardson unknowingly had bolted past Major Emil Reed, the POW from Dallas whose wife was a good friend of the Ranger's sister-in-law. Reed had been inside the front gate peering through binoculars toward the dim artillery flashes to the northwest.

18

Pandemonium Erupts
in the Night

7:46 P.M.

Pitching grenades, the Rangers, like cogs in a well-oiled machine, poured into Cabanatuan camp through the front and back gates. Pandemonium erupted. A raucous din from the cacophony of battle noises reached a peak. Bands of tracer bullets from GI weapons rendered iridescent geometric patterns as they flew toward the Japanese area of the compound. Grenade explosions shot fiery orange balls into the black sky. Frantic orders were shouted in Japanese. Dim figures dashed about helter-skelter. A hut burst into flames, casting eerie dancing shadows throughout the camp. Above the racket could be heard the screams of Japanese soldiers punctured by grenade fragments or victims of aimed bullets. Although outnumbered by perhaps two to one, the Rangers had the distinct advantage of gaining total surprise and of each man having been briefed on his precise mission, while the Japanese were milling about in mass confusion—even panic.

When the fireworks had broken out, Lieutenant Merle Musselman, a company surgeon who had been captured on Bataan, and another POW were sitting on the steps of the camp dispensary, whiling away the humid night with talk of home. Suddenly, the two men tensed as stray bullets began whizzing past. Musselman and the other man took cover and pondered what to do. Both were convinced that the Japanese had started slaughtering the prisoners.

A few minutes later, Musselman's thoughts flashed to his one hundred patients in what passed as a surgical ward. Not certain what he could do to help once he arrived, the doctor ran as fast as his weak legs would carry him the few hundred feet to the ward. Going inside, he was shocked. All the patient beds were empty. Musselman had no way of knowing that American Rangers had already entered the facility and cleared out the patients, lugging a few of the weaker men on their backs.

Leaving the ward, Lieutenant Musselman collided with a heavyset figure carrying a rifle.

"Get the hell to the front gate!" the Ranger shouted.

Musselman needed no encouragement.[1]

Hard on the heels of Sergeant Ted Richardson, who had blasted off the front gate lock, Leland Provencher, the Minnesota farm boy, and Private First Class Charles S. Swain of Beaver Dam, Wisconsin, charged toward their assigned target, the barracks containing Japanese officers. They sent bursts of fire from their Browning Automatic Rifles (BARs) into the building, then charged inside and hosed down the rooms with their weapons as frantic Japanese scurried in vain for cover.

After Provencher and Swain silenced the officers' barracks, they dashed back outside and heard a voice calling out in English: "Don't shoot! Don't shoot! I'm an American."

Leland Provencher remembered: "We saw this dim figure approaching us only a few yards away. We knew it had long been a favorite trick of the Japanese to speak English in battle to lull our fellows into a false sense of security. So I started to blast him—then had a sudden change of heart. This fellow, an American sailor, had been tending the generator in a building next to the Jap officers' barracks. Only the good Lord knows why we didn't shoot him."[2]

In the meantime, Lieutenant Mel Schmidt led his men through the front gate, and they dashed down the dirt road bisecting the stockade. Along the way, their rifles, Tommy guns, and BARs spat a constant stream of bullets into the huts and barracks on the western, or Japanese, side of the compound. Schmidt's platoon was to wipe out the guards in the POW area, search the barracks, and direct all prisoners who could walk to the front gate.[3]

As Schmidt and his men bolted into the POW area, a lone enemy soldier happened to be sitting on the roof of a barracks and he was screaming at the top of his lungs. A burst of Tommy gunfire silenced him. From behind a structure, another Japanese soldier, shouting "banzai!" charged at Private First Class Alexander Truskowski of Port Washington, New York, who calmly raised his Tommy gun and sewed a stitch of bullets into the man's belly.[4]

While many Rangers loosed blistering fusillades of fire into the barracks known to hold the guards and Japanese transient troops on their way north, Staff Sergeant Manton P. Stewart of Goose Creek, Texas, and a comrade edged up within twenty yards of the two corrugated tin sheds that the Alamo Scouts had reported contained trucks and possibly a tank or two. Stewart kneeled and placed a bazooka on his shoulder, and his loader promptly inserted a rocket in the rear of the weapon, then tapped Stewart on the shoulder to indicate it was ready to fire. Taking aim at one shed, Stewart started to squeeze the trigger when his eye caught a movement in the nearby shed. Two trucks, loaded with Japanese soldiers, apparently were going to bolt from the stockade to escape the unexpected man-made whirlwind that had descended upon them.

Quick as a cat, the Texan shifted his aim and fired a rocket. An orange ball of fire split the night as the missile tore into the truck. Seconds later, another rocket blasted the second truck. Both vehicles burst into flame. Japanese soldiers who survived leaped from the vehicles. A few, saturated by burning gasoline, were human torches, and their screams penetrated the grating sounds of the gunfire on all sides. Others, dazed by the blasts, staggered around. Silhouetted by the brilliant fires, they were cut down by Ranger guns.

In the meantime, Manton Stewart fired three more rounds through the walls of the second shed. Presumably, one or two tanks were inside, but Stewart and the others had to rush off to complete their mission before the charred structure could be inspected inside.

7:47 P.M.

George Steiner, an airman captured on Bataan, happened to be outside at the time the Rangers reached the POW area. He was bewildered. There were battle noises that were strange to him. As he looked on in amazement, an intruder fired a missile from a stovepipe-like apparatus, disintegrating a guard tower. The POW had not known that such a thing as a bazooka existed.

Steiner remembered: "I was awestruck and peed in my pants. I jumped into a smelly drainage ditch from our latrine and was crawling to get out of sight, when one of the big fellows (Rangers) grabbed me and pulled me out. I didn't know who in the hell he was. This soldier spoke English, and he told me to get the hell to the front gate, that a prison break was on. I had gangrene in my right leg and foot so bad that I had a hard time even walking, but the adrenaline was pumping so hard that I ran for the gate in high gear."[5]

Elsewhere in the enclosure, POW Robert Body, who had been planning to escape that very night, left his hut after the uproar broke out and collided with a soldier in a strange-looking uniform. By the light of a burning hut, he could tell his garb was green.

Body recalled: "I thought it was a Jap and that he was going to shoot me. Instead, he hollered, 'Get to the gate.' I was confused and didn't know which gate he meant so I decided, to hell with the gate. I barged right through the barbed-wire fence, tearing my tattered clothes and cutting a deep gash in my nose. But I didn't give a damn. I wanted out of there!"[6]

When the heavy firing erupted, Sergeant Bill Seckinger was with a group of four other POWs. Bullets were whistling past outside. All the men belly flopped to the floor. A canteen on the window sill was struck by a stray bullet, fell, and hit Sergeant Hasso Short on the head. Quickly, Short wormed his way across the floor and asked the question that was on the minds of all: "What in the hell is going on?"

Little Jose Archibeque, a medic who was known for keeping a sense of humor amid the horrors of the prison camp, had landed in the center of a nest of ants when he hit the floor. Archy piped up: "Come on, let's get the hell out of here! I'd rather face bullets than these damned ants!"

William Seckinger recalled: "While bullets were flying through the thin walls of the hut, Marine Sergeant Harry Pinto kept calling out our names, just to make certain that none of us had been hit. Someone on the floor yelled, 'It looks like they're going to get us all!' We were convinced that the Japs had begun to wipe out all of us POWs.

"Then we heard a voice call out in an unmistakable Southern drawl, 'Yaw'll are free! Head fer the front gate!' No Jap could sound like that, we decided. So we leaped up and, foolishly, stopped to collect our pitiful personal possessions before going outside."[7]

All the while, Rangers were dashing from hut to hut, shouting at the top of their lungs: "We're Americans! This is a prison break! Get to the front gate!"

Their pleas often got no response. Having endured nearly three years of brutality, starvation, and the constant specter of death, and having seen the harsh fate of men who protested or tried to escape, most of the haggard prisoners had adopted a kind of muteness, a stupified mentality. They had pressed themselves to the brown, stinking soil or lay face down on the split bamboo floors of the huts and barracks when the sounds of violence and the shouting had begun. Even after the shooting had stopped, large numbers of the prisoners were too petrified, numb, or physically unable to move.

Slowly, the suspicions inhabiting wasted bodies and tortured minds began to wear off. Now the Green Angels were gently lifting them to their feet. The POWs had not known such kindnesses since before their capture ages ago. Some burst into tears. Weakened prisoners began to hobble on bare, swollen feet through the front entrance. In their confusion, some POWs embraced and kissed their saviors, whimpering: "Thank you! Thank you! Thank you! Thank God, you've come!" Most of the POWs were barefoot and clad only in underwear.

Rangers dashed into barracks, hoisted bedridden men onto their backs, and headed for the front gate. One POW scrambled off the back of a Ranger and declared: "I can walk. I'm an American *soldier*!" He took two halting steps and collapsed.

Staff Sergeant Julian B. Brown of Madison, Florida, may have been the first POW to hobble through the dark main gate. There he bumped into Captain Bob Prince. A survivor of the Death March and Camp O'Donnell, Brown had sworn for nearly three years that he would kiss the first armed American soldier he saw. Now, he fulfilled that pledge, lunging forward and bussing Prince on the cheek before limping off toward the Pampanga River.

In one barracks, Navy Lieutenant George Green of Auburn, Alabama, a former Manila stockbroker and a reserve officer, had been racked with arthritis for months and could not get out of his bunk. Hearing the Ranger shouts, Green forgot about his arthritis, scrambled out of his bunk, and hobbled unassisted all the way to the front gate.

Elsewhere, E. C. Witmer, Jr., was lying in his bunk when the din of battle erupted. In the bunk next to him was a POW named Jackson. Witmer recalled: "We thought the Japs were shooting the prisoners.

Mr. Jackson, who had but one leg, and I hit the drainage ditch back of our building. I landed smack on top of Jackson. Even though he had but one leg, he moved faster than I could. If you think you're about to be killed, you don't let a little matter like having only one leg slow you down."[8]

From another hut, an English civilian shuffled up to a Ranger. Satisfied that the green-clad figure was indeed an American, he grumbled, "Well, you Yanks got us into this bloody mess here, so it's bloody well right that you get us out of it!"[9]

Nearby, Corporal Marvin W. Kinder of Fortville, Indiana, had hold of a POW's scrawny arm and was leading him out of a barracks. Suddenly, the bewildered man began struggling.

"I have to go back inside and get the documents I hid."

"No, we have to keep moving."

"But I need my documents to court-martial a man who ate my cat. It was a beautiful cat. He ate my cat!"

Then the POW began crying profusely. Kinder gently lifted him and headed for the front gate.

In the meantime, Alamo Scouts Lieutenant John Dove, a veteran of numerous missions behind Japanese lines in New Guinea and on Leyte, was caught up in the mass confusion, going from hut to hut to locate the ranking American officer in the camp and escort him and other POWs to the front entrance.

Dove recalled: "On the way, I crossed a little bridge and caught a glimpse of a foot moving in the ditch under it. I called to the man, but got no reply. Obviously, he was scared to death. Then I pulled on his leg, but he refused to budge. Knowing that the POWs were weak, I thought I might hurt him if I kept pulling, so I lifted the small wooden bridge from its base and talked him into heading for the gap in the fence. He muttered something like 'I thought you were a Jap and was going to kill me.' Then he broke into tears and hugged and kissed me."[10]

Finally, in a barracks, Lieutenant Dove located the officer he was seeking, Colonel James W. Duckworth of San Francisco, California, who had operated a field hospital on Bataan. Duckworth, too, seemed slightly bewildered and appeared suspicious of the heavily armed figure in green who stood before him. Dove asked the colonel to head for the main gate, adding that if he, the senior POW officer went, large numbers of other confused prisoners would follow.

"Well, let me get my walking stick," Duckworth said.

"No time, colonel," Dove answered with a sharp tone in his voice. "Get going—now!"[11]

When Duckworth, a white-haired, distinguished looking man, neared the front gate, he fell into a hole and broke his arm. In excruciating pain, he grimaced, scrambled out of the excavation, and began urging the POWs to get through the entrance as rapidly as possible.

In one barracks, Corporal James Herrick came upon an older POW lying on a bunk and staring toward the ceiling.

"Come on, pal, we got to get going," the Ranger said softly.

"No, no," replied the other in a barely audible tone. "I'm a goner. Help get the other fellows out."

Herrick leaned forward and gently picked up the prisoner, who was mostly skin and bones. Placing the man on his back, the corporal hurried outside and headed for the front gate.

James Herrick remembered: "About halfway to the gate, I heard the POW give out with a faint gasp and then he seemed to go limp. At first I thought he might have been hit by a stray bullet. So I set him down and felt his pulse. There was none—he was dead of an apparent heart attack. The excitement had been too much for him, I guess. It was really sad. He was only a hundred feet from the freedom he had not known for nearly three years."[12]

In a few instances, some of the less weak prisoners carried or escorted their incapacitated comrades to the main entrance. One POW providing this help was Cecil "Red" Easley, the Texan who had been involved in the carabao-butchering raid a couple of weeks earlier.

He remembered: "I was one of the 'healthy' POWs, as my weight had gone up to about 110 pounds after we had eaten the carabao steaks and the food we had pilfered after the regular Jap guards pulled out earlier in the month. So I lifted my pal, Cecil Hay, who was from Harlingen, Texas. He was so weak he could not walk. I carried him to the gate piggyback, and at the same time, led another friend, Jimmy Pittman of Dublin, Texas, who was almost blind from malnutrition."[13]

7:51 P.M.

Alone, in twos and in tiny knots, a steady stream of POWs was edging through the main gate. Staff Sergeant August Stern was carrying a

POW on his back and had moved some distance past the entrance when he came to what he thought was a small stream. While trying to wade across, Stern fell to his knees, but he managed to keep hold of his POW.

August Stern remembered: "I got a whiff of the stinking odor and realized that I had fallen into a drainage ditch that carried sewage from the camp. I was so angry that I started cursing and swearing and calling the Japs all kinds of names. My POW said to me, 'Please don't be angry. I am a Catholic priest, Lieutenant Hugh Kennedy.' I quickly apologized for using God's name in vain. He said, 'Son, you are forgiven, because there is a time and place for everything—and *this* is the time and the place.' "[14]

7:52 P.M.

While the firing and explosions were raging inside the compound Captain Jimmy Fisher, the Ranger doctor, was crouched in the darkness about fifty yards from the front gate. He told the two medics with him, Sergeant Jack Nelson and Corporal Bob Ramsey, "Okay, boys, let's get up to the gate. They might need us there." Moving forward, the three medical men became separated.

At the same time, three Japanese soldiers at the far end of the huge compound fired three shells from a mortar in the direction of the front gate, more than five hundred yards away. The three "coughs" as each projectile left the tube were heard by the close pals, Corporal Francis Schilli and Corporal Roy Sweezy, both of Lieutenant Frank Murphy's platoon, which was still outside the barbed-wire fence.

Francis Schilli recalled: "We not only heard the pops as the shells flew out of the mortar, but we saw the flames that shot upward from the barrel. All of us opened fire on the Japs at the mortar, and no more rounds were shot from it. As it turned out, we were a little too late."[15]

As Sergeant Jack Nelson neared the gate, the three shells fired by Japanese mortar exploded nearby. Nelson flopped to the ground and heard someone shout, "Man down ahead!" He scrambled to his feet and dashed a short distance forward, where a figure was crumpled on the ground. It was too dark to know who the Ranger was, and no one was wearing rank insignia.

"Where've you been hit?" Nelson asked.

"Stomach," was the gasped reply.

Moments later, First Sergeant Charles H. Bosard of Warren, Minnesota, approached. Bosard's task had been to remain near the front gate and help direct the emerging POWs.

"Better find Captain Jimmy (Fisher) right away; this fellow's been hit pretty bad."[16]

The man on the ground whispered weakly, "I am Captain Fisher."

Lying along the road a short distance away was Technical Sergeant Alfred Alfonso, the Alamo Scout and Hawaiian-Filipino of Maui, Hawaii. Bleeding profusely from a mortar shrapnel wound to the lower abdomen, Alfonso was writhing in agony. One of Fisher's medics, Corporal Morton T. Estensen of Gaylor, Minnesota, limped up. Estensen himself had been nicked by a sliver from the exploding shells, but he managed to inject Alfonso with morphine to relieve the riveting pain.

Two other Alamo Scouts, Lieutenants Tom Rounsaville and Bill Nellist, had been standing near the gate, where they were to form a rear guard once all the POWs were out of the compound. One of the mortar shells exploded behind them, and both men instinctively did belly flops. Nellist, reflecting that they had had a narrow escape, climbed to his feet, but his pal Rounsaville remained on the ground.

"Are you hit?" Nellist asked.

"Yeah, I'm bleeding."

"Where are you hit?"

"In the ass."

Lieutenant Nellist whipped out his trench knife and cut a bloodstained swath from his comrade's trousers seat. "I can see a piece of metal sticking out," Nellist said. "I'll try to pull it out."

While Rounsaville gritted his teeth, Nellist tugged at the sharp fragment, but he was unable to extract it.[17]

Sprawled nearby and being treated by a medic was Private First Class Jack A. Peters of Mesquite, Texas, who had been hit by a mortar shell fragment that cut the insides of both thighs. It was a painful wound, but not life-threatening.

7:59 P.M.

Among the Alamo Scouts, whose job it was to escort the first freed POWs to the Pampanga River, were Corporal Andy Smith and Sergeant Harold Hard, veterans of numerous behind-the-lines operations in New

Guinea. Within a few minutes of the first shots, a crunch of humanity had developed at the front gate, with small-arms fire and grenade explosions providing background music.

Harold Hard recalled: "I managed to quickly round up a good-sized number of POWs as they hobbled, bewildered, out through the gate. My orders were to start immediately for the Pampanga with them. So we set out into the night. One prisoner could not get up a three-foot bank, and when I put my hands around his arms to help him up I found he had no muscles at all—only bones. My hand encircled his entire arm."[18]

Andy Smith remembered escorting a batch of freed POWs: "I told them to follow me to the river, but if they were unable to keep up, that they should stop and sit down and wait for other Rangers to come by and pick them up. Some were barefoot and wearing only white underwear. We had gone only a couple of hundred yards, when bullets, apparently fired by the Japs, hissed past us. Everyone hit the dirt, but no one was hit. I told the POWs to remove any outside white clothes, for I felt the Japs had spotted all the underwear. Without a word, the prisoners got up, took off their white underwear, cupped it in their hands, and continued on, barefoot and naked.

"When we reached the Pampanga, I told the POWs to sit down. Then I handed each one a Camel cigarette and lighted it for him. It was the first American smoke they had had since Bataan and Corregidor. One POW burst into tears."[19]

Meanwhile, along the trail leading to the Pampanga, Corporal Jim Herrick came upon a fellow Ranger escorting a frightened POW, who said he was too ill to continue and begged to be allowed to return to the dark camp to die.

Herrick recalled: "I told him we couldn't abandon him. So I took off my fatigue jacket and asked the other Ranger to take his off, too, and we used our rifles and jackets to make a stretcher. In his haste, my comrade had forgotten to remove his bayonet from his rifle, so when I grabbed the weapon to pick up the POW, I cut a deep gash in my hand, which made carrying the load for more than a mile quite painful."[20]

8:01 P.M.

As expected, the heavy firing at Cabanatuan camp kicked up a fuss along the banks of the Cabu River several hundred yards to the northeast.

Japanese scouts edged forward to reconnoiter the bridge, which blew up in their faces when the planted time bomb exploded.

Captain Juan Pajota had hoped the explosion would demolish the span to prevent Japanese tanks from crossing the stream, but only about thirty feet of the bridge had been destroyed. However, Pajota breathed a sigh of relief when his men reported the time bomb had blown such a gaping hole that tanks could not get over the span.

Within minutes, a platoon of Japanese soldiers charged down the road, screaming, "banzai!" Reaching the bridge, they tried to leap over the large hole. A withering fusillade of fire erupted from the concealed guerillas, and many in the enemy contingent were mowed down. Undaunted, the Japanese commander, applying his army's customary battle doctrine, sent a second, then a third group to charge over the bridge. All of them were chewed up or driven back by murderous gunfire.[21]

8:06 P.M.

Near the front gate, Captain Bob Prince held a hurried discussion with a few of his officers and noncoms, who felt that all of the POWs had been evacuated. However, Prince headed for the prisoner section to search for stragglers. With a .45 automatic in one hand, he entered the dark POW structures and shouted in each one, "Anybody here?" There were no replies.[22]

Like the other Rangers, Prince was convinced that all the POWs were out of the camp. However, it would be discovered much later that they had failed to locate one POW, a Canadian civilian, sixty-six-year-old Edwin Rose. Only a few minutes before the assault was launched, Rose had sauntered wobbly out of his barracks and headed for the latrine on one of his frequent dysentery-induced emergency calls. The Toronto native was deaf as a post, enfeebled by beriberi, and nearly blind. Entering the latrine, he sat down and, after performing his ritual, apparently fell asleep. In the half hour that followed, he would be totally unaware of the racket and organized turmoil erupting throughout the camp.

8:13 P.M.

Now back at the front gate, Captain Bob Prince glanced at his watch. It seemed like a lifetime since John Murphy's platoon had fired the first shots to open the attack—actually, only twenty-eight minutes had elapsed and 250 Japanese soldiers had been killed in the compound and 511 freed POWs were being escorted northward to the Pampanga River. According to plan, Prince pulled out his Very pistol and fired a red flare high into the black sky, the signal for all Rangers and Alamo Scouts to withdraw from within and around the camp.[23]

8:15 P.M.

Corporals Roy Sweezy and Francis Schilli, the devout farm boys and inseparable pals, were with a squad of John Murphy's platoon on the back side of the camp. Seeing the red flare, the squad began trotting along outside the fence, heading for the front gate. Squad members felt no immediate danger: Not a shot had been fired for fifteen minutes.

Suddenly, the quiet was broken by the sharp crack of two rifle shots coming from within the enclosure. Both bullets ripped into Sweezy's chest, and he pitched forward, collapsing in a heap. Other squad members flopped down and tried to locate the source of the firing, but silence returned. Schilli crawled to Sweezy's side. By the light of moon rays seeping past the rolling clouds, Schilli could see that his friend's uniform was saturated with blood and his face was ashen.

Schilli remembered: "Roy Sweezy obviously was dying. So I took a small amount of water from my canteen, put a few drops on his forehead and baptized him in our Catholic tradition. Then two Filipinos came along and told us to go on, that they would carry Roy's body."[24]

8:32 P.M.

Guided by a bright moon and escorted by the Rangers, the POWs were shuffling zombies, driven on by the prospect of freedom. The straggly column was stretched out for a mile, and progress was so slow that Colonel Mucci began to fear that all of the prisoners would not reach the Pampanga until after daybreak.

Even though the POWs had been snatched from under the noses

of the Japanese, Mucci and Captain Prince knew that the peril was far from over. Off toward the Cabu River, they could hear the gunfire as Juan Pajota's guerillas battled to hold off the Japanese force. There were still many miles to be traveled through enemy territory, and disaster could lurk anywhere along the route.

19

Stealthy Trek
by Carabao Caravan

It was 8:45 P.M., only one hour since the stockade assault began, when Captain Bob Prince, who was bringing up the rear of the long column, reached the south bank of the shallow Pampanga River. This was the stream that Colonel Mucci had worried might turn into a raging torrent should a tropical storm erupt before the arrival of the Rangers and the prisoners. For the next half hour, Rangers waded back and forth, carrying or shepherding POWs.

Waiting on the north shore were twenty-six two-wheeled carts with a carabao to pull each one. These conveyances and beasts had been rounded up by the Filipino villagers at the request of Henry Mucci within the past twenty-four hours.

Bob Prince remembered: "In order to collect all these carts and carabao so rapidly, the Filipinos had to fan out over the countryside for a radius of at least ten miles. Almost every farmer had a cart and carabao, and all of them willingly parted with these precious possessions, by which they eked out a living."[1]

Just past 9:15 P.M., with everyone across the Pampanga, Captain Prince fired a second red flare, the signal to guerilla Captains Juan Pajota and Eduardo Joson at the roadblocks to pull their forces back to Plateros. Joson and his men began withdrawing, but Pajota and his force were still locked in heavy combat at the Cabu River bridge northeast of the POW camp and could not pull back without endangering the prisoners and Rangers.

Cecil Easley remembered: "We POWs were very nervous about all the shooting we could hear coming from the Cabu River. We thought

203

the Japs might break through with tanks, because we had seen eight or ten tanks go past the camp a couple of days earlier. However, most of the POWs were very quiet and were probably in shock. And a few of them were simply plain crazy after their nearly three-year ordeal."[2]

Henry Mucci realized that there was not a minute to be lost, so he promptly lead the column on toward the barrio of Plateros, where the Rangers had been royally wined and dined only twenty-four hours earlier. The trek to Plateros was painfully slow. Although the ponderous carabao were moving in high gear, that high gear was about two miles per hour.

Under the circumstances, there inevitably was periodic confusion on the dark trek. Corporal James Herrick and two other Rangers were escorting one group of three carts, each loaded with two or three infirm POWs. When the conveyances reached a fork in the trail, the first cart took the right branch.

Herrick recalled: "One Filipino guerilla with us began talking excitedly in Tagalog. Fortunately, one of the POWs in the other two carts understood that dialect, so we Rangers learned what had happened— the first cart had taken a wrong turn and was heading in the direction of Japanese forces to the east. Since we had to remain as quiet as possible and could not shout, two Rangers had to catch the cart and help turn it and the carabao around, no easy task unless the carabao *wanted* to turn around."[3]

Meanwhile, Lieutenant Bill Nellist and his Alamo Scouts were deployed along the north bank of the Pampanga, serving as a rear guard to halt or slow down any pursuing Japanese troops. With Lieutenant Tom Rounsaville and Sergeant Alfred Alfonso wounded and already in Plateros, there were only eleven Scouts to blunt any Japanese efforts to storm across the Pampanga and onto the heels of the withdrawing Ranger and POW column.

Shortly after 10:00 P.M., the first Rangers and freed prisoners, led by Henry Mucci, trundled into Plateros. Others followed in a steady stream. A degree of bedlam erupted. Excited natives again greeted the Americans with open arms. Despite the urgent efforts of Ranger officers to keep down the noise, there was much talking, much laughing.

While Colonel Mucci was preparing to start the column on the next leg of the journey surgery was being performed in the Plateros "hospital," a schoolhouse that had been converted by a local physician, Dr.

Carlos Layug, who had been serving with Juan Pajota's guerillas. As a medical officer, Layug had been captured on Bataan, survived the March of Death and a few weeks at the O'Donnell hellhole. Along with thousands of other Filipino soldiers, Lieutenant Layug had been released on the condition that he was loyal to Emperor Hirohito.

Layug returned to practicing medicine in Manila. After a few months, he was tipped off that he had fallen into disfavor with the conquerors and was suspected of aiding Filipino guerillas. So the doctor and his wife fled to central Luzon, where he volunteered to serve with Pajota's irregulars.

Now, in the converted Plateros schoolhouse, Dr. Layug, working by the flickering light of kerosene lanterns, prepared to operate on Alamo Scout Sergeant Al Alfonso, known to his comrades as Opu. Working with Layug in the operation was a surgeon POW, Lieutenant Merle H. Musselman of Nebraska City, Nebraska. Although he had just arrived and been a free man for only two hours, Musselman insisted on helping out in the makeshift operating room, which had burlap sacks hanging over the windows to conceal the dim light.

Mortar-shell fragments were removed from Alfonso's abdomen, and the two surgeons agreed that his chances for full recovery were good if he could reach American lines and be given medical treatment in a field hospital.

Ironically, the next surgical patient, Captain Jimmy Fisher, had worked with Dr. Layug in setting up the schoolhouse as an emergency hospital when the Rangers arrived in Plateros the first time, thirty-six hours earlier. There were no anesthetics, so Fisher was administered morphine to reduce the pain. He remained semiconscious throughout the complicated surgery.

Midway through the procedure, Layug and Musselman knew that Fisher's chance for survival was minimal. The shrapnel had done extensive damage to his stomach and intestines. Certainly, the Ranger would not live unless he reached an American field hospital, yet a jolting overland trek might kill him. So the surgeons sewed Fisher back up and hoped for a miracle.[4]

Unseen high in the star-spangled sky over Nueva Ecija Province were eleven P-61 Black Widows, individually on the prowl for Japanese troop-carrying trucks and tanks that might be a threat to the westward withdrawal of the Rangers and POWs. These crack pilots of the 547th Night Fighter Squadron were graybeards. Most of them were twenty-six to thirty years of age, far older than the average fighter pilot in other outfits. A few of the P-61 pilots had seen combat with the Royal Canadian Air Force and England's Royal Air Force before the United States got into the war.

Each Black Widow had been assigned a specific sector, so all roads leading toward Cabanatuan camp or the Rangers' withdrawal route were being alertly patrolled. Just before 9:00 P.M., a P-61 cruising over the Rizal Road, the heavily traveled thoroughfare fourteen miles west of Plateros, spotted blips on its radar and circled for another look.

"There're five Jap trucks and a tank heading south," the radar observer called out over the intercom system. Since the enemy convoy, which could be loaded with troops, was on the same road Colonel Mucci's column would have to cross on the way back to American positions, the pilot prepared to attack.

The Black Widow banked in a wide arc and dropped to about five hundred feet. Then, with throttles wide open, the speedy craft zoomed along the road toward the convoy. Peering through night binoculars, a technological feature of the Black Widows, the pilot clearly could see the enemy vehicles when they were still two miles away. Closing fast, he aligned all four .50-caliber machine guns and four 20-millimeter cannon on the unsuspecting enemy vehicles and pressed the button.

All of it controlled by the pilot, the awesome firepower poured a torrent of incendiary bullets and shells into the five trucks and the tank. Through the high-tech binoculars, which permitted him to see five times as sharply as the average pilot without the refinement, the pilot saw Japanese soldiers leap from the burning trucks and scramble into the countryside. Scores of others no doubt were cremated when the vehicles burst into flame.

Yet another dangerous threat to the Rangers and POWs had been eliminated.[5]

Meanwhile, back at dark and silent Cabanatuan camp, Edwin Rose, the elderly, stone-deaf and nearly blind Canadian, was wandering around in a confused state of mind. After performing his latrine ritual, Rose had apparently slept through the violence and turmoil swirling in and around the camp.

When Rose had finally awakened, perhaps around midnight, he sensed that something had changed dramatically, even though he could not see or hear. He was mystified, sensing that everyone, Japanese and POWs alike, had vanished. A few huts were smoking as though they had been on fire—he could smell the smoke. He tripped over a clump lying on the ground. Stooping, he felt the limp form; it was a Japanese soldier, seemingly a dead one.

Unaware that there were some 250 other Japanese corpses strewn about, Rose shuffled back to his hut to await daylight.

It was about 10:30 P.M. when the savage firefight that had raged along the Cabu River suddenly ceased. Quiet descended. Apparently, the Japanese had given up efforts to cross the bridge and rush to the POW camp only a half mile away. Now Juan Pajota sent word to his fighting men to start pulling back to Plateros. It had been an impressive victory for the Filipino guerillas, earned at the cost of numerous casualties in their ranks.[6]

Meanwhile at Plateros, Colonel Mucci led the first contingent of walking POWs and their Ranger escorts toward Balincarin, a barrio four and a half miles to the northwest. Captain Bob Prince remained in Plateros to shuttle other groups along. At the same time, Bill Nellist and his tiny band of Alamo Scouts pulled back from the Pampanga River to provide a rear guard at Plateros.

When Captain Prince was about ready to leave Plateros with the last carabao carts filled with infirm men, he was approached by Lieutenant Merle Musselman and another freed POW, Chaplain Hugh Kennedy of Scarsdale, New York. The surgeon and the man of God told Prince that they would remain behind with Jimmy Fisher, even though their refusal to evacuate the barrio could mean their death if Japanese forces were to barge onto the scene.

A few minutes later, the last carts trundled out of Plateros, with Bob Prince bringing up the rear to make certain that no confused prisoners would saunter away or inadvertently be left along the road. One POW, Paul Jackson of Long Beach, California, who had been a navy pay clerk, refused to ride in a cart, even though he had a peg leg, one carved by a fellow inmate at Cabanatuan.

"I walked into that damned camp," he declared, "and, by God, I'm sure as hell walking out of it!"

Henry Mucci remembered: "The spirit of some of the POW old-timers was remarkable. There was an old man who could hardly hobble, but he insisted on walking unaided. He told me, 'I made the Death March from Bataan, so I can certainly make this one!' "[7]

Back at Plateros, Alamo Scout Lieutenant Bill Nellist was holding a solemn discussion with Dr. Carlos Layug and Lieutenant Merle Musselman, the surgeons who had operated on Captain Jimmy Fisher. The three men had to reach an agonizing decision: what to do with the critically wounded Ranger doctor. Clearly, he could not be left in Plateros, for the Japanese no doubt would soon be scouring the region in search of the liberated prisoners. Would Fisher survive the trek to Balincarin? That was a chance that would have to be taken.

Gentle Ranger hands lifted Fisher from his cot and placed him on a large wooden door that had been removed from a house in Plateros. Six men lifted the burden and, as smoothly as possible, they began trudging toward Balincarin.

In the meantime, the carabao caravan of Rangers and POWs reached Balincarin, where Filipino guerillas had rounded up eleven more carts and the carabao to pull them. This brought the number of two-wheeled conveyances to about fifty. POWs who had walked the nearly seven miles from Cabanatuan camp were exhausted, and their bare feet were swollen, blistered, and bloody. The extra carts were needed to carry these men. After a brief rest, Henry Mucci started the column toward the barrio of Mataas na Kahoy, about a mile to the northwest.

Progress was slow and painful. POWs who could still shuffle along stumbled and fell. Rangers, themselves near exhaustion, picked them up and gave them cigarettes and words of encouragement.

"Just a few more miles, fellows," Mucci's men would lie. "Hang in there! Only a few more miles!"

After collecting eleven more carts and carabao in Mataas na Kahoy, the motley convoy headed generally westward along dirt roads that had been packed down over the decades by the hooves of thousands of carabao. Just over a mile from Mataas na Kahoy, the carabao caravan neared the Rizal Road, the main artery for Japanese forces going north. Colonel Mucci halted the column and sent scouts to reconnoiter the road. Two nights earlier, the Rangers had scampered across the thoroughfare like so many jackrabbits between Japanese traffic convoys. Now, however, it was quite a different situation: In excess of five hundred POWs and scores of carabao-drawn carts had to get over the highway without being detected. There was potential for disaster.

When his scouts returned, they told Mucci that it would be impossible to cross the road to the immediate front because the carts could not negotiate a steep embankment on the far side. So the colonel reached a prompt decision: The convoy would have to travel on this Japanese main thoroughfare for three-quarters of a mile and risk detection.

While most of the caravan, stretched for a mile and a half, waited anxiously in the darkness, Lieutenant Bill O'Connell was ordered to send bazooka teams to establish roadblocks five hundred yards to the north to halt any Japanese convoy coming from that direction and two thousand yards to the south to confront any enemy force heading northward.

A few minutes past 3:30 A.M., Colonel Mucci received word from O'Connell that the roadblocks were in place. No one held any illusions that a few bazookas would turn back an all-out effort by a Japanese force to crash through to the carabao convoy. But Mucci had no alternative: At 3:34 A.M., he waved the first cart onto the Rizal Road.

Henry Mucci remembered the danger vividly: "The Gods of War were smiling on us. That long column of slow moving carabao pulling carts loaded with POWs had to use the road for more than an hour before swinging out into open country. We sent Rangers on some ponies we found, two miles up and down the highway, to warn us if the Japs were coming. Luckily, they didn't come. That time we spent on the customarily busy road was the longest hour I had ever sweated out in my life."[8]

Earlier, during the long halt in front of the Rizal Road, Alamo Scout Lieutenant John Dove noticed that many of the POWs far back in the column had grown nervous. Others had climbed from their carts and were meandering around. Many were concerned that the Rangers up ahead had run into trouble, and that all hell might break loose.

Dove recalled: "During the wait, I saw a dark object in a rice paddy, for we had good moonlight. I walked out to see what the clump was. It was a confused POW who had wandered out there and fallen asleep. I woke him up, and he had a hard time getting to his feet. So I picked him up; he was skin and bones, probably didn't weigh more than a hundred pounds. I crowded him into a cart with two other POWs, and I kept my eye on him."[9]

While Henry Mucci was leading his carabao caravan across open country toward the northwest, at about 2:00 A.M., Lieutenant Bill Nellist and his Alamo Scouts, along with eight Rangers and a small force of Filipino guerillas, marched wearily into Balincarin. Lieutenant Merle Musselman, the POW who had helped operate on Captain Jimmy Fisher, arranged for the seriously injured man to be put on a cot in a nipa hut. All through the grueling trek from Plateros, Musselman had been keeping his patient under close observation, regularly monitoring vital signs.

Now, Musselman told Lieutenant Bill Nellist, "Unless we can get Captain Fisher to a hospital, and soon, he is a goner."

Although they were in the midst of Japanese territory, it was decided that an airstrip would be hacked out near the barrio and a radio message would ask for an airplane to land and take Fisher to an American field hospital in the vicinity of Guimba. Alamo Scout Private First Class Gilbert Cox was one of those given the task of rounding up a large number of natives to help build the improvised airstrip.

Cox remembered: "It was really amazing. Every native man, woman, and child for miles around came out to level a stretch of rice paddies. They used shovels, hoes, rakes, and even large spoons and their bare hands. They began work at about 3:00 A.M., and never rested for a moment until the strip was complete in five hours. Sadly, no airplane showed up."[10]

20

Hamburgers, Tears, and Freedom

Dawn was beginning to shatter the slate gray sky over Luzon when Colonel Mucci halted the column. Captain Bob Prince, still bringing up the rear, was a mile and a half away. At this point, Mucci decided to break radio silence, and his communications man, Staff Sergeant Norton S. Most of Hawley, Minnesota, tried to reach Sergeant James Irvine, who had been waiting by his radio set in the command car outside Guimba for nearly seventy hours. Now, for undetermined reasons, Most could not make electronic contact, so Mucci ordered the caravan to push onward.

Although the constant marching in the past three days had severely tested the physical mettle of the Rangers, Mucci had walked the greatest distance of them all. Almost on a regular basis, he strode up and down the long, stretched-out column, exhorting the Rangers and the POWs to hang in there.

"All right, men, only three more kilometers, just three more!" he would call out.

Eventually, his tired Rangers joked when they saw Mucci approaching: "Here comes 'Old Three Kilos More!' "

It was typical dry GI humor; the Rangers loved their colonel.

Two hours after sunrise, tired men in the column heard the faint purr of powerful engines off in the distant sky. Then they saw the specks, which grew larger as they drew nearer. A surge of concern swept through many in the convoy: Had the Rangers and POWs been discovered and were these Japanese planes approaching?

Suddenly, there was enormous excitement: These were American planes, swift P-51 Mustangs, which zoomed in low over the marching men, waggling their wings. Like mother hens hovering over their brood, the P-51s circled protectively. Other fighter planes could be seen and heard on all sides, strafing and bombing Japanese troops and vehicles that had been caught on the roads or out in the open.

Recalled former POW George Steiner: "We were jubilant over the appearance of our airplanes, and the sound of their strafing was music to our ears. Many POWs were still deeply worried, however, because we still had a long way to go through Japanese territory."[1]

Meanwhile, back at Cabanatuan camp, which was strewn with Japanese corpses, the stone-deaf and nearly blind Canadian, Ed Rose, awakened after daylight and soon became convinced that the POW camp had turned into a ghost camp. His calls to comrades went unanswered. So the elderly man began edging toward the front entrance, which was about a hundred yards from his barracks, and walked out through the gate to the road, which was barely discernible to his limited vision.

Pausing briefly, Rose decided to head in the direction of the Cabu River, but after going perhaps three hundred yards, his instincts told him to get off the thoroughfare and strike out cross-country. Soon, he came upon a path and began hobbling along it, not having the slightest notion in which direction he was traveling.

Suddenly, he faintly discerned four or five armed men scramble from thick vegetation, and moments later, he was aware that they were aiming rifles at him. Perhaps they were demanding that he identify himself, but clearly Rose was not a Japanese. Dame Fate had smiled on the Canadian; the Filipino guerillas he had encountered escorted him to a nearby barrio where he would be safe until he could be handed over to the Americans.

It was about 8:00 A.M. when the carabao convoy came to a halt before a barrio. Rangers and POWs alike, dead-tired and sleepy, grumbled. They wanted to push on. A Filipino guerilla who had been scouting ahead of the column returned to Colonel Mucci who asked, "What's the holdup?"

The Filipino said that about a hundred armed Huks had control of the barrio and that they were not going to permit the Rangers and POWs to pass. The Communist-led Huks were especially resentful over the fact that Major Bob Lapham's Filipino guerillas were guiding Mucci's group.

Mucci had been thrust into a dilemma not covered in West Point textbooks. Tough fighting man that he was, the colonel's first inclination was to tangle with the Huk force blocking his way. Yet that could result in many Ranger and POW casualties and hold up the convoy indefinitely. Then there was the political angle to be considered: Mucci had no desire to be caught in the bull's-eye of a squabble between guerilla groups over control of the Philippines after the war. Compounding the situation, the Huks were led by hard-line Communists, and Communists were supposed to be America's allies.

Mucci asked his Filipino guides if there were other trails leading around the barrio, and he was told that there were none. Now the colonel made up his mind.

Turning to the Filipino, he declared: "Go back to that barrio and tell those Huks that we're coming through if we have to blast our way through!"

It was a bluff: Mucci's Rangers were stretched out for a mile and a half and all of them were weak from physical strain and lack of sleep.

Mucci knew—or hoped he knew—that he had an ace in the hole: The Huk force did not know how many Rangers he had with him, nor was it aware that Mucci's contingent had no machine guns or artillery. The colonel waved the convoy forward and within minutes, it was rolling through the barrio. Lining both sides of the dirt road were the Huks, who glared menacingly at the passing parade. Not a single Huk stepped forward to aid the POWs or offer words of encouragement to them.

Just after 9:00 A.M., the caravan reached the barrio of Sibul, where Mucci ordered another brief respite. Typically, the natives eagerly produced fresh drinking water and a wide array of vegetables for the Rangers and freed prisoners. As if by a magical wave of a wand, the villagers also produced 19 carabao and carts, bringing the total number of the two-wheeled carriages to 106.

Again Sergeant Norton Most tried to contact Guimba, and this time, he reached James Irvine in his command car. Through a coded message, Henry Mucci informed Sixth Army headquarters that his column would soon be approaching the north-south National Highway, and he asked that enough trucks to carry about four hundred POWs and ambulances to hold some one hundred immobile prisoners be dispatched to meet the caravan.

In turn, Jim Irvine passed along exhilarating news. Since the Rangers had left Guimba on the evening of January 29, Walter Krueger's forces had driven forward and now occupied the town of Talavera, only eleven miles from Mucci's column.

At Balincarin, far to the rear of Mucci's cart convoy, Ranger Captain Jimmy Fisher was lying on a cot, his life steadily ebbing. Seated next to him was his top medic, Sergeant John Nelson. As with the other medics, Jimmy Fisher was a beloved figure—friendly, considerate, compassionate.

Fisher had been in a coma off and on since dawn. At about 11:00 A.M., the wounded man opened his eyes slightly and started to say something. Moments later, Captain Jimmy Fisher was dead.

Outside Balincarin at the stroke of noon, Lieutenant Bill Nellist and his Alamo Scouts, eight Rangers, and a couple of hundred Filipino civilians stood around an open grave on a little knoll where there was a palm grove about one hundred yards square. Father Hugh Kennedy, the POW who had chosen to remain behind with the grievously wounded Ranger, conducted the funeral service.

After Fisher's remains were covered in his grave, the Filipinos put up a crudely lettered sign at the entrance to the grove of palms: Doctor Fisher Memorial Park.[2]

Five miles inside Japanese territory, near the National Highway, Henry Mucci's caravan met up with an oncoming convoy of GI trucks and ambulances, escorted by an infantry company. When the drivers halted and stepped down to the ground, they were engulfed by jubilant POWs.

"Christ, are we glad to see you!" one shouted, hugging a dust-caked driver.

It was a scene of minor pandemonium. More trucks and ambulances arrived, guarded by armored weapons carriers with GIs manning their machine guns. As the carabao column kept coming in accordion fashion, freed prisoners struggled off the carts and hobbled toward the young soldiers who had come to get them for the final lap to American lines. Fighter planes and Piper Cubs buzzed over the POWs like a swarm of happy hornets.

The exhausted Rangers, their mission accomplished, dropped

where they stood, sleeping over one another, curled up next to straw stacks or lying flat on the ground. Scores, perhaps as many as two hundred Filipino civilians, alerted by the Bamboo Telegraph, descended on the site. They stared at the inert forms of the sleeping Rangers, thinking that they were dead.

Beside the dusty road, the liberated prisoners sat, still dazed, or, seized spasmodically by surges of emotion, they laughed and talked loudly or burst into tears. Some remained mute. Many munched on tomatoes given them by Filipinos or hamburgers that the relief trucks had brought in.

"If this is a dream," one skinny POW declared, "then don't wake me up!"

Nearly all the freed men tried valiantly to regain the soldierly pride that the Japanese had smashed during thirty-two months of brutality. Several of the POW officers and senior noncoms had retained their faded badges of rank, worn proudly on ragged shirts above shorts that had been patched and repatched. Some wore old campaign hats, some overseas caps with company insignia, and one had retained his prewar pie-plate helmet.

The first meeting of the POWs with the trim officers of the "new" United States Army that had landed at Lingayen Gulf three weeks earlier was a tense, courageous effort to span the dead years. Many POWs gave the newly arrived officers the regulation salute, hoping no one would notice their quivering hands. A few of the prisoners limped past an American flag flying from a short pole attached to a truck fender. Enfeebled Staff Sergeant Clinton Goodbla of Longview, Washington, broke into tears. Most of those with him did likewise.

Boyish-faced GIs, many of whom had been attending high school proms back home when the tragedies at Bataan and Corregidor were unfolding, stared in awe at the bony apparitions: POWs who limped from beriberi brought on by lack of proper food; men whose bodies were laced by tropical ulcers; men who lay helplessly on litters, staring into space; men without arms and legs.

Soon it was time to shove off for the five-mile ride to American lines. Gentle hands helped the POWs into trucks and lifted the litters with their immobile men into the backs of ambulances. Three miles later, the POWs saw an amazing sight: Lining the road on both sides and cheering loudly as the Ghosts of Bataan and Corregidor passed were swarms of GIs who had returned to the Philippines with MacArthur.

When the vehicle convoy reached Guimba, six barefoot POWs carrying the regimental flag of the U.S. 26th Cavalry, which had fought to the bitter end on Bataan, climbed off a truck. This flag, piped in gold, had never touched the ground in three years of Japanese occupation of Luzon. Its first bearer was killed as he went into battle on Bataan. It was sewn for a time inside a pillow provided by a Filipina housewife, then flown by a band of three thousand Filipino guerillas before being smuggled into Cabanatuan camp, where it was hidden for months.

Singing "California, Here I Come," the six barefoot men marched up to General Oscar Griswold, commander of the U.S. XIV Corps, and presented the historic battle flag to him.

With tears in his eyes, the hard-nosed general said: "This is the most touching incident of the war. I accept this flag for the United States government in humility, in the presence of the brave soldiers who carried it. To you men, the American flag has never ceased to fly over Bataan and Corregidor."

In the meantime, many miles behind the Rangers and POW column, Lieutenant Bill Nellist was leading his band of Alamo Scouts across the dry flatlands toward Guimba. Their mission as rear guard for Mucci's caravan had been completed. The long trek from Plateros had been uneventful until about halfway home when the Scouts were halted by a heavily armed band of Communist-led Huks.

Gilbert Cox remembered: "The Huks were very nasty. Said we couldn't get through. All of us thought we were going to have to shoot our way through. Then Lieutenant Nellist walked up to the Huk leader and said, 'You sons of bitches better get out of the way or we'll have the whole United States army hunt you down like rats.' They got out of our way and we reached our lines without incident—but thoroughly exhausted."[3]

Soon, the liberated prisoners reached the 92nd Evacuation Hospital where the "new" United States Army's efficiency and planning astonished them. They were registered and given showers. Seriously ill or injured cases went into the wards at once. Others were taken to tents. All received Red Cross kits and they played with the contents like children playing with dolls.

Each doctor's or nurse's hand that touched a POW was one of such feeling that many of the men who had held up so staunchly and proudly until now broke down and wept. When this occurred, the medical people would go right on, giving no indication they had seen the breakdown.

For other POWs, their long dream of liberation became a reality when they had their first breakfast under freedom. Private Alfred Jolly of San Francisco, a young soldier who had lost an arm on Bataan, ate six eggs, a large helping of ham, seven biscuits with jam, and an entire can of sliced grapefruit. He washed it down with five cups of coffee.

"This will probably make me sick as hell," Jolly told a reporter. "But I don't give a damn!"[4]

Private Jolly proved to be an apt prognosticator.

Just before noon on February 1, a dusty jeep, bearing the five stars of a general, halted in front of the 92nd Evacuation Hospital, which had once been a large schoolhouse. Out stepped Douglas MacArthur, his jaw set grimly. He had come to greet the gaunt Ghosts of Bataan and Corregidor, although many of the mobile POWs had been trucked to another camp earlier that morning.

When MacArthur entered the reception room, haggard veterans, their faces lined from nearly three years of abuse, moved toward the general, trying to raise enfeebled arms in salutes and reaching out to touch him. A few broke out in sobs. Clasping the hand of one man after another, the Southwest Pacific commander made no effort to conceal his deep emotions.

"God bless you, General," one whispered hoarsely.

"Thank God you came back!" said another.

His voice choking, MacArthur said, "I'm a little late, but we finally made it."[5]

For all, MacArthur had an encouraging word. "Eat all you can now," he urged. "You are a little better off than the last time we met (referring to the starvation diet on Bataan)."[6]

MacArthur immediately recognized Lieutenant Colonel James Green, a veteran of nearly four decades in the army, and he recalled promoting Green to corporal thirty-five years earlier. Although wobbly, Green insisted on standing at attention, even though MacArthur gently admonished him several times to "please sit."

Navy Lieutenant Carl Baumgardner, former manager for Radio

Corporation of America in Manila, reminded the general that the last time the two had met, he had asked MacArthur to attend an American Legion dinner.

POW Lieutenant Colonel Thomas R. Wilson declared, "The Rangers and Alamo Scouts have done a wonderful job."

"Indeed they have!" MacArthur replied. "I'm going to decorate every one of them!"[7]

MacArthur spoke longest with an old friend, Lieutenant Colonel Alfred Oliver, who had been the army's chief chaplain in the Philippines. White-haired Oliver was still wearing a neck brace as the result of a severe beating by Japanese soldiers several months earlier. At that time, they were trying to force him to identify Miss U (Margaret Utinsky), the underground leader, and her contacts in Cabanatuan camp.

MacArthur suggested: "Chaplain, in your next sermon take your text from Lazarus arisen from the dead."

Major Paul R. Wing, a former Hollywood photographer who had won an Academy Award for his work on *The Lives of a Bengal Lancer*, told the general, "Those Rangers gave me more drama in thirty minutes than I expect to see in all the rest of my life."

Wing, who had been captured on Corregidor, declared that "Hollywood never produced a picture with any more dramatic climax. Those boys (Rangers) saved 511 lives, because I'm sure the Japs were going to murder us."[8]

When MacArthur entered one of the wards to visit the weakest of the rescued men, Captain Ben King of Austin, Texas, a tall army artillery officer, said, "General, please let me go back to Corregidor with you. I'd like to lead a platoon ashore."

Bystanders noticed a lump in the general's throat. Moments later, he replied, "We are going back all right—and we'll take you with us."[9]

Outside the 92nd Evac, scores of war correspondents and photographers swarmed around Colonel Henry Mucci. Despite his extreme weariness, he patiently related time and again the story of the raid that freed the pawns of war. Typically, Mucci deflected credit from himself to Captain Bob Prince and the Rangers who had assaulted the stockade and escorted the POWs to safety. He also heaped praise upon the Alamo Scouts and the Filipino guerillas. "Make no mistake about it," he emphasized. "We couldn't have pulled it off had it not been for the Scouts and the guerillas."

Minutes later, war correspondent/photographer Carl Mydans of *Life* magazine was seated on a stool at a rickety table under a clump of trees near the 92nd Evac. Renowned for being in the thick of the action, Mydans knew intimately the ugly face of war. When the Japanese had charged into Manila in late December 1941, Mydans had been taken into custody and jailed for several months before being exchanged for Japanese newsmen. Now, in front of his battered portable typewriter, he was groping for words to describe the Cabanatuan rescue operation.[10]

Mydans began to type: "Every American child of coming generations will know of the 6th Rangers, for a prouder story has never been written. . . ."

Epilogue

Twenty-four hours after Colonel Henry Mucci's Rangers and the Cabanatuan POWs reached the safety of American lines, the telephone jangled in the Seattle, Washington, home of Mr. and Mrs. A. A. Prince. Minutes earlier, the couple had heard fragmentary radio reports of a daring raid on a Japanese prison camp in the Philippines, and they conjectured that their son, Bob, might have been involved.

Mrs. Prince answered the telephone and a newspaper reporter asked: "Have you heard about your son, Captain Robert Prince?" Her heart leaped into her throat. Had he been killed? Wounded? Captured? Then the caller told about Captain Prince leading the raid on the Cabanatuan stockade, and his mother broke out in tears of pride—and relief.

For hours, the telephone rang incessantly. The elder Prince told one journalist: "Well, Bob's role doesn't surprise me. It was his duty, and he did it."[1]

News of the Cabanatuan mission was plastered on front pages across the United States, and stirring accounts were broadcast by hundreds of radio outlets. In Connecticut, Mrs. Elizabeth Mucci, widowed mother of Colonel Mucci, told a flock of reporters who besieged her home, "I'm not particularly surprised by Henry's adventure. He always wanted to be a soldier since he was only big enough to carry a broomstick as a gun."

In Chicago, white-haired Mrs. Mary Zelis hurried to the Church of the Immaculate Conception, where she had prayed every day for her son, Louis, during the thirty-two months he had been a captive. Kneeling at the altar, she gave thanks for Louis's delivery.

220

In Oakland, two days after she was notified by the War Department that her brother had been killed fighting on Leyte, Mrs. Miriam L. Picotte wept again—this time with happiness. Her husband, Captain Caryl Picotte, had been rescued.

In Seattle, Mrs. Matilda Englin, mother of Sergeant Milton Englin, told reporters that she gave credit for his rescue to "the power of prayer—and to General MacArthur." A devout Catholic, Mrs. Englin added: "I kept asking God to send Milton back to me—and I also prayed for General MacArthur, because I knew if anyone here on earth could help my boy, it would be the general. He said he would save those boys, and he did."

Mrs. Englin then wrote a letter to Mr. and Mrs. A. A. Prince, whom she did not know, in Seattle: "God bless the family of Captain Robert Prince who so heroically rescued my son from three years under Japanese cruelty. My prayers will always include you and yours."

In Oklahoma City, Mrs. Grace Hubbard, wife of Major Ralph W. Hubbard, was at a children's hospital reading to polio victims. A radio newscast elated her. She dashed out of the building, ran all the way to Culbertson School, barged into the first-grade class with tears streaming down her cheeks, and called out to her son, Joe: "Your daddy's been rescued! He's safe!"

In Dallas, the mother of Staff Sergeant Theodore Richardson, who had shot the lock off the Cabanatuan gate, stared in disbelief at a photo of her son in a local newspaper. Actually, the picture was that of Captain Bob Prince, who had mistakenly been identified in the caption as Richardson. Mrs. Richardson, who had not seen her son in three years, cried out, "Good Lord, what have they done to Theodore!"

Meanwhile in Manila in early February 1945, savage fighting was raging. Although General Tomoyuki Yamashita had declared Manila an open city after MacArthur's Lingayen Gulf landings and pulled his troops back to Luzon's northern mountains, Rear Admiral Sanji Iwabuchi, who was not under Yamashita, ordered his twenty-one-thousand-man Imperial Navy force to defend Manila to the death.

While the house-to-house, no-holds-barred struggle was in progress, Margaret Utinsky, the underground leader known as Miss U, hitched a ride into Manila in a GI truck. For the past few months, she had been a guerilla lieutenant in the mountains after having been tipped off about her imminent arrest by the Kempei Tai.

On the outskirts of the burning city, an American military police-man halted the truck. Miss U dismounted and strode forward, her .38-caliber pistol resting in its holster on her right hip.

"You can't go in there, lady," he said. "It's too dangerous."

"Too dangerous!" she snapped. "Well, what do you think I've been doing for the past three years?"

Instantly, she realized that the young GI knew nothing about the Philippine underground and had no inkling about her critical role in smuggling food, goods, medicine, and money into Cabanatuan camp.

Eager to get on her way, Margaret said, "I'm going on in."

The rattled MP called for an officer, and when he appeared, Miss U gave him a terse rundown on her activities during the Japanese occupation and why she had to get into Manila. The officer gave her permission to go into the city.

By now, her truck was gone, so she walked briskly ahead. The MP private called out a parting shot: "Lady, do you have an official permit to carry that pistol?"

Margaret made a beeline for the Malate Convent to renew old acquaintances with Morning Glory (Father John Lalor) and the other Irish priests, all of whom had been such key cogs in her underground machine. She was jolted over the ugly sight that greeted her eyes. Seeking vengeance after learning of the priests' clandestine activities, the Japanese had put the torch to the convent complex. The garage, in which tons of supplies had been stored before being shipped to the POW camp, was only ashes. Around the once beautiful, immaculately manicured grounds were strewn Filipino corpses and pieces of bodies.

Although Miss U knew that the five priests had been on the Japanese death list that the Apostolic Delegate's young Filipino spy had seen at Fort Santiago, she was badly shaken to learn of the murder of Father Lalor, Father Patrick Kelly, Father Joseph Monaghan, Father John Henaghan, and Father Peter Fallon. Because of their efforts in the face of constant peril, many POWs at Cabanatuan were alive to return to their homes.

There was more bad news: Much of Miss U's underground network had been wiped out in recent days, betrayed by Filipino collaborators. Her loyal agents had been tortured for a week, put to death in a gruesome manner, and hurled into an unmarked communal grave.

A few days after Margaret arrived in Manila, U.S. Navy Lieutenant

Thor Johnson entered the city just as a graves registration unit was digging up the mass burial site. Fourteen corpses were removed, including that of the lieutenant's father, Ernest Johnson (code name Brave Heart), who had conducted his underground work from the Manila hospital where he had been a long-term patient. The corpses were wearing blindfolds and had been shot in the back of the head.

These were the remains of patriots who had been highly active members of either Miss U's network or the one headed by Claire Phillips (High Pockets), or belonged to both clandestine groups. They included Ramón Amosategui (Sparkplug), the wealthy Spaniard who had provided the truck that carried goods smuggled into Cabanatuan camp; Enrico Paravino (Per), who had collected large amounts of money from fellow Italians in Manila and served as a courier; Juan Elizalde, who had been a driving force in the network, and two nuns.

Although her heart was heavy, Margaret Utinsky had joyous times in the days ahead when she met several Americans who had been freed in the Rangers' raid on Cabanatuan camp. One of these was Colonel Alfred Oliver, who had been a main contact inside the POW enclosure. Chaplain Oliver, too, was nearly overcome with emotion to finally meet his underground collaborator face to face. Before Miss U and the chaplain departed to go their separate ways, he wrote on a piece of paper:

It is the opinion of the undersigned that Lieutenant (Margaret) Utinsky did more than any other one person for the morale and physical well-being of the Allied prisoners held at Cabanatuan.[2]

Elsewhere in Manila, Claire Phillips (High Pockets) was liberated from her Japanese dungeon by the Americans. Her survival bordered on the miraculous. Although the Kempei Tai had compiled much evidence linking her to espionage activities, they left her in jail for many weeks instead of executing her.

High Pockets was also grief-stricken over the deaths of so many persons with whom she had worked to smuggle food, medicine, money, and letters into Cabanatuan camp. She was especially distraught to learn that Father Heinz Buttenbruck, the kindly German priest who had informed her of the death of her husband John at Cabanatuan camp, had been arrested, tortured, and put to death.

After Margaret Utinsky and Claire Phillips returned to the United

States, each was awarded the Medal of Freedom, the nation's highest civilian decoration, for her aid to the Cabanatuan POWs. Later, Hollywood produced a movie about Claire's adventures during the war. Starring a top big-screen actress, Ann Dvorak, the film was entitled *I Was an American Spy*.

Meanwhile, Colonel Henry Mucci and the Rangers, Alamo Scouts, and four combat photographers who conducted the Cabanatuan mission were decorated for their historic achievement. Mucci had been recommended for the Congressional Medal of Honor, but he and Captain Robert Prince were awarded Distinguished Service Crosses, the nation's second highest award for valor. The other officers received Silver Stars and the enlisted men, Bronze Stars. Although Filipino guerilla chiefs Juan Pajota and Eduardo Joson had played crucial roles in the venture and were members of the U.S. Army, they were awarded only Bronze Stars.

Shortly after returning from the raid that electrified the free world, Bob Prince, nine other Rangers, and two Alamo Scouts were notified that they would return to the United States for a nationwide tour to boost the morale of defense-plant workers. Taking off in a C-54 cargo plane from Tacloban, Leyte, the instant celebrities flew to Hamilton Field, outside San Francisco, after a series of refueling stops during the nine thousand-mile journey. For the next four days, they rode a train to Washington.

For five days, the Cabanatuan-rescue men engaged in countless sessions with high Pentagon officials, members of Congress, and news reporters. A couple of the soldiers had lunch with the vice president of the United States, Harry S. Truman. Then, on March 8, they were escorted into the Oval Office of the White House by four-star General Joseph "Vinegar Joe" Stillwell, who had gained fame fighting the Japanese in the vastness of the Burma jungles.[3]

"When we entered the Oval Office, my knees felt like jelly," recalled Bob Prince. "The other fellows later told me they felt the same way. After we had all shaken hands with him, President Roosevelt put us at ease and chatted for about ten minutes. Our first remarks after we left the White House were how old and tired the President looked. A month later, he was dead."[4]

From the beginning, the nonstop tour was a blur of cheering

crowds, radio appearances, newspaper reporters and photographers, handshaking governors and big-city mayors, and as many as ten war-plant speeches each day.

On April 7, after thirty hectic days and nights on the road, the Cabanatuan raiders scattered to their homes for short furloughs. There they were again besieged by the media. In Seattle, Bob Prince summed up the view held by most Rangers and Alamo Scouts involved in the rescue mission: "People everywhere try to thank us. I think the thanks should go the other way. I'll be grateful for the rest of my life that I had a chance to do something in this war that was not destructive. Nothing for me can ever compare with the satisfaction I got from helping to free our prisoners."[5]

Shortly after the Rangers and Alamo Scouts concluded their na-tionwide safari and returned to the Philippines eighty-three days after leaving there, Mrs. Eleanor "Bodie" Fisher, wife of the medical captain killed on the Cabanatuan raid, received word from the Red Cross that her application for immediate overseas duty had been accepted. Writ-ing to a close friend from her parents' home in Philadelphia, Bodie Fisher said: "You must know that my prayer is that they will send me to the Philippines, or wherever else it may be that the 6th Rangers are stationed."[6]

Except for the most extreme illness or injury cases, the Americans freed from Cabanatuan were returned to the United States as rapidly as possible. Many flew on available aircraft. But the largest group, some 280 men, sailed into San Francisco Bay on the transport ship *General A. E. Anderson* after a thirty-day trip. Many emotions gripped the POWs, one of which was concern over how America would accept them. Would they be branded as cowards for the surrender of Bataan and Corregidor?

Soon their qualms were laid to rest. Ships, boats, tugs, yachts, and other craft circled the *Anderson* as it cut through the harbor. A cacoph-ony of sound erupted: bells, whistles, sirens, and a band that broke out in a stirring rendition of "California, Here I Come." As the ocean liner passed under the graceful Golden Gate Bridge, which was jammed with thousands of people furiously waving tiny American flags, the POWs saw huge banners that read: "Welcome Heroes of Bataan and Correg-idor" and "God Bless You Heroes." Minutes after *General Anderson* docked, the former POWs gathered on deck to pray, thanking God for their rescue.

Pushing through shouting, jostling throngs, the former prisoners boarded busses that carried them to Letterman Hospital outside San Francisco, where they were reintroduced to clean sheets. Early the next morning, the VIP treatment resumed. Riding in a caravan of shiny army sedans, the POWs were hailed in a gigantic parade in downtown San Francisco. Some one hundred thousand cheering people lined both sides of the street along the route. It seemed to the honorees that every band in California had turned out—all of them playing as loudly as possible.

When the cavalcade reached the city hall, the POWs alighted and stood before a platform loaded with civilian dignitaries and high military brass. There were prayers, welcoming speeches, and a vocal rendition of "God Bless America." It was heady stuff, almost too much to cope with for the returnees.

Back at Letterman Hospital, most of the men telephoned home and held joyous, tearful verbal reunions. Other POWs were jolted. Wives were dead. Families had moved and could not be located. Children had died. Wives had abandoned offspring or put them in orphanages. After locating his wife, one man found that she had been living with a boyfriend since the Bataan tragedy. Another POW learned that both his father and mother had died, and that his brother and sister had confiscated his part of the inheritance.

In August, while the POWs were struggling to readjust to freedom, General MacArthur was appointed to command an impending invasion of mainland Japan, and the world stood on the brink of the greatest massacre since the days of Ghengis Kahn. Set for November 1, 1945, Operation Downfall would begin with a sea and airborne assault on Kyushi, followed by landings on other Japanese islands. MacArthur informed the Joint Chiefs that American forces alone would suffer in excess of one million casualties before Dai Nippon was brought to its knees.

Then, on August 6, a lone B-29 Superfortress, piloted by twenty-nine-year-old Colonel Paul Tibbetts, dropped what was later described to an awed world as an atom bomb on the Japanese industrial city of Hiroshima. Casualties were enormous: 60,000 killed, 20,000 injured, perhaps 160,000 left homeless. Yet these casualties were but a fraction of the number that would have been killed and wounded on both sides had American troops been forced to invade Japan.

At noon on August 15, Emperor Hirohito, the ruler regarded as a god by most Japanese, took to Radio Tokyo to announce that the empire was surrendering. The declaration stunned the Japanese people and touched off a flurry of ceremonial hara-kiri suicides by generals and admirals.

Two days later, in bleak Mukden, Manchuria, emaciated Jonathan Wainwright and several other American generals captured on Bataan and Corregidor were standing morning roll call at their POW enclosure. Wainwright had been subjected to periodic beatings and humiliations during his long captivity, including having to bow to any Japanese private he encountered. Now, the camp commandant, Lieutenant Hishio Marui, read aloud from a piece of paper, and the interpreter relayed the message in English: "By order of the emperor of Japan, the war has been brought to an amicable conclusion."

Wainwright and his generals exploded with laughter.[7]

Within hours of MacArthur's troops overrunning Cabanatuan camp shortly after the Ranger raid, GI graves registration units began the grisly task of disinterring the remains of the nearly three thousand American POWs who had died there of disease, maltreatment, and starvation or had been murdered by Japanese soldiers. Each American was reburied with full military honors at U.S. cemeteries elsewhere in the Pacific.

Even while the battle for Manila was raging in February 1945, other graves registration teams, aided by Filipino civilians, started the immensely difficult task of locating, disinterring, and identifying the bodies of some twenty-five hundred American servicemen who had died or been killed along the route of the Death March in April 1942. That task would continue for three years.

After the surrender, 3,128 Japanese military men, government officials, and civilians were put on trial in Manila and in Tokyo for "crimes against peace," and most of them were convicted and sentenced to long terms or death. In Manila, Douglas MacArthur's foes on Luzon, General Masaharu Homma in 1942 and General Tomoyuki Yamashita in 1944–45, were tried by a tribunal of American army officers in the huge reception hall of the Philippines high commissioner's residence. Homma and Yamashita were found guilty on the grounds that they had held command responsibilities for the atrocities inflicted upon American and Filipino POWs and the civilian population of the Philippines. General MacArthur reviewed the evidence and approved the verdicts.

In the early morning hours of February 23, 1946, Tomoyuki Yamashita was hanged at Los Baños, a town twenty-five miles south of Manila. A week later, Masaharu Homma was executed by gunfire in the same courtyard. Until his death, Homma swore that he had known nothing about the Death March until two months later, claiming that he had been occupied with planning and conducting the assault on Corregidor.[8]

American guerilla leaders were angry and saddened by the shabby postwar treatment of the Filipinos.

"Seldom in history has one people been so loyal to another or suffered so much for another as the Filipinos did for the Americans," Ray Hunt, the guerilla leader on Luzon, declared recently. "Throughout the struggle, the Filipinos shared our hardships, fought beside us, and risked their own and their families' lives for us. One million Filipinos were casualties. Yet, when the war was over, the United States turned its back on the Philippines."[9]

Confused Filipino guerilla survivors could never comprehend why their war-ravaged nation received a mere $3 million in recovery aid from their ally, the United States, while Communist Yugoslavia, aligned with America's postwar enemies, was granted $300 million.

Hardly had the ink dried on the surrender document signed by the Japanese aboard the battleship *Missouri* in Tokyo Bay on September 2, 1945, than the American home front went on an unprecedented binge of self-indulgence and the pursuit of pleasure. The Death March and the Japanese POW camps became ancient history, and most Americans didn't want to be reminded of those unpleasant events. So the Ghosts of Bataan and Corregidor, as with all POWs of the Japanese, tried to slip back into the mainstream of civilian life, aided only by their loved ones.

How had American POWs of the Japanese managed to survive the brutalities, disease, starvation, and hopelessness? One former inmate, William Delich, credited his survival to a will to live, a desire for revenge, and a sense of humor and the ability to laugh on occasion.

Ex-POW Samuel Grashio explained: "It is hard to kill a man by mere ill treatment if he is determined to live. I wanted to see my wife, family, and friends again. I always believed that God would not desert me."[10]

Numerous former Cabanatuan POWs returned to civilian pursuits. Lieutenant Merle Musselman, the doctor who had volunteered to remain behind with the mortally wounded Captain James Fisher, served for many years on the staff of the University of Nebraska School of Medicine. Colonel James Duckworth, the senior officer at Cabanatuan camp who broke his arm during the raid, resumed his civilian medical practice in Atlanta.

Other POWs continued their military careers, and some of them reached high rank. Lieutenant Colonel Harold K. Johnston gained four stars and became army chief of staff during the Lyndon Johnson administration. Among the ten POWs who made the daring escape to Australia in 1943, Captain Austin Shofner retired as a Marine Corps brigadier general, Lieutenant Samuel Grashio as an air corps colonel, and Major Steve Mellnik as a two-star officer. Captain Robert Taylor eventually became the U.S. Army chief of chaplains with the rank of major general.[11]

Although numerous men bridged the gulf between the horrors of Japanese POW camps and freedom, most of the returned prisoners bore emotional scars that time would never heal. Some had to be confined to what were then indelicately known as "funny farms." Many would be hit by panic attacks, anxiety, depression, and neuroses. Horrible nightmares would last a lifetime. A few committed suicide.

Former POWs' efforts to obtain treatment in U.S. Veterans Administration hospitals were often maddening exercises in futility. In the postwar years, staff psychiatrists had no grasp of the unique kind of emotional distress suffered by the POWs, so patients were sometimes released with the comment: "It's all in your mind." Many men racked by pain from maltreatment and starvation diets often received similar send-offs. On occasion, VA bureaucrats would demand nonexistent wartime medical records as proof that a POW's ailment was service-connected.

After dawdling for three years, Congress, in 1948, finally awarded financial compensation to the prisoners of the Japanese. A POW received one dollar for each day he had endured the horrors of the Death March, Camp O'Donnell, Cabanatuan, and other Far East hellholes. Two years later, an additional dollar and a half per day was authorized.

There ensued countless hassles between former POWs and faceless Washington bureaucrats over precisely how many days a survivor had actually been in Japanese captivity. James P. Boyd, who had escaped from the Death March after one day and risked his life as a guerilla for three years, claimed that he should be classified as a POW during that time. For many years, he dueled with federal agencies over the amount he should be compensated. Finally, Boyd received his lump payment—a U.S. Treasury check for one dollar, which he left uncashed, framed, and mounted on the wall of his home.

In the years ahead, former POWs, many of them in dire straits, demanded that the U.S. government press prosperous Japan for compensation, but they were told that claims against that nation had been settled by the 1951 peace treaty, which bars former American POWs from suing Japan for reparations.

As time passed and Uncle Sam adopted Japan as an ally and commercial partner, hundreds of the more than three thousand convicted war criminals were quietly released from Tokyo's Surgamo Prison, where they had been serving long terms. Most of these freed men promptly resumed leadership roles in Japanese government and business. Manoru Shigemitsu, who, as Japan's wartime foreign minister had signed the Tokyo Bay surrender document, was one of those released. A few years later, Shigemitsu again became foreign minister.

Among the war criminals given early freedom were the commandants of the O'Donnell and Cabanatuan POW camps, and numerous Japanese army men convicted of inflicting atrocities on Americans and Filipinos during the Death March. By January 1, 1959, all of the Japanese war criminals had been released. Except for those who had been executed, the severest punishment for the convicted men was thirteen years in the relative comfort of Surgamo Prison.

After the Cabanatuan mission, Henry Mucci, leader of the 6th Ranger Battalion, was promoted to full colonel and given command of the 1st Regiment of the 6th Infantry Division. Later, he was wounded in action, resulting in a medical discharge in 1946. Still youthful and energetic, Mucci accepted a position as Far East representative of an oil corporation and remained in that capacity until his retirement in 1977.

Bob Prince, who led the Ranger assault on the Cabanatuan stockade, left the army as a major in early 1946, and for many years globe-trotted as an executive with an apple marketing firm based in his native Northwest.

Thomas Rounsaville and John Dove, two of the Alamo Scouts lieutenants involved in the Cabanatuan mission, remained in the army and retired as colonels. William Nellist, the other Scouts lieutenant, returned to civilian pursuits in his home state of California after the war.

Captain Eduardo Joson, the Filipino guerilla chief, was elected governor of Nueva Ecija Province after hostilities concluded. Juan Pajota, promoted to major, continued fighting the Japanese in northern Luzon until the end of the war. The American guerilla leader, Major Robert Lapham, who had informed U.S. Sixth Army intelligence that the Cabanatuan POWs were in danger of being murdered, returned to civilian life and eventually retired as a vice president of the Burroughs Corporation.

General Walter Krueger, the Sixth Army commander who had given the green light for the Cabanatuan raid, retired shortly after the war. Jonathan Wainwright, who was plucked from his Manchurian jail in time to stand next to Douglas MacArthur at the Tokyo Bay surrender ceremony, returned to the United States a hero. He retired in August 1947, after forty-five years of service.

Five-star General of the Army Douglas MacArthur never forgave President Roosevelt for the messages he sent to Corregidor in early 1942, signals that MacArthur had interpreted as meaning military help was on the way to the Battling Bastards of Bataan. On April 13, 1945, MacArthur was informed by an aide, Colonel Bonner Fellers, that the president had died.

"So Roosevelt is dead," the general mused to Fellers. "Now there was a man who would never tell the truth when a lie would serve just as well."[12]

Throughout the war, MacArthur had to fight with only 12 percent of America's manpower and production. Nonetheless, he made eighty-seven amphibious landings and four paratrooper assaults, all of them successful, cutting Japanese escape routes and lines of communication.

Field Marshal Alan Brooke, chief of the Imperial General Staff during World War II and England's most decorated soldier since Wellington and Marlborough, wrote at the conclusion of hostilities: "MacArthur has outshone (General) George Marshall, Ike Eisenhower, (George) Patton, (Bernard) Montgomery, and all other American and British generals."[13]

Never in history has there been a major commander so economical in the expenditure of his men's blood as Douglas MacArthur. Comparisons are startling. During the six-week battle of Normandy, General Eisenhower lost 26,266 men killed or wounded. Between the start of MacArthur's counteroffensive in New Guinea and his return to Philippine waters two years later, his hit-'em-where-they-ain't tactics held his casualties to 27,684. In a single fight at Anzio, Italy, 72,306 Allied men fell.

Who was to blame for America's monumental debacle in the Philippines and at Pearl Harbor in the early days of the war in the Pacific? Blessed by twenty-twenty hindsight, some critics have pointed the finger at U.S. military professionals who, they declare, had been taken by surprise. Actually, the culprits were the people of the United States and shortsighted politicians in Washington who held fast to the belief that the way to keep America out of war was to remain militarily weak, even though scheming aggressors were on the march around the world.

Notes and Sources

Chapter 1. Deep in Hostile Territory

1. Author interview with Colonel Henry A. Mucci (Ret.).
2. Ibid.
3. Author interview with William E. Nellist.
4. Author correspondence with Gilbert J. Cox.
5. Author interview with William E. Nellist.
6. Ibid.
7. Author interview with Robert W. Prince.
8. Author interview with Cecil E. "Red" Easley.

Chapter 2. Roosevelt Abandons the Philippines

1. Stephen E. Ambrose, *Eisenhower* (New York: Simon & Schuster, 1983), p. 138.
2. *The New York Times*, January 4, 1942.
3. National Archives, Modern Warfare Section, Washington, D.C.
4. *Washington Times-Herald*, January 10, 1942.
5. USAFFE-War Department messages, December 27–28, 1941, MacArthur Memorial, Norfolk, Virginia.
6. Ibid., January 3–5, 1942.
7. Francis B. Sayre, *Glad Adventure* (New York: Random House, 1957), p. 222.
8. Stephen E. Ambrose, p. 138.
9. Dwight D. Eisenhower Diary, Eisenhower Library, Abilene, Kansas, January 19, 1942.
10. Ibid., January 23, 1942.
11. Ibid., January 29, 1942.
12. Three years later, while being held in a Manila prison for trial as a war criminal, General Masaharu Homma wrote in his diary: "It is reported that Mr. Tojo will be here (in prison) before long. There is nothing more unpleasant than this. To have to see his face every day will be more than I can bear."

Chapter 3. Legion of the Living Dead

1. Author interview with Vice Admiral John D. Bulkeley (Ret.).
2. Author correspondence with Captain Malcolm N. Champlin, USN (Ret.).

3. Sidney L. Huff, *My Fifteen Years with General MacArthur* (New York: Harper, 1964), p. 73.
4. Author interview with Vice Admiral John D. Bulkeley (Ret.).
5. Sidney L. Huff, p. 87.
6. Ibid., p. 96.
7. *The New York Times*, March 22, 1942.
8. Author interview with Bill Begley.
9. Author correspondence with Michael Gilewitch.
10. Author provided William Galos recollections by Thomas Gage, who had belonged to 34th Pursuit Squadron.
11. Seventy-seven years earlier to the day, on April 9, 1965, General Robert E. Lee surrendered his Confederate army to General Ulysses S. Grant at Appomatox Courthouse, Virginia.
12. In March 1943, Lieutenant Colonel Garnet Francis, not knowing if his wife, Lieutenant Earleen Francis, was alive, was transferred from Cabanatuan camp to Santo Tomás internment camp in Manila, where she was a prisoner. Thinking her husband was dead, Earleen happened to run onto him and fainted.
13. Courtney Whitney, *MacArthur: His Rendezvous with History* (New York: Knopf, 1956), p. 51.
13. Ibid., p. 56.

Chapter 4. Sixty Miles of Atrocities

1. Author communication with Colonel Samuel C. Grashio (Ret.)
2. Ibid.
3. Author interview with Leon D. Beck.
4. Author correspondence with Major Richard M. Gordon (Ret.).
5. Author provided William Galos's recollections by Thomas E. Gage.
6. Author correspondence with Leon Wolf.
7. Author interview with Michael Gilewitch.
8. Ibid.
9. Author provided recollections of Lieutenant Colonel Emil P. Reed by his daughter, Mrs. Elizabeth Redwine.
10. John Toland, *But Not in Shame* (New York: Random House, 1961), p. 340.
11. Author interview with Michael Gilewitch.
12. Author interview with Bill Begley.
13. Ibid.
14. Author interview with Leon D. Beck.
15. *Medical Opinion and Review*, August 1949.
16. Sidney Stewart, *Give Us This Day* (New York: Norton, 1956), pp. 72–73.
17. Author interview with Leon D. Beck.
18. Leon Beck's first sergeant had seen him in the line of corpses and later reported Beck as dead and buried.

19. Leon Beck fought as a guerilla on Luzon for nearly three years.
20. Author communication with Lieutenant Colonel Ray C. Hunt (Ret.).
21. Author interview with Robert J. Body.
22. The precise Death March totals would never be known. These figures were based on U.S. Army educated estimates.

Chapter 5. "Situation Fast Becoming Desperate"

1. Japanese War Crimes Documents, USA vs. Masaharu Homma, MacArthur Memorial, Norfolk, Virginia.
2. Author correspondence with William R. Evans.
3. Louis Morton, *Fall of the Philippines* (Washington: U.S. Government Printing Office, 1953), p. 462.
4. Ibid., p. 463.
5. Jonathan Wainwright, *General Wainwright's Story* (New York: Doubleday, 1946), p. 95.
6. Author correspondence with Jerry L. Coty.
7. Jonathan Wainwright, p. 101.
8. Ibid., p. 102.
9. After the war, Eunice Young remained in the army until 1949, when she transferred to the air force, retiring as a lieutenant colonel in 1961. In 1991, Colonel Young was inducted into the Steuben County Hall of Fame in her native New York. American nurses captured on Corregidor were imprisoned at Santo Tomás, a former university in Manila. The Angels of Corregidor were liberated when the U.S. Army arrived in February 1945.
10. "Corregidor's Last Breath," *Coast Artillery Journal*, August 1943, p. 2.
11. Jonathan Wainwright, p. 137.
12. Ibid., p. 139.
13. Colonel Paul Bunker cut a small swath from the lowered American flag and concealed it under a false patch on his shirt. When he was in a Formosa POW camp months later, Bunker became very ill, so he removed the piece of Old Glory and put it in the care of a fellow prisoner. Two years later, the swath was presented to U.S. Secretary of War Robert Patterson. Colonel Bunker died in the prison camp from hunger, abuse, and disease.
14. "Corregidor's Last Breath," p. 3.
15. Author contact with Thomas E. Gage.

Chapter 6. "You Are Enemies of Japan!"

1. In postwar war criminal trials, Captain Tsuneyoshi was sentenced to death for his role in the Camp O'Donnell atrocities. Later, the sentence was commuted to life at hard labor, and even this punishment was set aside and he became a free man after serving a few years in prison.
2. Author provided Lieutenant Colonel Emil Reed's recollections by his daughter, Elizabeth Redwine.

3. The Japanese captured much war booty on Bataan and Corregidor. A con-
    siderable amount of it failed to function for the Americans during the
    conflict, so it may have been of dubious value to the Japanese. Taken from
    the Americans were 27,412 rifles, 844 trucks, 1,132 passenger cars, 31
    tanks, 1,161 pistols and revolvers, 218 machine guns, 68 automatic rifles,
    2,071 grenades, 9,371 bayonets, 6 million rounds of small-arms ammu-
    nition, plus huge amounts of oil.
4. Author interview with Brigadier General Austin C. Shofner, USMC, (Ret.).
5. After the war, Lieutenant Colonel Shigeji Mori was sentenced to life in
    prison for maltreatment of Cabanatuan prisoners. A few years later, his
    sentence was commuted and he was released.
6. Author interview with Michael Gilewitch.
7. "Triumph in the Philippines—Enemy Occupation," unpublished manu-
    script by Robert Smith, pp. 19–21.
8. Author interview with William Delich.
9. Ibid.
10. Ibid.
11. Lieutenant Colonel Harold K. Johnston kept two sets of books for the
    Cabanatuan commissary. The actual record included the food smuggled
    in by Miss U's underground, while the phony books, the ones shown to
    the Japanese, did not disclose the "illegal" food.
12. Author interview with Charles Di Maio.
13. Douglas MacArthur had been a baseball star at West Point and remained
    a fan of the sport. His "hit-'em-where-they-ain't" expression came from a
    fabled remark by "Wee Willie" Keeler, a major league hitting star in the
    early 1900s. When asked by reporters for the secret of his success, Keeler
    replied, "I hit 'em where they ain't!"

Chapter 7. Miss U and Her Underground

1. Two years later, Chief Godofredo Monsod was betrayed and executed by
    the Japanese.
2. After the war, Mario Garcia was elected mayor of Cabanatuan.

Chapter 8. Secret Radios and Boxcar Smugglers

1. Sidney Huff, pp. 9–10.
2. *The New York Times*, May 25, 1943.
3. Thomas Lanphier was awarded the Navy Cross and received a personal
    letter of congratulations from President Roosevelt. Thomas's brother,
    Charles, was freed from his POW camp by American troops. After the war,
    Thomas Lanphier eventually became vice president, planning, for Ray-
    theon Corporation in Lexington, Massachusetts.
4. Author interview with William Milne.
5. A zoot suit had greatly exaggerated lapels, trousers that gathered tightly

at the ankles, and an extremely long coat. The zoot suit was usually worn with extra-wide-brimmed hats and key chains that hung almost to the ground. It was often a status symbol among young gang members.

6. Chaplain Robert Taylor was often the target of good-natured ribbing because his name was the same as that of a leading Hollywood superstar.

7. Chaplain Alfred Oliver never fully recovered from the broken neck, and he had to wear a brace for many years.

8. Author interview with William Delich.

9. Author provided recollections of Lieutenant Colonel Emil Reed by his daughter, Mrs. Elizabeth Redwine.

Chapter 9. An Audacious Escape

1. The Geneva Convention provided for the humane treatment of prisoners of war. The first Geneva Convention was signed in 1864 by all countries in Europe, the United States, and by some nations in Asia and South America.

2. The two Filipino guides, Victorio and Ben, chose to remain in Mindanao as guerillas. As soon as Commander Melvyn McCoy and Major Steve Mellnik got back to the United States, they went to Saranac Lake, New York, to see President Manuel Quezon, who was ill with tuberculosis (he died a year later). Quezon granted full pardons to Ben and Victorio.

3. Author communication with Colonel Samuel C. Grashio (Ret.).

4. Ibid.

5. Paul Marshall and Robert Spielman were given guerilla commissions and remained on Mindanao for the rest of the war. Spielman married the daughter of a Spanish-American War veteran who had been in the Philippines for many years.

6. Author communication with Colonel Samuel C. Grashio (Ret.).

7. Colonel Sam Grashio retired from the air force in 1965. He then became an assistant to the president of his alma mater, Gonzaga University, in Spokane, Washington, retiring from that position in 1977.

8. *The New York Times*, January 28, 1944.

9. Ten years after the war, a Strategic Air Command (SAC) facility near Abeline, Texas, was named Dyess Air Force Base in honor of the Bataan hero.

Chapter 10. Manila's Notorious Club Tsubaki

1. Myron Goldsmith, *Manila Espionage* (Portland, Oregon: Binford and Mort, 1947), p. 103.

2. Dialogue in this chapter was conducted by the participants in Spanish, English, Japanese, Tagalog, or a mixture of these languages and dialects.

3. Much of the background of Club Tsubaki was obtained by the author's interview with retired U.S. Navy Petty Officer Charles Di Maio, who had

been a good friend of Claire Phillips before his capture on Corregidor, and he had talked with her at length after the war.

4. Myron Goldsmith, p. 106.
5. Ibid., p. 119.
6. Author interview with Charles Di Maio.

Chapter 11. Alamo Scouts and Rangers

1. Author interview with Colonel Gibson Niles (Ret.).
2. Ibid.
3. Author interview with Colonel Robert S. Sumner (Ret.).
4. Author interview with Colonel John M. Dove (Ret.).
5. Author correspondence with Colonel Thomas Rounsaville (Ret.).
6. Ibid.
7. Author correspondence with Andy E. Smith.
8. Author interview with Robert W. Prince.
9. Ibid.
10. Author correspondence with Charles Bosard.

Chapter 12. Thumbs Down on a POW Rescue Scheme

1. Courtney Whitney, p. 144.
2. Huk strength estimates from *Intelligence Activities*, October 23, 1944, No. 81, pp. 3–4. National Archives.
3. Author communication with Lieutenant Colonel Ray C. Hunt (Ret.).
4. Theodore A. Agoncillo, *The Fateful Years* (Quezon City: R. P. Garcia, 1965), pp. 663–672.
5. Author communication with Lieutenant Colonel Ray C. Hunt (Ret.).
6. William Halsey, p. 202.

Chapter 13. Eagles Soar Over Cabanatuan

1. Author provided unpublished recollections of William C. Seckinger.
2. Ibid.
3. This incident was told to Admiral William Halsey when he visited Clark Field nine months later.
4. William Halsey, p. 203.
5. Author provided unpublished recollections of William C. Seckinger.
6. Blind Mrs. Robert Yearsley apparently was never suspected by the Japanese of being part of Miss U's covert operation.
7. General MacArthur always used A-Day, N-Day, or other initials for his assaults. He told aides that General Dwight Eisenhower in Europe had "monopolized" the term D-Day.
8. Author interview with Colonel Robert W. Garrett (Ret.).

9. Philippine guerillas had flown U.S. flags on occasion, but only briefly for fear of detection by the Japanese.

10. Author interview with Colonel Robert W. Garrett (Ret.).

11. *Time* magazine, October 26, 1944.

12. Although General MacArthur's invasion fleet had fewer ships than did General Eisenhower for Normandy, MacArthur's armada had more firepower.

13. Over the years since the war, Douglas MacArthur critics, mostly those ten thousand miles from the Philippines, have claimed the general waded ashore several times at Leyte Gulf in order for photographers to shoot good pictures. Actually, MacArthur waded ashore, not at one, but at three different Leyte invasion beaches miles apart, usually while the fighting was still hot.

14. Author provided Lieutenant Colonel Emil Reed's recollections by his daughter, Mrs. Elizabeth Redwine.

15. Ibid.

Chapter 14. Hell Ships and Vanishing Guards

1. Author correspondence with Colonel Robert S. Sumner (Ret.).

2. Ibid.

3. Author correspondence with Colonel Henry J. Stempin (Ret.).

4. Ibid.

5. Ibid.

6. Ibid.

7. Henry Stempin was freed by Russian troops at a POW camp at Mukden, Manchuria, on August 17, 1945.

8. William Manchester, *American Caesar* (Boston: Little, Brown, 1978), p. 405.

9. When General Yamashita, the "Tiger of Malaya," surrendered at the close of the war, GIs quipped that he had become the "Pussycat of Luzon." Actually, had it not been for the A-bomb, Yamashita's force in northern Luzon could have extracted a heavy American toll for many months before it was dug out of the mountains.

10. Author provided recollections of Lieutenant Colonel Emil Reed by his daughter, Mrs. Elizabeth Redwine.

11. Author interview with Marine Brigadier General Austin C. Shofner (Ret.).

12. Author provided unpublished recollections of William C. Seckinger.

13. Author interview with Cecil Easley.

14. During the Vietnam War, in November 1970, Colonel Arthur "Bull" Simons led a team of U.S. Special Forces (Green Berets) in a daring helicopter assault to liberate American POWs held in a camp near Hanoi. Unfortunately, the POWs had been moved earlier.

15. Author correspondence with Leo V. Strausbaugh.

16. Author provided unpublished recollections of William C. Seckinger.

Chapter 15. A Perilous Mission

1. Author correspondence with Robert W. Lapham.
2. Dates and times in the planning and execution of the Cabanatuan raid are from a U.S. Sixth Army intelligence summary, February 22, 1945.
3. *Saturday Evening Post*, April 7, 1945.
4. Author interview with Robert W. Prince.
5. Author interview with Colonel Robert W. Garrett (Ret.).
6. Author provided the gist of Colonel Mucci's remarks by Ranger historian Harry Pearlmutter.
7. Author interview with Robert W. Prince.
8. Author communication with James B. Herrick.
9. Author interview with Colonel John M. Dove (Ret.).
10. Author provided background and some details of the P-61s' role in the Cabanatuan raid by the U.S. Air Force Historical Research Center, Maxwell Air Force Base, Montgomery, Alabama, microfilm roll AO826.

Chapter 16. Cross-Country Dominos

1. A few days after returning from the Cabanatuan raid, the same 832nd Signal Service Battalion photographers parachuted onto Japanese-held Corregidor with the U.S. 503rd Parachute Infantry Regiment.
2. The map Captain Robert Prince used on the Cabanatuan raid was loaned to the author and used for reconstructing the operation.
3. Author correspondence with James B. Herrick.
4. Ibid.
5. Author interview with Colonel John M. Dove (Ret.).
6. Author interview with Colonel Henry A. Mucci (Ret.).
7. Author correspondence with James B. Herrick.
8. Author interview with Colonel Henry A. Mucci (Ret.).
9. Author provided unpublished recollections of William C. Seckinger.
10. Author interview with Master Sergeant George R. Steiner (Ret.).
11. Author correspondence with Robert J. Body.
12. Author interview with Colonel Henry A. Mucci (Ret.).

Chapter 17. Creeping Up on a Dark Stockade

1. Author correspondence with August T. Stern, Jr. During the Vietnam War, his son, August III, a squad sergeant in a rifle platoon of the 101st Airborne Division, saw heavy combat. When the younger Stern received his first respite, he gained permission to fly to the Philippines to see the shrine to the 6th Rangers that had been erected at Cabanatuan camp. No one in that region knew about the shrine, but young Stern finally located an el-

derly farmer who took him to the ground where his father had helped rescue 511 POWs twenty-five years earlier.

2. Summary of the 547th Night Fighter Squadron's role in the Cabanatuan rescue mission, Historical Research Center, Maxwell Air Force Base, Alabama.
3. Author correspondence with Cecil Easley.
4. Author communication with Cleatus G. Norton.
5. *Yank* magazine, March 2, 1945.
6. Author communication with Cleatus G. Norton.
7. Author interview with Leland A. Provencher.

Chapter 18. Pandemonium Erupts in the Night

1. Author interview with Robert W. Prince.
2. Author correspondence with Leland A. Provencher.
3. Author interview with Melville B. Schmidt.
4. Author communication with Alexander Truskowski (Troy).
5. Author correspondence with Master Sergeant George R. Steiner (Ret.).
6. Author correspondence with Robert J. Body.
7. Author provided unpublished recollections of William C. Seckinger.
8. Author communication with E. C. Witmer, Jr.
9. *The New York Times*, February 2, 1945.
10. Author interview with Colonel John M. Dove (Ret.).
11. Ibid.
12. Author correspondence with James Herrick.
13. Author correspondence with Cecil Easley.
14. Author communication with August T. Stern, Jr. After the war, Stern joined the Baltimore, Maryland, fire department, where he remained for forty-five years. In light of his role in the Cabanatuan rescue mission, it seemed to be quite appropriate that his years in firefighting would be on a rescue team.
15. Author correspondence with Francis Schilli.
16. Author correspondence with Charles H. Bosard.
17. Author interview with William E. Nellist.
18. Author correspondence with Harold N. Hard.
19. Author communication with Andy E. Smith.
20. Author correspondence with James B. Herrick.
21. Since the Rangers had to withdraw promptly, it would never be known precisely how many Japanese were killed within the POW enclosure. A few may have hidden or fled, but so swift was the assault that Ranger leaders believe the entire garrison had been wiped out.
22. Author interview with Robert W. Prince.
23. Ibid.
24. Author correspondence with Francis R. Schilli.

Chapter 19. Stealthy Trek by Carabao Caravan

1. Author interview with Robert W. Prince.
2. Author correspondence with Cecil Easley.
3. Author communication with James B. Herrick.
4. Former Rangers have told the author that they felt that Lieutenant Merle Musselman should have received the Congressional Medal of Honor.
5. Microfilm roll AO826, U.S. Air Force Historical Research Center, Maxwell Air Force Base, Alabama.
6. No specific records were kept, but Captain Juan Pajota's guerillas suffered ten to twenty-seven casualties in the fight at Cabu bridge.
7. Author interview with Colonel Henry A. Mucci (Ret.).
8. Ibid.
9. Author correspondence with Colonel John M. Dove (Ret.).
10. Author communication with Gilbert J. Cox.

Chapter 20. Hamburgers, Tears, and Freedom

1. Author correspondence with Master Sergeant George R. Steiner (Ret.).
2. Captain James C. Fisher was awarded posthumously the Silver Star and the Purple Heart. After the war, his remains were disinterred at Balincarin and buried at the U.S. Military Cemetery in Manila.
3. Author correspondence with Gilbert J. Cox.
4. *Chicago Tribune*, February 2, 1945.
5. *The New York Times*, February 2, 1945.
6. *Washington Star*, February 3, 1945.
7. *St. Louis Post-Dispatch*, February 2, 1945.
8. Major Paul Wing's blonde and beautiful daughter, Toby Wing, was a budding Hollywood starlet during and after World War II. The mother and father of another movie star, Brenda Marshall (who later married actor William Holden), were interned by the Japanese at Santo Tomás in Manila throughout the war.
9. *Time* magazine, February 8, 1945.
10. Carl Mydans's wife, Virginia, was a prisoner of the Japanese in Santo Tomás.

Epilogue

1. *St. Louis Globe-Democrat*, February 2, 1945.
2. Oliver note on file at U.S. Military History Institute, Carlisle, Pennsylvania.
3. Not long after introducing the Rangers and Alamo Scouts to President Roosevelt, General Stillwell was rushed to Okinawa to replace General Simon Bolivar Buckner, who had just been killed in action, as commander of the U.S. Tenth Army.
4. Author interview with Robert W. Prince.

5. *The New York Times*, April 8, 1945.

6. Author in possession of Mrs. James "Bodie" Fisher's original letter.

7. Jonathan Wainwright, p. 276.

8. After General Masaharu Homma was sentenced to death, his wife made a tearful plea to General MacArthur to spare her husband's life. MacArthur later would say that refusing Mrs. Homma's request was an exceedingly difficult decision.

9. Author communication with Lieutenant Colonel Ray C. Hunt (Ret.).

10. Author correspondence with William Delich and with Colonel Samuel C. Grashio (Ret.).

11. On April 24, 1993, General Austin C. Shofner was honored as a "Distinguished American" by the Tennessee chapter of the National Football Foundation in ceremonies at Knoxville.

12. William Manchester, p. 362.

13. Viscount Alan Brooke, *Diaries* (London: Collins, 1957), p. 321.

Index